Major General
Philip Kearny

ALSO BY ROBERT R. LAVEN

A Burned Land:
The Trans-Mississippi in the Civil War
(McFarland, 2019)

Major General Philip Kearny
A Soldier and His Time in the American Civil War

Robert R. Laven

McFarland & Company, Inc., Publishers
Jefferson, North Carolina

LIBRARY OF CONGRESS CATALOGUING-IN-PUBLICATION DATA

Names: Laven, Robert R., author.
Title: Major General Philip Kearny : a soldier and his time in the American Civil War / Robert R. Laven.
Description: Jefferson, North Carolina : McFarland & Company, Inc., 2020 | Includes bibliographical references and index.
Identifiers: LCCN 2020012667 | ISBN 9781476680286 (paperback) ∞
ISBN 9781476639024 (ebook)
Subjects: LCSH: Kearny, Philip, 1815–1862. | Generals—United States—Biography. | United States—History—Civil War, 1861–1865—Campaigns. | United States. Army. Cavalry—Biography.
Classification: LCC E467.K24 L38 2020 | DDC 355.0092 [B]—dc23
LC record available at https://lccn.loc.gov/2020012667

BRITISH LIBRARY CATALOGUING DATA ARE AVAILABLE

ISBN (print) 978-1-4766-8028-6
ISBN (ebook) 978-1-4766-3902-4

© 2020 Robert R. Laven. All rights reserved

No part of this book may be reproduced or transmitted in any form or by any means, electronic or mechanical, including photocopying or recording, or by any information storage and retrieval system, without permission in writing from the publisher.

On the cover: General Philip Kearney (i.e. Kearny), 1862, Hartford, Conn., Taylor & Huntington, No. 2 State 1862 July (Library of Congress)

Printed in the United States of America

*McFarland & Company, Inc., Publishers
Box 611, Jefferson, North Carolina 28640
www.mcfarlandpub.com*

Acknowledgments

Invariably, the primary works that I used for the Civil War consisted mostly of the Official Record War of the Rebellion that was compiled shortly after the war. In some instances, it provided a wealth of information to be gleaned, and in others it revealed discrepancies between what some officers did not report or were seemingly vague in reporting. For some officers the Official Record was simply a means to highlight their case, particularly the Union officers, who always had to concern themselves with the Congressional Conduct of the War Committee.

The other work that offered a wealth of personal experience and was a little flowery and a bit biased at times was John De Peyster's biography of Kearny. Even though the work was very pro–Philip and pro–Union, it does reflect the time in it was written; however, it did have some revelations about Kearny's family relationships. This work offered a number of low-hanging fruit and some insight into Kearny's thinking. It led to the interesting correspondences of people, including his relationship with Winfield Scott, and also that of young Gustave Schurmann, who would relate his experience as an orderly serving the general. The work of Thomas Kearny was also valuable in illuminating Kearny and his relationship with his family and the officers he served with.

Living in St. Louis, I worked for the Department of Defense and was afforded the opportunity to work on the old Arsenal Grounds. I became familiar with its association with Jefferson Barracks and the influence it would have on many of the players who would participate in that internal conflict. I have visited often to look over the facility and visit the Missouri Civil War Museum, where I am a member, and visit with the staff there who work to preserve the sites in and around St. Louis. I also had the opportunity to use the research facilities at the Missouri History Museum Library in St. Louis, allowing me to peruse the Papers of Stephen Watts Kearny, Philip's uncle, which would prove most useful and informative. These papers helped provide information that suggests

Acknowledgments

the possibility of Philip Kearny's consideration to command the Army of the Potomac.

The Combined Arms Research Library (on-line) in Fort Leavenworth was also helpful in researching Kearny. To all those libraries I owe my appreciation. The visits to the battlefields around Richmond and Manassas brought about a greater understanding of field positions, as well as hindsight concerning the forces and ground that Kearny had to deal with. Preservation that is entrusted to the National Park Service is greatly appreciated. Having worked for the Park Service I understand their difficult task, particularly for those sites, like Seven Pines or Chantilly (Ox Hill), where there is simply very little of those battlefields left.

Special consideration must be given to those people from the Fairfax, Virginia/Ox Hill Battlefield preservation group and Ed Wenzel. I also thank those I met at the 2015 Virginia Signature Sesquicentennial event who went out of their way to assist me in some of the research, particularly the Philip Kearny GAR Post No. 10, Richmond, Virginia. Also, I must mention the continuing support I have received from the Missouri Civil War Museum and their contribution to Civil War studies. Finally, thanks to all who were there to give advice and whom I may have missed.

Table of Contents

Acknowledgments   v
Preface   1

    I. Beginnings   5
   II. Influences   10
  III. A Soldierly Figure   17
  IV. Valley of the Sun   32
    V. Camp Seminary   46
  VI. Williamsburg   56
 VII. Seven Pines   67
VIII. Pivot at Gaines' Mill   77
  IX. Glendale   86
    X. Malvern Hill   97
  XI. A Long Roll of Thunder   104
 XII. Manassas, August 29: Pope Engages   113
XIII. Manassas, August 30: Longstreet Attacks   129
XIV. Requiem   138

Epilogue   155
Appendix A: Lost Letter of Lt. Philip Kearny   161
Appendix B: Extracts from Official Reports— Mexican War   163
Appendix C: Documents, Reports, etc.— American Civil War   169
Appendix D: Kearny Testimonials   173

Table of Contents

Appendix E: Kearny and First New Jersey Regiment   181

Appendix F: Kearny Assigned to III Corps, 3rd Division   183

Appendix G: Union and Confederate Order of Battle (Selected Units)   185

Chapter Notes   189

Bibliography   195

Index   199

Preface

One summer, many years ago, I was working as a park ranger for the National Park Service along the George Washington Memorial Parkway bike and pedestrian pathway in Virginia. This bike path stretches from Mount Vernon to the Lincoln Memorial, and part of my duties often took me from Mount Vernon to Alexandria, Virginia. There I often found myself on the Strand on the Potomac River, at a local sandwich shop of the same name. Just a few blocks to the south along that waterfront was located an old naval station where rusting hulks of unused naval paraphernalia of another era lay languishing with the tide.

My thoughts carried me to another place in time and I realized that it was at this site that the old U.S. military wharves once stood during the American Civil War. At that time, I really only noticed the site insofar as it ran parallel to the bike path. I later realized, while researching this book, that I once rode my Park Service bicycle on the same ground that Philip Kearny and his men embarked from Alexandria on sail and steam transport to the York Peninsula. Down on the Virginia tidewater, Kearny would return to Alexandria as Major General of the III Corps' First Division. Here one could literally step off the steamers at the wharf and immediately board the train cars of the Orange and Alexandria Railroad, located close by along Duke Street, to depart the city.

Alexandria is now a thriving city in the midst of the U.S. capital, Washington, D.C., with small shops and restaurants. In 1861–62, Alexandria looked different: it was a bustling seaport and military base, covering the area where that sandwich shop now stands. It was a pro–South city, organizing the 17th Virginia from the local populace of the town to serve in the Confederacy. Seeing such activities close by the Union capital, the Union military authority moved quickly, and the city was immediately occupied by Union forces at the beginning of the internecine conflict.

Alexandria was soon an armed military base described in this way at the time by local observers: "[B]lock by block, the town was defined by various Federal military installations while the surrounding area was

Preface

secured with fortifications." The city bristled with forts and cannon, and another war correspondent described it this way: "Its streets, its docks, its warehouse, its dwellings, and its suburbs have been absorbed to the thousand uses of War."[1] It was from here that Kearny's entrance into the war began, and it was likely from here that he eventually left for his home in New Jersey.

I came upon the notion of writing a book on Kearny while I was working on a book about the Seventh Wisconsin Regiment, which was part of the Union Iron Brigade. Kearny's interaction at Second Manassas with John Gibbon, who commanded that Brigade, gave me pause to think that not much material was devoted to this particular general in the Union Army. Not regularly referenced like U.S. Grant or William T. Sherman, or even George McClellan or John Pope, Philip Kearny was probably one of, if not the best prepared officer to lead a modern continental army in the field. There has always been a debate over the quality of Union versus Confederate officer material, and here was one soldier in the Union ranks who seemed to really stand out.

Here was a well-qualified and experienced officer who had served in a number of theaters of war when the Union seemed to have few to fit that bill. I find very interesting that during Kearny's relatively brief Civil War career, someone like eminent historian Douglas Southall Freeman, who has described in detail what the South had to offer, would single out Major General Kearny in his work *Lee's Lieutenants*. Freeman points out, in a number of chapters of that work, that the Confederates had more respect for the one-armed-devil than any other Union officer. In fact, Kearny seemed to affect some of the Confederates officers' response and actions in the fight around Richmond. That is high praise from a great American historian, an acknowledged expert of that conflict.

This narrative brings alive a soldier and his times, an American Odyssey from the shores of America to Europe and Africa and back to America to Mexico and the Pacific Northwest and back again to the shores of the Potomac. Here was a soldier who was always in the midst of battle leading his men to the front line. By his experience, he would instill into his men a confident fighting spirit, and his men were aware that he would always be there. Kearny understood the math of combat; he sought the offensive and recognized that in order to win a war there could be nothing less than victory. As Freeman referenced, "He was the type of all great soldiers. And like successful soldiers of the past, he could order men to their death as a matter of course."[2] He was of the type who, when the sound of the guns arose, seemed to have a quality that was irrepressibly positive, witty and

Preface

buoyant of spirit. Kearny sought action, and he believed that to remain stagnant in battle as in life would lead to an outcome that was simply unacceptable. His own motto was this: "It is sweet and seemly to die for one's country."

As will be clear, Philip Kearny always led from the front, as he was acutely aware that his presence was necessary to inspire his men in the face of close-order combat. It should be kept in mind that Kearny never had the initial formal training that many of his associates had at West Point Military Academy. Kearny would learn from experience, and as we will see, at the side of many officers who had cut their teeth in the War of 1812, including his distinguished uncle, Stephen Watts Kearny. He was probably fortunate that his training was in the field, for in many regards this allowed him to bring no preconceptions other than what was taught to him in his early life and the French School at Samur. Experience in and out of the saddle would serve him well, along with what seemed to be his belief that he was invincible.

The fact that the American Civil War occurred cannot be denied, but yet there are those who would like to remove any reminders of it. Yes, slavery was a stain, but to destroy those who believed in a less centralized government should not be disregarded as a central aim of the war. It is now left to us the writer and historian to continue to speak, to raise our voices over the partisan politics and the disease of present-mindedness that dismisses our past and elevates dissension that only divides all of us. Methodology teaches that one should evaluate anything within the broadest possible context, to think historically. Do we really want to dismiss our past or condemn it only to find that we might actually relive it at another great loss of life and liberties?

A word about names. It should be pointed out that at many places the Kearny name is often spelled Kearney. This should not be the case, and John Watts De Peyster takes pains to point this out. "This family were very particular about the spelling of their name, and if such a thing were possible the General would turn in his grave with indignation if he knew that his name was written and printed with two E's, *Kearney* instead of *Kearny*."[3] I am aware of at least two places where this mistake is evident today: a street name at Jefferson Barracks, Missouri, and a town in the state of Nebraska.

I

Beginnings

When the American Civil War began, it was believed that the Confederate States had an advantage in the area of a professional officer corps superior to what the North had to offer. It is true that many of those Southern officers trained at northern military academies before returning to their respective states. It should be observed that even with the South's apparent professional advantage, the North could count on a diverse cadre of officers with considerable experience. All these soldiers, North and South, had one thing in common: they all considered themselves Americans in the same sense that they saw themselves in the mold of all the Founding Fathers of independence. This single notion of independence was on all their minds when war broke out in 1861.

With an initial poor showing by the Northern forces early in the war, it can be argued that this idea of Southern leadership being somewhat superior to Northern can also be regarded as a myth, perpetuated by the seemingly stunning victories of those early years. We should be reminded that prominent historians like Douglas S. Freeman, no apologist for the Southern cause, remarked, "The South was thought by most public men to be opulent in leadership."[1] Freeman believed that this thinking may have been a mistake, for he goes on to point out in his work *Lee's Lieutenants* that "on cold reappraisal ... some generals have diminished in stature."[2] What Freeman was leading up to was that in further analysis it could be argued that there were Union officers of quality, and that had it not been for the attrition of combat early in the war, it was merely a matter of time before Northern officers would define the war.

The Union Army, at the beginning of this internecine strife, was perhaps one of the smallest armies in the world at that time; with just under 20,000 soldiers, it could not be expected to put down the Southern uprising. Many regiments were understrength, so the officer corps at the beginning of the conflict was limited. Some of the most promising officers in the United States Army held their allegiance to their respective Southern

Major General Philip Kearny

states, and they resigned their commissions to serve the Confederate cause. Those events of late 1860 and early 1861 helped to impede the strength of the Union forces.

Beginning a war presented difficulties to both North and South. President Lincoln seemed to recognize this aspect when he said something like both sides were equally green. Surprising as it may be to both layman and professional, what was wanted most, particularly by Northern politicians, was a combat-ready and most of all lucky general officer. This, then, presents us with the realization that the Southern Confederacy did not really have the advantage that was once thought. In fact, Freeman argues that the state of Virginia could barely field enough officers for fourteen regiments, including retirees.[3] He also argues that this was the case, not just in Virginia, but throughout the entire Confederate realm of Southern states.

Where does this leave the Northern officer corps? There was very real teething pain early on, but this was to be expected. The quality was actually there as events were to unfold. One the best and at times most glaring examples was in the person of George McClellan. For many he is a complex problem, and volumes have been written about him. For example, American historian Samuel Eliot Morrison remarks that McClellan's strategic sense was sound and that he traded tactic for tactic in his advance up the peninsula before Richmond. Even his eventual adversary Robert E. Lee thought McClellan was the most capable against him. What did he lack? This situation presents our initial argument and leads us to our subject, Philip Kearny and the juxtaposition between these two will be explored.

Philip Kearny did not come from a martial background. Indeed, his prominent family believed that serving in the military was something others would do. He did have an uncle of considerable recognition, Stephen Watts Kearny, who went against that trend and would become Commander of the Army of the West in the Mexico War. His uncle, probably by this example, had an influence on Philip. Stephen Kearny was aware that there had been certain family members who had loyalties toward England at the time of the American Revolution. Stephen believed that the time had come to cement the family name firmly in the Republic, so he enlisted during the War of 1812 or the Second American War for Independence. By this act, Stephen Watts Kearny set an example that his nephew Philip would take notice of and certainly emulate.

Philip Kearny was born, according to available records, on June 2, 1815, but Susan (née Watts) Kearny, Philip's mother, indicates the family Bible says June 1, 1814, which collateral circumstances would go to prove

I. Beginnings

was the correct date. Philip's home would be at No. 3 Broadway, in the First Ward of the city of New York, which, together with the adjoining building, No. 1, was formerly owned by his great-uncle, Hon. Archibald Kennedy, then a captain in the British Navy. Kennedy married Miss Anne Watts, eldest sister of Hon. John Watts, Jr., maternal grandfather of Philip. Born into wealth and privilege, Philip Kearny did not even have to consider a career that would include military service, but his path would almost be parallel to that of his distinguished uncle, Stephen Watts Kearny. He attended school at Northampton and later Columbia College, where he chafed with boredom at his curricula. In fact, Philip's father and grandfather tried to steer young Philip toward higher education and away from the adventure of a military life; the influence that the stories of adventure that his uncle experienced seemed to attract a young boy's imagination and only heightened his desire to learn more.

He was the only child of Philip and Susan Watts Kearny, and when he was only nine years old, Philip's mother died. This would impact his life in ways not even Philip would realize. Like his mother, he was shy and reclusive, but he initially tried to fit in socially with the New York elite. His father probably did not know how to deal with a motherless child. His concern was mostly financial, and he was famous as one of the founding members of what we today recognize as the New York Stock Exchange. It was in this business atmosphere where he became a successful and influential businessman his aristocratic heritage notwithstanding.

Philip Watts Kearny had considerable influence in the social and cultural community of New York City. His son Philip was expected to follow suit, go to a fine university with New York ties, and pick up the mantle of business or an even higher calling: his grandfather encouraged the young Philip to enter the ministry. In 1830, Philip Kearny came to reside with his grandfather John Watts. "Even at that time Kearny was very peculiar, proud and shy, and averse to those associations which youths of his age generally form from impulse rather than from judgement."[4] In the circles of the well-to-do along the avenues of New York, young Philip came to dislike the staid day-to-day activity of his neighbors and probably even of his father. Alone and without the mediating influence of a mother, Philip did indeed have to create a world within himself, and he would eventually find it in the martial history so foreign to most around him.

From the 1820s, Philip lived with his grandfather until he went off to college. It was understood by Philip's father that the grandfather would provide Philip an inheritance contingent on whether he went to college. Philip would soon attend Columbia University and would graduate from

Major General Philip Kearny

there in 1833. His grandfather had hoped that the young man would continue a path in business, or if nothing else pursue a religious order. The young man had made up his mind and none of the hopes or wishes of his family were going to change it. When his grandfather died, he inherited a large fortune, and being of adult age, he could now decide how best to pursue his life.

Philip now decided to follow his own path, and it was a path that did not sit entirely well with some. Philip had a longing to become part of the U.S. military at a time when the military was not considered a proper place for someone of Philip's social standing. But even as a boy he was thrilled with stories and books of martial lore, and probably had to read them out of sight of his father and grandfather. His inspiration for the study of war led him to Marshal Tilly of the Thirty Years' War, and to Count Lippe of Prussia. When reflection is made upon why these two were chosen for study, it is understandable that Philip Kearny learned that war could only be fought on the offensive and not in a defensive manner. What he learned by these individuals in military history was to move on the enemy's line of march.

There had been some benefits of living under his grandfather's roof. Sometimes prone to being sickly, Philip Kearny seemed to gain confidence and strength under his grandfather's guidance. It helped that he had someone of like mind in the study of military history in his cousin John Watts De Peyster, who, while there in the home, was his constant companion in mock battle. "Almost all the

Major General Philip Kearny was born into wealth and privilege; he went against family wishes and joined the military. Always confident and poised, he was probably the most experienced general in the Union army at the start of the American Civil War. His motto was "Dulce et decorum est pro patria mori" (It is sweet and honorable to die for your country) (Library of Congress Prints and Photographs Division, Washington, D.C.).

I. Beginnings

leisure time of both was spent in mimic campaigns, with armies composed of from four to six thousand leaden soldiers."[5] From the harmless play of two young men, John Watts would get to know his cousin well and would serve with him in the coming internecine strife during the Peninsula Campaign.

Whether or not because of his uncle's association with training the new U.S. Dragoons, Philip believed his course would be in the cavalry. Having completed a college education at Columbia University in New York, Kearny sought a commission in the regular army. He was following in his uncle's footsteps and was eager for an assignment in the west. He sought a commission and was granted one as 2nd lieutenant. "Upon the receipt of his commission, Philip Kearny immediately abandoned the enjoyments of all luxuries placed at his command ... and started for the west."[6] Despite all the attempts of his father and grandfather to convince Philip of doing something other than military service, his intent on a military career was not dented. Soon he was traveling by ship and paddle wheeler along the shores of the Mississippi River for Jefferson Barracks.

In the 1830s, St. Louis, Missouri, was a dusty, dirty but booming mercantile and trading city crammed with a myriad of steam-driven paddle wheelers along its river wharfs, as teamsters and stevedores worked the line to unload the seemingly unceasing goods coming off the boats. Twelve miles south of the city, along the Mississippi River, was the burgeoning military complex known as Jefferson Barracks. Founded in 1826, in large part by the work of his uncle Stephen Watts Kearny, it became the most important training and supply base at what at that time was the entrance to the American frontier. Commissioned a 2nd lieutenant of U.S. Dragoons in 1836, Philip Kearny was among many young officers who would pass through the Barracks, many of whom would play prominently in the sectional strife. Soldiers like Robert E. Lee, James Longstreet, John Pope and Ulysses S. Grant would all go to Mexico together, and then eventually face off against one another in the coming civil conflict.

II

Influences

In the mid–nineteenth century, Stephen Watts Kearny would become prominent in the U.S. Army and to his nephew. Born to a well-to-do New Jersey family in 1794, Kearny was related to several important families in New York City. He grew up in Newark, New Jersey, and attended Columbia University. He soon grew bored with the sheltered environment of home life and the formal education of eastern privilege—a condition his future nephew, Philip Kearny, would also experience and chafe at. Both men came to the same decision: they would reject the cultured world of the east and set a course to help build and protect a burgeoning nation on the move.

Stephen Kearny's career in the U.S. Army began with his experience in the War of 1812, when he bravely distinguished himself with Winfield Scott at the battle of Queenstown Heights, in Canada. Although the battle was an American defeat, Kearny was exhilarated with the adventure. Kearny even impressed his captors with his keen wit and engaging repartee and was eventually released. When war ended in 1815, he went on to be stationed in the new Louisiana Purchase acquisition and the American west, and in so doing came into contact with William Clark, of Lewis and Clark fame, in St. Louis, Missouri. He would soon marry into the Clark family, marrying Clark's step-daughter and settling for a time in St. Louis.

When Stephen Kearny was assigned to the western frontier, he would begin at the then remote area of Missouri at Fort Belle Fontaine, about 12 miles north of the city of St. Louis on the Mississippi River. It was here that Stephen Kearny would come under the influence of generals Henry Atkinson and Henry Leavenworth, who were there to establish an American military presence and establish military posts. This assignment at Fort Belle Fontaine would be the jumping-off point for expeditions that would lead north and west and would define the life of Stephen Watts Kearny as an explorer and a pathfinder. No doubt the tales he heard as a young boy

II. Influences

of his uncle's experiences would inspire the imagination of young Philip Kearny in far-off New York.

Stephen Kearny would prove his worth as an explorer when in 1820 he led an expedition from Camp Missouri (Fort Atkinson) near Council Bluffs, Iowa, overland to the confluence of the St. Peters and Mississippi rivers, a location he referred to as Camp Cold Water, following in the steps of some distinguished American officers who had gone before.[1] Stephen Watts Kearny was not the first to explore the area. Zebulon Pike had passed there in 1807, making his way up the Mississippi trying to find its source. In 1817, Major Stephen Long's expedition also passed by and recorded that the site might be favorable for a military post. Major Long considered that the area of the St. Peters River and the Mississippi River may be an important commerce point on the upper Mississippi River. Also, considering the number of tribes inhabiting the region, the location would give the government an important site for establishing its presence and keeping an eye on possible British influences on the Indians.

Stephen Watts Kearny was from a distinguished American family that traced back to before the American Revolution; this soldier and adventurer was an inspiration to young Philip Kearny (Library of Congress Prints and Photographs Division, Washington, D.C.).

The Long expedition proved to be the first serious military excursion into the newly acquired upper Louisiana Purchase and its upper Mississippi River region. Major Long knew of the Pike Expedition, and based on its findings, the U.S. government needed to learn more. The British were still considered hostile in their Canadian holdings and still had considerable influence on the local tribes, particularly Ojibwa and Sioux tribes. The U.S. government was concerned about British influence on the local Indian tribes and needed to learn more. It possibly could be said that Stephen Long was one of the first government operatives—a spy in the employ of the U.S. government—to report on intelligence issues facing the country in its newly acquired Northwest Territories.

Major General Philip Kearny

Indeed, Major Long's expedition of 1817 into the upper Mississippi country would provide valuable information for the Kearny party to work with. Long made his journey up the Mississippi in a six-oar skiff, making notes on locations for possible military outposts, and it was at the confluence of the Mississippi and St. Peters rivers he made a particular observation. "At the positions most exposed viz.... At the junction of the Mississippi & St. Peters.... I would advise the erection of regular fortifications on a respectable scale.... They should each be furnished with quarters and other appendages necessary for the accommodation of at least two companies in addition to the permanent force respectively stationed at them."[2] Long also believed that the post should be "constructed of durable materials and in other respects possess a permanent as well as formidable character."[3] After Long's recommendation, Henry Leavenworth was sent north to adequately establish a post.

Stephen Watts Kearny made his journey overland across the open prairie and cottonwood-lined streams in the summer heat of mid-continental North America.

> From the opening statement in Kearny's journal it appears that the task was entrusted to Captain Magee, of the Rifle Regiment, Lieutenant Talcott, of the Engineers, and fifteen soldiers. Lieutenant-Colonel Willoughby Morgan, of the Rifle Regiment, Captain Kearny, of the Second Infantry, and two unior officers accompanied the party. Four servants, an Indian guide, his wife and papoose, eight mules and seven horses completed the outfit. The journey from post to post took twenty-three days, and during the latter part of it the explorers had but vague notion of their whereabouts. Their arrival at Camp Cold Water, the destination, produced a great sensation in that garrison, inasmuch as they were the first white persons to cross from the Missouri to the Mississippi River at such distance above the confluence.[4]

It was a defining experience for Captain Stephen Watts Kearny, and would define the respect he would acquire of the land and its environs. On numerous occasions his party encountered ravenous mosquitos and other insects that provided the party with no quarter. They encountered elk and badgers and were utterly mesmerized by the sudden storms that seemed to manifest from nowhere. "[July 8] During last night we experienced a severe storm of rain, accompanied by Thunder & Lightning, which from our exposed situation, in the open Prairie, we find by no means agreeable."[5] But Kearny's assignment was to acquire the confluence of the Mississippi and St. Peters rivers, and using Long's maps and journal notes, he was determined to do just that, no matter what the difficulties were.

II. Influences

By 1819, at about the time Kearny was planning his expedition across what is now Iowa, Colonel Henry Leavenworth was making his way up the Mississippi River with a detachment of troops. Leavenworth reached the site late in that year. "Lt. Col. Henry Leavenworth with a detachment of 7 companies of the 5th Regt. Infantry was ordered to repair to the mouth of the St. Peters [Minnesota River] in the spring of 1819 and commence the erection of Works."[6] He then set about laying out the fort design and structures. "The outfit consisted of 98 soldiers, 20 boatmen, with the requisite supplies, in 17 batteaux and other craft. They arrived 14 Aug., 1819, at the mouth of the St. Peter's (Minnesota) River, and forthwith threw up the cantonment which later became Fort Snelling."[7]

By the time Stephen Kearny arrived at the mouth of the St. Peters River, the construction on the fort had begun. Colonel Leavenworth found that location on the river bottom opposite a standing bluff on the other side of the St. Peters was poorly drained, but he continued building huts for a new fort. This was the post Stephen Kearny brought his expedition to on July 25, 1820, where he was welcomed by Commander Leavenworth, on a site below Pilot Knob on poorly drained soil that was prone to flooding. It was a military location less than desirable in its effects, and was noted thus by Major Stephen Long.

It was here where Kearny and his men did some exploration around the Falls of St. Anthony. Kearny was not entirely impressed with the falls because he had seen Niagara Falls when he was stationed there during the War of 1812. "I must confess they did not strike me with that majestic & grand appearance I had been induced to expect from their description by former travelers—They are, however, very beautiful & probably on account of having frequently seen the immense Falls of Niagara & the high pitch I had wrought myself up to, of witnessing in the savage country a body of water (at a particular point) held in veneration by the neighboring Tribes of Indians, & to which many of them at this day offer their tribute, may account for my disappointment."[8]

Kearny was more impressed with what affect the falls had on the local tribes and wrote, "[T]he Indians consider these Falls as a Great Spirit, & when passing make presents & pay their adoration to them—Some give tobacco; some, whiskey, & all, what they themselves are most fond of— a Drum and sticks were once thrown in & the present accompanied by the remark that as the Great Spirit appeared to be fond of noise."[9] Stephen Kearny had a keen interest in the ways of the American Indian. He would have contact with a number of plains tribes throughout his military career and had good relations with these people, all the while taking into consideration the concerns of an expanding nation and his responsibilities and duties as a soldier.

By 1825, the conditions that Colonel Leavenworth and his troops had experienced at Camp Coldwater were basically as bad as what those troops had encountered in the lowlands at the confluence of the St. Peters and Mississippi rivers in 1820. Stephen Long relates, "[I]n June following he [Leavenworth] was induced to remove from this cantonment in consequence of sickness which prevailed among his troops, which he supposed was occasioned by the lowness of the situation ... and to the badness of the water."[10] This site and the subsequent site of Camp Coldwater did little to help until Josiah Snelling, subsequent commander, decided to remove the camp site to the heights above.

The situation at Fort Belle Fontaine, in Missouri, had not been much better than that at Camp Coldwater. Fort Belle Fontaine had been around since 1806, established shortly after the Lewis and Clark expedition in 1804. It suffered from the same maladies that Leavenworth encountered up river, and it did not improve over time. Located near Portage de Sioux, the fort was well situated for intervening in tribal disputes but was less suited for outfitting military forces for the expeditions the government now wanted to carry out. Fort Belle Fontaine was first a Spanish military post. After the Louisiana Purchase, by a treaty made between the United States government, signed by William H. Harrison and representatives of the Native American Sac and Fox tribes, on November 3, 1804, the fort became a fur trading post of the United States government.

Fort Belle Fontaine was an early addition to the list of forts on the U.S. western frontier. It was established in 1806, at the mouth of Coldwater Creek, which was then called La Petite Riviere, by General James Wilkinson, then governor of the Territory of Missouri. The fort was used by the Army through 1828. Its location was less than ideal, and its decaying condition and the changing military needs of the region convinced the War Department to abandon the fort and relocate its cantonment. The United States government wanted a larger post in order to supply soldiers and settlers as they began to establish settlements and military posts further west.

Up to this time there had been little U.S. military presence west of the Mississippi River. "Until 1818 no effort had been made to establish army posts beyond the Mississippi."[11] With the abandonment of Fort Belle Fontaine, a new post would be necessary. In July 1826, a deed was signed to transfer 1,702 acres of the Commons associated with the Village of Carondelet to the U.S. Secretary of War for the purpose of establishing a

II. Influences

permanent military reservation to replace Fort Belle Fontaine. On July 10, Major Stephen Watts Kearny, with four companies of the 1st United States Infantry, set up camp near a place called Sylvan Springs up from the Mississippi River. It was near this spot, ideally situated near the Mississippi River, that the cantonment of Jefferson Barracks was established in honor of the recently deceased former president and one of the creators of the Declaration of Independence.

The location of the post was on a rise some 50 feet above the west bank of the Mississippi River. One of the particulars of the place was a spring that brought clear, fresh water, and it was not far from where the fort's buildings would be erected. Under the command of Henry Atkinson, the forces at Fort Belle Fontaine began their gradual removal to the new post at Jefferson Barracks. A sprawling complex with much more acreage than Fort Belle Fontaine, Jefferson Barracks would become a training ground and staging area for movement of U.S. interests heading west. It was Stephen Watts Kearny who actually established the site, and although Major Kearny brought the first troops to the new installation, the command of the new post was retained by Gen. Henry Atkinson.

One of the most significant reasons for the locations of these posts on the Mississippi and Missouri rivers was not only the commerce and communications of these highways but the influence of the Indian tribes on them. From Ft. Snelling on the upper Mississippi to Jefferson Barracks at St. Louis, the most anti–U.S. tribe was the Sac and Fox, located at the confluence of the Rock and Mississippi rivers in Illinois Country. Occupying an area that included the mouths of the Rock and Des Moines rivers, the Sac and Fox maintained a strong control of the region for hundreds of years and had good relations with the British authority from Canada. The British wanted to prevent the new United States from moving farther north, particularly since establishing the Northwest Ordinance of 1787. In fact, the British authority encouraged the Sac and Fox to attack United States garrisons along the upper Mississippi during the War of 1812.

It finally all came to a head when in 1832 the Sac and Fox, under Black Sparrow Hawk (Black Hawk), refused to relocate from their ancestral lands and attacked encroaching settlers who were destroying their crops and fencing off their lands. At Jefferson Barracks, General Henry Atkinson was forced to lead a military expedition to put down the attacks and subdue Black Hawk and his warriors. At Bad Axe, Wisconsin, the forces of Atkinson overtook the Sac and Fox band under Black Hawk and a bloody massacre took place, at the end of which Black Hawk acquiesced to Atkinson's demand to surrender.[12] This was one of the last uprisings

Major General Philip Kearny

of the Eastern Woodlands Indians, and the U.S. Army was assigned to transport the leader Black Hawk to Jefferson Barracks. To the credit of the U.S. government, Black Hawk of the Sac and Fox was accorded good treatment under a young Army officer by the name of Jefferson Davis as he was escorted down river to the Barracks. It was soon after this uprising that Stephen Watts Kearny and Philip Kearny's paths crossed.

Stephen Kearny was instrumental in the founding of the post at Jefferson Barracks. As the nation now grew, Kearny's future was interconnected with whatever direction and decisions the leaders in Washington decided. The strategic advantage of Jefferson Barracks would lead to the founding of other posts farther afield in areas that would be advantageous for movement of Americans farther north and west. It would also signal that the Permanent Indian Frontier that was being considered could now be established, leading the U.S. government to fund continuing expeditions to improve relations and keep watch on its frontier borders.

For Stephen Watts Kearny, his service in the U.S. Army continued unabated. In 1836 he was promoted to colonel and appointed to the First Dragoons. In 1842 he was appointed to command the Third Military Department, which was headquartered at St. Louis, a position he held until his assignment to command the Army of the West at the beginning of the Mexican War. This Army of the West consisted mostly of recruits from Missouri and Kansas, and followed the same route of the Santa Fe Trail that had brought the 1845 expedition back from Bent's Fort on the Arkansas River. This time, the Army crossed the river and headed toward the Mexican province of New Mexico.

This American army took military possession of New Mexico and California and accomplished the first military march across the North American continent, a land march of great distance across a desert region. Kearny provided a temporary civil government for the possession of Santa Fe and its territory after its abandonment by Mexican officials. From here he set out to cross the Mojave Desert, and after considerable hardship confronted and defeated Mexican forces outside San Diego, at San Pasqual. He returned to Leavenworth in 1847, and then as brevet major general was sent to Mexico City to oversee the peace after the treaty settlement in 1848.

III

A Soldierly Figure

When Philip Kearny's grandfather died, the way was open to Philip's joining the military. In March of 1837, Philip Kearny was given a commission of 2nd lieutenant of the 1st Dragoons, commanded by his uncle, Stephen Watts Kearny. The elder Kearny had already established himself as one of the best cavalry commanders in the U.S. Army, training units at Jefferson Barracks and Ft. Leavenworth. The idea that Philip would now serve under his command raised his interest with anticipation. Philip Kearny's excitement was probably palpable as he made his way by steamer down the eastern seaboard to New Orleans. There he and the other recruits boarded a paddle wheeler up the Mississippi River, arriving in the spring of 1837. His uncle, now a senior officer, recalled his arrival, noting in his diary: "June 6th, 62 recruits under West & Kearny, who left New York on the 26th April. They came by way of New Orleans."[1]

Stephen Watts Kearny's responsibilities did not really allow him to spend time with his nephew after his arrival. Colonel Stephen Kearny was soon on his way with troops to Fort Des Moines and eventually to Fort Leavenworth, where he would take command of the post soon after the death of the fort's founder Henry Leavenworth. "In 1836 he was promoted to the Coloncey of the first Dragoons ... and until 1843 [1842] was stationed at Fort Leavenworth."[2] There he would be stationed until 1845, commanding Fort Leavenworth and Jefferson Barracks, but it would not be the last time he and his nephew would come together. The expansion of the nation, the establishment of the Permanent Indian Frontier, and the threat of territorial disputes would bring uncle and nephew together in an expedition that would define the country in the mid-nineteenth century.

Philip Kearny soon had the opportunity to interact with the Indians of the frontier. On July 27, 1837, he left Fort Leavenworth with a patrol of dragoons to show the flag and visited an Ioway Indian village at the junction of the Nebraska and Missouri rivers. It was a peaceful visit; the Ioway were impressed by the dragoons, and of course they admired the discipline with which the horses were presented. It was good experience and exposure for the young officer. In 1839, Philip was assigned to the staff of General Henry Atkinson at Jefferson Barracks, where he continued his training. It was while he was here that General Atkinson informed Kearny of his selection to go to France and attend the Royal School of Cavalry.

In Washington, D.C., Joel Roberts Poinsett, Secretary of War, conceived of the idea of sending young officers to the Royal School of Cavalry at Saumur in France. One of those selected was the aspiring Philip Kearny. "Pursuant to orders, Philip Kearny left his regiment to proceed to Washington D.C., 21st May, 1839, to proceed to France on special duty."[3] It was a choice assignment and it would develop young Kearny in the arts of war through exposure to how one of the premier military forces of the time conducted war. This exposure was instrumental in developing Kearny's view on the deployment of infantry and the use and effectiveness of dragoons. Kearny believed that this was an opportunity to make a statement as to the differences between French and U.S. cavalry and present those findings to Mr. Poinsett.

Saumur, France, is located some seventy miles southwest of Paris. It was once the stronghold of the Huguenots before their expulsion from France in the 17th century. The school was located just outside the city, and it is here that Philip Kearny arrived for his introduction in the art of cavalry warfare. The Royal Cavalry School was located here during the French Revolution and played a significant role in training the legions of Napoleon's Chasseurs à Cheval. The three young Americans who arrived here soon began their instruction in horsemanship and the best method to use and deploy the cavalry. Philip Kearny described his intentions to learn in six months the French language, the use of the sword and other arms pertaining to cavalry, and the practice (or pratique) of riding. He hoped for the opportunity to serve in Africa, and soon events would provide just that. The conflict between France and Muslim tribesmen in Algeria afforded an opportunity for actual hands-on combat experience.

This would be no textbook or schoolroom assignment. If anything, it would prove to be lessons in the saddle on campaign. Kearny arrived at a moment when France's North African colony of Algiers was rife with some Arab elements of dissent that had called for jihad against the infidels of Europe. Always troublesome, this area was near the home of the Barbary pirates who had terrorized European and western trade for centuries. Many of the Arabs in the mountainous areas, under the auspices of the Ottoman Turks, were active in slave trading, including enslavement of white captives. As a matter of fact, the U.S. Navy had confronted those

III. A Soldierly Figure

areas, under Stephen Decatur, almost 25 years before. Now France was on the move in North Africa.

Well before Philip Kearny arrived in France, "In May–July 1830, General Bourmont landed a French army, and captured Algiers."[4] In 1839 some Arab tribes under Wahabi leader Abd-El-Kader (Servant of the Almighty) rose up against French control around Algiers. This prompted the French government under King Louis-Phillipe to act. Limited to control along the Mediterranean coast, the French now decided to move against this force, which had taken position in the Atlas Mountains. On the southern coast of France, ports made ready as transports began to load military stores for removal to the North African coast of Algiers.

Since the heady days of Napoleonic France, the country had returned to the control of a monarchy. In 1815, the Empire of France ceased to exist and a mixed monarchy and republic came into existence after the Congress of Vienna. In this difficult blend, the one constant was the French military, which had the experience of the Napoleonic victories wrought from the early Republic and from the Empire. Now under the auspices of monarchy, the French Army continued to hone its skills, and found the Mediterranean area of Algiers fertile ground to promote its officer cadre and continue to develop its military forces. The Ottoman Turks experienced difficulties in maintaining control over the client states in their far-flung empire, including Algeria, which gave the French an opportunity.

Assigned to the expedition command under Marshal Valee, Kearny and the French forces sailed from the southern French ports along the Mediterranean in early fall. In fine spirits, young Kearny was excited with the anticipation of a fine adventure waiting for him in North Africa. The rugged Atlas Mountains cross North Africa west to east, across Morocco through northern Algeria, ending with the Dorsals in Tunisia. An ancient mountain range with an altitude of nearly 8,000 feet, it prevents the Sahara Desert from running over the lush greenery of the coastal cities, such as in Algeria. It's in these high defiles that the Muslim Arabs launched their raids on the French, and it was here that the force Kearny was with would enter to engage.

This expedition set out from the Gulf of Bougia, on the African continent in the Department of Constantine, in October 1839. The object was Les Portes de Fer or the Iron Gates. Once past the gates, the French Army would be in the hostile environs of Abd-El-Kader's territory and would have to drive enemy forces before them. Before the expedition arrived and even while it was in transit, the so-called Mahdi Kader was devastating the environs around Algiers. The land around Algiers was situated in the

Major General Philip Kearny

Metidjah Plain. The mountain of Sahel occupied the rear of the city, and from here one could look out over the Metidjah Plain toward the Lesser Atlas Mountains, an interval of varying distance of some 15 to 25 miles.

The province of Constantine eventually became part of the Department of Algiers under French military command. In the area in and around the Sahel and the Metidjah, Muslim insurgents would not hesitate to raid French-controlled villages and local caravans, carrying off captives. The horrified captives were often sold into slavery, or kept as prisoners in less than ideal conditions and held for ransom. The French conquest of Algeria seemed to have taken place for a number of reasons, dictated by important political and economic considerations and the continued problem of piracy. The war with the Arabs would be a nasty fight and would continue into 1840 and beyond; here Kearny would earn his spurs in combat, giving him valuable experience as one of the first U.S. Army officers to combat with Muslim antagonists.

The commander-in-chief of the French force was Marshal Valee. Under him the Duke of Orleans commanded a light horse division. To this staff was assigned Lieutenant Philip Kearny, attached as honorary aide-de-camp. Kearny was soon campaigning to see actual service and was soon attached to the Chasseurs. "It was a fortunate thing ... that although he had an honorary positions on the staff of the Duke of Orleans, for actual service, his place was with the First Chasseurs d'Afrique."[5] In May of 1840 Philip Kearny was with the First Chasseurs when they ran up against Abd-El-Kader's forces at a place called Mouzaia at the foot of the Atlas Mountains. His manner of fighting on horse was described as "charging with his sabre in one hand, his pistol in the other, and his reins in his teeth."[6] The battle continued all day but was ultimately successful. One French officer recalled: "Kearny rode up to my tent during the battle—a striking soldierly figure—one armed much as we might expect a French General to look."[7] Fighting in the mountains through the summer, Kearny continued to impress the French Command; had he not been an American, he would surely have been made an officer in charge of pursing the tribal brigands. But in the fall of 1840, Kearny's assignment in France came to an end with his orders to head back to the United States.

Kearny honed his understanding of warfare and its applications. It might even be said that Kearny was one of the first to understand the complexity that war was to become. The chance of Kearny to attend the school at Saumur, and to actually to take that instruction and apply it in combat in the mountains of North Africa, allowed Kearny to observe and analyze how forces could be applied and the importance of open maneuver. The

III. A Soldierly Figure

hit-and-run tactics of the Muslim militants was not lost on Kearny. He soon became a proponent of swift action and deep penetration of enemy positions to defeat an adversary. Advance on the enemy's lines of march was seen as essential.

Another thing the youthful Kearny learned was how to know your enemy. He observed how the Arab leader was deceptive in his maneuvers, testing the French forces sent against him. From this experience, Kearny continually advocated direct contact and keeping up pressure on the enemy. Kearny would put his experience in North Africa to use in his assignments in Mexico against Santa Anna's lieutenants, and in the Pacific Northwest, where the hit-and-run tactics of Pacific Indians was somewhat similar to what he had faced in North Africa. Kearny was impressed with how the French conducted their operations, and stated in a letter to Poinsett that the tactics were perfect and conducted in a manner less harassing and destructive of soldiers. (See Kearny's letter to Secretary Poinsett in Appendix A.)

The high plains of the Western United States spreads out in an undulating sea of mixed grasses that almost beckons a person to seek out what is in that vastness that confronts him. Fort Leavenworth sits above the Missouri River on the very edge of that vastness and is almost swallowed by it. The fort was situated up the Missouri River above growing towns like St. Joseph and Independence, Missouri. The fort was also within reach of the Oregon and Mormon Trails. At the fork of the Kansas and Missouri rivers sits the small landing of Westport (Kansas City) and Independence, Missouri, a jumping-off point for the Santa Fe and Oregon Trails, a fitting-out station to begin the arduous journey. The trails filtered away from the banks of the Missouri River, heading into the unknown perils of Indian lands and the western mountains.

The path of the Oregon Trail started out as an Indian path used by various tribes to pursue game, particularly bison, and otherwise maneuver across the Rocky Mountains. It was soon utilized by mountain men pursuing fur pelts, and by teamsters moving freight wagons to the British possessions in the Pacific Northwest in the 1820s and '30s. Soon this trail would become a highway for thousands of Americans settlers seeking better lives. "Economic depression in 1837 and 1841 left desperate farmers and businessmen looking for new opportunities. Politicians urged people to go west, where a stronger American presence might help wrest disputed the Pacific Northwest from British control."[8] The economic difficulties in the east and the Americans moving west prompted the U.S. government to seek a more vigorous accounting of just what the nation was facing out west.

Philip Kearny and his uncle Stephen Watts Kearny were reunited at

Major General Philip Kearny

Fort Leavenworth in May 1844. After returning from his sojourn to North Africa and France, Philip was assigned to be aides to the aged Major General Alexander Macomb, commander-in-chief of the United States Army, and Major General Winfield Scott, with a short assignment at Carlyle Barracks in between. Lieutenant Kearny was probably elated when he finally was relieved from those assignments and was assigned to Fort Leavenworth. He saw his service to his country as action, so the paperwork and political assignments, and the posturing that went with it in Washington, D.C., were more than stifling for him.

Meanwhile, Stephen Watts Kearny was reaching the apogee of a fine military career. Colonel Kearny was not only commander of Fort Leavenworth, but was also commander of the Third Military District, which included Jefferson Barracks. His responsibility was such that no action related to military, Indian and other movements west could take place without first coming across his desk. With an eye on the Permanent Indian Frontier, Colonel Kearny was given the task to show the flag on the frontier and remind the native inhabitants and others who was in command and assert American Manifest Destiny.

This authority presumably came from President James K. Polk. Polk, who was elected the 11th president of the U.S. in 1844, believed that the country needed to settle the Oregon question and secure U.S. boundaries. Polk was also concerned with the presence of foreign governments in the area and soon would give approval for the military expedition. This assignment would encourage Colonel Kearny to survey the interior of the new nation as specifically a military expedition. He would go west along the Oregon Trail and return from the Rocky Mountains by way of the Santa Fe Trail around the Permanent Indian Frontier. This assignment would build on the previous expedition routes of Zebulon Pike, Stephen Long and Colonel Henry Dodge.

The undefined boundary of the Western United States was considered by the U.S. government as the Permanent Indian Frontier. This frontier consisted of the high plains bordering the Rocky Mountains to the west and the Arkansas River to the south. The Arkansas River was the de facto border with the new nation of Mexico. This Indian country had to be investigated and the new forts and posts bordering this region, many established between 1820 and 1840, would be entrusted with safeguarding the area, particularly those trails leading to the far west and the Pacific. This Indian country would soon become the focus of the governing officials who wanted to remind all bordering the region that it was under the faithful watch of the U.S. government.

III. A Soldierly Figure

This expedition would be not only a geographic mapping and scientific adventure, but would also be a military show of force. With the growing numbers of people headed west on this trail and the Mormon Trail, it was decided to show the tribes inhabiting the plains that this belonged to the United States and all movement along the trails was under U.S. protection. The point of interest was to reach the South Pass, which was regarded as the summit for moving across the Rocky Mountains. "Its object was to awe the savages and thus afford protection to the emigrants who were crossing the plains in great numbers on their way to settle in Oregon."[9] It was also a point where the frontier between the U.S. and British Canada was at best tenuous. The U.S. government wanted it to be known that they had a presence there, and wanted all to be aware of this through Colonel Stephen Watts Kearny's expedition.

Since the Lewis and Clark Expedition in 1804, this would be the first serious U.S. military expedition going west towards the South Pass of the Great Divide Basin. There had been numerous north and south expeditions along the Mississippi River, and it should be noted that the U.S. had sent out expeditions before. Zebulon Pike had traversed west toward Santa Fe within reach of Pikes Peak, but had never reached it. He had then decided it could not be reached, and proclaimed that that part of the high plains as the Great American Desert. More information was required, particularly the routes that settlers were now taking to the coast. The Oregon Trail was of particular interest, and it was here that the expedition would make its course.

Previously there had been one expedition that fell somewhat short of its journey west and was not considered an entirely military expedition. This expedition, called the Yellowstone-Missouri Expedition, was led by General Henry Atkinson and was, in essence, a military expedition until it arrived at Council Bluffs, where it was abandoned due to logistical problems with the steamboats. "The failure of the steamboats was a material factor in causing the troops to winter at Council Bluffs and abandon the project of ascending further up the river."[10] The one thing that was not given up on was the geographic and scientific element of this expedition.

This scientific element of the expedition was led by Stephen H. Long, the same person who had recommended the fort site at the confluence of the Mississippi and St. Peters (Minnesota) rivers. At the same time Long was heading west, Stephen Watts Kearny was headed to the site on the St. Peters River in 1820. Major Long had previously selected that fort site, and it would be Long's journal and notes of his 1819–1820 expedition, which was developed out of U.S. concern over British interest in the west, that

Major General Philip Kearny

The caption to this engraving reads, "View of the Rocky Mountains on the Platte 50 miles from their Base." The illustration appeared in an account of the Long Expedition, 1819-1820. S. Seymour, artist; F. Kearney engraver (Library of Congress Prints and Photographs Division, Washington, D.C.).

Colonel Kearny would use on his expedition in 1845, to cross the Platte River expanse and see what obstacles might be there. "Its modern repute rests in part on the fact that it was the first well-equipped scientific expedition to cover the expanse of land from the Missouri river to the sources of the South Platte, Arkansas, and Canadian rivers in present Colorado and New Mexico."[11]

With this information in hand, the expedition of 1845 prepared itself to leave Fort Leavenworth in the spring. This expedition would come to be called the South Pass Expedition and would explore the North Platte River, as Long had explored the South Platte, to Fort Laramie. Along the way observations would be made of the land and elevation, along with a record of Indian life and the geography of the landscape up to South Pass. On the agenda of General Kearny and not officially stated was to make known to the British in the Pacific Northwest that the U.S. planned to see to the safety of the immigrants now spilling into the region. It was also designed to reinforce the point that the United States would expect the British to safeguard those immigrants as it continued to negotiate territorial boundaries, such as the 49th parallel as the future boundary with British Canada.

III. A Soldierly Figure

This military operation would be under the command of Stephen Watts Kearny, and it would cover much of the interior of central North America. "Its object was to awe the savages and thus afford protection to the emigrants who were crossing the plains in great numbers on their way to settle in Oregon."[12] The staff of this expedition consisted of: Lieutenant Henry S. Turner, adjutant and acting assistant adjutant-general of the Third Military Department on the expedition and at the headquarters in St. Louis; Lieutenant William Benjamin Franklin, topographical engineer; and G.J. De Camp, surgeon. With this expedition were five companies of dragoons commanded by Captain Philip St. George Cooke, Captain Benjamin D. Moore, Lieutenant William Eustis, 1st Lieutenant Philip Kearny, and Lt. Richard Ewell.[13] It was a comfortable fit for the young Kearny, and he saw the high plains desert as very much like the arid areas of the Atlas Mountains in Algeria.

This was a combined operation of units from both Fort Leavenworth and Fort Scott. Setting on the Plains along the so-called Permanent Indian Frontier, both Forts Scott and Leavenworth covered the important roads to Santa Fe, New Mexico, and the growing travel along the Oregon Trail. U.S. dragoons were stationed near these trails and oversaw this Indian Frontier, and now would combine in a force to show the flag. Fort Scott would provide Company A of the First U.S. Dragoons for the expedition. Starting out from Fort Leavenworth, the expedition would showcase a number of officers and men who would serve together in the upcoming Mexican War and against one another in the coming American Civil War. Under the command of the newly promoted Captain William Eustis, the Fort Scott dragoons made their way north to Fort Leavenworth from the Leavenworth-Fort Gibson Military Road.

By mid–May of 1845, the expedition headed west to meet up with the Oregon Trail. "The line of march followed was that which is called the 'Oregon Trace,' along the North Fork of the Platte River."[14] The party soon began to observe the differences that surrounded them as they made their way along the banks of the Platte River. Colonel Kearny realized the vulnerability of the slow-moving caravans of emigrants making their way west across the wide-open spaces of the undulating prairies. Stephen Kearny, as commander, made note of the need for way-posts along the trail as the expedition moved along the Platte. Many of the travelers found the Platte a very unusual stream. Coming out of the Rockies, this broad stream was at the mercy of how much water the mountains could send it. The expedition took note of this and recorded, as they stopped one night, "The Platte River, upon the right bank of which we are encamped, is by far the greatest curiosity that we have seen. It seems to be nearly a mile wide, and yet it is so shallow that one may wade across it."[15]

The military party's destination was the trading post at Fort Laramie, and the plains rose imperceptibly as the party moved steadily westward. The description of the plains as a Great American Desert only applied as this expedition passed the Sand Hills in far west Nebraska, just north of the North Platte River. They soon became captivated by great expanse of the prairies and noted: "The prairie is a heaving, swelling ocean of grass, mingling mistily with the sky, like an unbounded sea. In the ravines—or rather troughs of this sea—are occasional streams, or perhaps series of water-holes, bordered with a thin skirt of trees. All else is grass."[16] As intermittent thunderstorms pelted the travelers, the land seemed to open up all around them.

Lt. Philip Kearny must have thought how familiar some of the surroundings were after his experience in Algeria. The mountains he understood well, but the prairie must have been something new to him. As they moved through the lands of the Cheyenne and Arapahoe Indians, among the familiar monuments that came into and passed from the emigrants' view were Chimney Rock and Scotts Bluff, where they camped. There were occasional encounters with some of those plains tribes along the river, looking for goods and trade. One soldier remembered that the party's baggage train, from a distance, must have "presented an appearance of a small blackish head followed by a whitish tail."[17] Dragoon Captain Cooke described the expedition in this way: "The squadrons were gliding two abreast, along gentle curves, over the fresh green grass … with horses matched by company, blacks, grays, and chestnuts."[18] As the party of travelers made their way along the trail across the gently rolling plain, windswept and rain-soaked, they eventually came into sight of Fort Laramie.

Fort Laramie was a remote trading post near the Platte, and a continuing symbol of the mountain men and their fur trade with the local tribes from decades previous. The fort was a convenient place for Indians and traders to barter and profit, and was fortuitously placed for travelers heading to the Oregon country. The Laramie Mountains rose to the west and framed the post, and it made an impression. "Fort Laramie, for an outpost, is a pretty place. It is situated in a large basin through which a clear large stream, called Laramie Forks, flows, skirted with cotton-wood trees … the blue peaks of mountains seen in the west—all these form a scene which, come upon in so wild and desert a region, looks odd, interesting, and beautiful."[19] Colonel Kearny recognized the fort's strategic significance, and it would be consistently manned by U.S. troops from that time forward.

III. A Soldierly Figure

The importance of the expedition was not lost on Stephen Watts Kearny in its impact on the local tribes and the influence of the government's military presence. At Fort Laramie, Colonel Stephen Kearny held a large council with a number of Sioux Indians. The meeting had its desired effect. Kearny wanted to impress upon the tribes that the U.S. government and its military were now controlling the region those tribes inhabited. He also wanted to send a message, through those tribes, to the British authority in the Northwest that the United States had no intention of leaving its settlers unprotected as they moved into Oregon Territory.

The expedition observed how the local tribes lived and made note of how the bison herds made a significant impact on how they lived their lives. "We have passed several large collection of lodges ... for the Indians still come here ... to intercept the Buffalo when they come down from the prairie to drink in the Platte and roll their huge carcasses in the sand and the mud."[20] The men and officers also observed the tribes' way of living, commenting on the conical tepees and the tripods formed by three poles and the accouterments that hung from the center, which the men believed originated from early French influences on those tribes. For the local inhabitants, the presence of Colonel Stephen Watts Kearny was well recognized and, most importantly, well respected by the tribes of the region. He was often referred to by those tribes as Horse Chief of the Long Knives.

Skirting north of the Laramie Mountains, after leaving Fort Laramie, the expedition came upon the Sweetwater River as the Oregon Trail started toward the Great Divide Basin. Some two hundred miles from the fort, the travelers found themselves now among the Rocky Mountains entering the Sweetwater watershed. In days they had made their way up the river and described it: "The Sweet water is rather an interesting stream. For some thirty or forty miles of its course it runs along the base of a chain of granitic hills."[21] This was an astute observation for a party not familiar with modern geologic principles, but contributing to a foundation for eventual physiography and the study of geomorphology.

Excitement now was growing as the Kearny Expedition was nearing its destination. As they moved up the Sweetwater, a curious edifice now presented itself, towering ahead of them. This was the ominously named Devils Gate, a geographic feature now known to be associated with antecedent geomorphic formations. This means that the Sweetwater had superpositioned itself and had cut through the end of a partially exhumed mountain range.[22] To the men of the expedition, it appeared like a large loaf of bread cut in two. For Philip Kearny, it was something like seeing the Iron Gates in the Atlas Mountains in Algeria.

Major General Philip Kearny

When the expedition finally reached South Pass, it was hardly perceptible, as it did not present a defile like that of Devils Gate. The pass presented more of a plateau as they came upon what eventually would be recognized as the Great Divide Basin. One soldier remarked that he "found the country uninteresting stunted with sage bushes."[23] They recorded the position by latitude and longitude but did not stay long, for Colonel Stephen Kearny had another assignment as important as the trek to the Great Basin Divide, if not even more so. They were not going back on the same route they had come; instead, the expedition would be heading south, skirting the Front Range of the Rockies, to visit a contentious area: the de facto border with Mexico.

Understood by Colonel Kearny and implied by the U.S. government was a military understanding that the expedition would investigate an area that President Polk wanted to know more about. Along with the border, the U.S. government wanted to better understand the situation within the Undefined Indian Territory. Most important was the area along the rivers adjacent to Mexico, particularly on the border of the Arkansas River and its environs. There was no river that ran north and south from the Great Divide Basin; rivers flowed primarily from west to east on the high plains. Kearny and his mounted dragoons made their way south from South Pass through the Great Divide Basin and by way of the High Plains Plateau that faced the jutting range and flatirons of the Rocky Mountains. One phenomenon that impressed the dusty riders was that at times, coming off the front range of the Rocky Mountains, a sudden thunderstorm would arise that would spread a shaft of rain that all could view from a distance but which would not cover them as they moved along the range in sunshine. At other times, as the sun shined around them, rain would drench the column as it moved away from thunder and lightning.

The party was making its way toward Bent's Old Fort on the Arkansas River. Previous expeditions had traversed this area. These military expeditions, under Zebulon Pike and Stephen Long, agreed that this steppe offered little and should be bypassed, giving it the sobriquet "the Great American Desert."[24] There was little to sustain them except for intermittent hordes of bison plying the short grasses. By the snowcapped summit of the 14,000-foot Pikes Peak, which rose prominently above the Front Range, the mountains gave off a purple hue as the party moved parallel to the them, seeking the Arkansas River and Bent's Fort. It was late summer by the time Colonel Kearny made the Arkansas River, and by traveling east, he soon came into sight of Bent's Fort, just ahead on the river's north bank. The expedition's dragoons were a welcome sight at Bent's Fort. The

III. A Soldierly Figure

big traders' caravans returning from New Mexico saw Colonel Kearny's force as an indication that the U.S. government considered the area important and welcomed the added protection.

Bent's Fort was a very remote trading post founded by the brothers Bent and Cerian St. Vrain, and it had been serving Santa Fe Trail travelers since 1833, before the Kearny Expedition got there. Being the only post on the Arkansas River, it was a place where Mexicans, Americans, and Indians gathered to trade and rest before continuing their journeys. Occupying a commanding point on the trail, its adobe walls and solitary tower could view travelers from a good distance. It now was part of the U.S., and with the continuing tensions now rising between the U.S. and Mexico in regards to Texas and disputed boundaries by all parties, Bent's Old Fort was an isolated and remote eye on the border. It would be a somewhat short respite for the military party, but an important one, for news of the presence of Colonel Kearny's force would certainly get back to officials in Santa Fe and Mexico City.

The Kearny Expedition was not long at Bent's Fort. Having rested for a time, the uniformed contingent was soon making its way back down the Santa Fe Trail to Fort Leavenworth. Late in August, it passed the red-tinted sandstone of Pawnee Rock, and some of the men knew that Fort Leavenworth was not far. In early September 1845, a dusty cloud could be seen coming up from the southern prairie toward the post. A column of horse soldiers, the Kearny Expedition, made its way into the Fort Leavenworth, dirt-covered but successful. It had been a remarkable accomplishment: the expedition had covered over two thousand miles, gathering a great deal of information on the land and the Indian tribes inhabiting it, and securing a route for travelers with no real confrontation with any of the tribes in the undefined Indian Territory.

All this was done in the remarkable time of about 99 days, with no loss of any of his men, a remarkable accomplishment in the annals of western expeditions, eclipsing all others. It's a testament to the men and to their leader, Stephen Watts Kearny, that this expedition established U.S. authority on the High Plains. In a letter written by Philip Kearny to Secretary Poinsett in 1840, then Lieutenant Kearny compared his experiences in the Atlas Mountains of Algeria as a model for how the U.S. government might deal with the plains tribes inhabiting the Permanent Indian Lands. He believed that rotating young officers through French Africa might be useful, and that some utility might be gained through it. The arrival at Ft. Leavenworth would be the last time Philip Kearny would be with his uncle and the last time he would see him, as tensions with Mexico soon boiled over.

The stark remoteness of Bent's Old Fort can be seen in this print. The fort marked the boundary of U.S. territory with Mexico and was on the Santa Fe Trail in 1845 (Library of Congress Prints and Photographs Division, Washington, D.C.).

In 1846, war broke out between the U.S. and Mexico after confrontation along the U.S. and Texas border. Stephen Watts Kearny was given orders to recruit an army of mostly Missourians and set out to move on Mexican authority in the Santa Fe region of Mexico. The Army of the West, as Kearny constituted it, made its way along the Santa Fe Trail with a retinue of nearly 1,500 soldiers made up of farmers and frontiersmen, including the famous scout Kit Carson. Securing Santa Fe and ousting the Mexican authority, Kearny established a post (Fort Marcy) in Santa Fe overlooking the area. Eventually Colonel Kearny made his way to California, and after a desperate fight near San Diego (San Pasqual), established U.S. presence there.

After returning to his post as commander of the 3rd Military District in St. Louis, Stephen Watts Kearny was sent on a mission to Mexico in 1848, as the military governor in Mexico City. Soon after arriving, he contracted an illness that incapacitated him. "General Kearny returned to

III. A Soldierly Figure

the United States in 1847, and for his services was commissioned a brevet major general. In 1848 he was sent to Mexico, had an attack of yellow fever from which he recovered, but contracted the seed of a disease which finally terminated his life. He died in St. Louis, Missouri, October 31st, 1848 and is buried in Bellefontaine Cemetery."[25] Still convalescing from the war, Philip Kearny mourned his esteemed uncle's death while considering what his future would hold. In 1849, in remembrance of General Kearny, the U.S. government established Fort Stephen Watts Kearny on the Oregon Trail in central Nebraska along the Platte River, on the same route he took during his 1845 expedition.

IV

Valley of the Sun

The tensions between the United States and Mexico became more noticeable when the United States acquired Texas in 1845. El Presidente Antonio Lopez de Santa Anna had been in a dispute with Texas since its war for independence in 1836. Now the United States government and Mexico were at odds over Texas, and tensions with disputes as to where the border would fall. "Mexico protested against the annexation of Texas and broke diplomatic relations with the United States. In July 1845 ... [President James K.] Polk ordered a detachment of the regular army under Zachary Taylor to take position on the Nueces River, the southwestern border of Texas, to protect the new state against possible Mexican assault."[1] The Mexican officials saw the U.S. movements on the border as an affront to Mexican sovereignty and as interference on Mexico's border.

The situation did not improve with Mexico, and the move by General Taylor was considered a provocation by the Mexican government. In Mexico itself, internal bickering between the president and the military ended in a military coup that removed President José Joaquín de Herrera. With further encroachment, the Mexican military skirmished with the Americans under Taylor at the disputed Rio Grande (Rio Bravo, as it was known to the Mexicans), and war was declared. "At noon on Monday 11 May 1846 the war message was sent to Congress.... Congress then declared, 'By act of the Republic of Mexico, a state of war exists between that Government and the United States.'"[2] With this development, Mexico put its military forces under the command of the one general whom Mexicans believed could restore Mexican pride: Antonio Lopez de Santa Anna. The choice of Santa Anna was probably the only viable one. His military record was a mixed one: his experience in Mexico's war for independence made him popular, while the war in Texas, although initially successful, ended with his defeat at San Jacinto.

When war with Mexico broke out in 1846, Philip Kearny found himself at home with his wife and children. By the spring of 1846, he had

IV. Valley of the Sun

resigned his commission, but when war broke out, Kearny sought to be reinstated. "No sooner, however, had the clash of arms resounded from the Rio Grande and the national banner been unfurled amidst the blaze of battle ... Kearny ... sought to recall his resignation, and applied to the government to be restored to his former rank and position."[3] Kearny was well known to Winfield Scott, so when Scott heard of Kearny's request, he acted to reinstate him into the service in the U.S. Army. It helped that Scott was well acquainted with Philip's uncle Stephen, and felt that a fine officer like Philip should be utilized in the coming war.

Kearny was once again back in the saddle, and there was no place he would have rather been. Once his company had been recruited, he decided that they would be outfitted with the best horses he could find. The South Pass Expedition and its two-thousand-mile trek had convinced him only durable animals would be useful. In the Illinois country, it was understood that a cadre of excellent horse flesh was available, and Kearny set out to locate some for the coming campaign. There he met an enterprising young lawyer by the name of Abraham Lincoln, who worked with him to acquire what he needed.

Outfitted as needed, Kearny made his way to his command, stopping in New Orleans. The populace noticed the presence of his dragoons, and it was noted in the *New Orleans Tropic*: "Lieutenant Philip Kearny, nephew of General Stephen Watts Kearny, arrived here ... with as fine a company of cavalry as was ever seen in New Orleans; the horses, ninety in number, are all greys.... The men are picked and noble-looking fellows."[4] Most of this martial splendor was actually paid from Kearny's own personal funds.

Philip Kearny did not directly go to Mexico with Scott's command; instead, his first assignment was with the forces of General Zachary Taylor on the Rio Grande near Brownsville, Texas. Taylor had a successful campaign against Mexican forces at Monterrey. He had advanced as far as Monterrey by September 1846 and defeated all forces against him, and by October had taken winter quarters. "Kearny, with his company, did not join Taylor until after the capture of Monterey, and the advance of the army of occupation to Saltillo."[5] Before this, Kearny and his dragoons had made uneventful sorties along the Rio Grande and came across little resistance.

In 1847 the campaign of General Winfield Scott was finally beginning to get underway. It had taken the form of an amphibious assault, in cooperation with the Navy, to land and capture the vital port of Vera Cruz. For this operation Scott needed as many experienced soldiers as he could find. Scott therefore, in November, requisitioned from Taylor about 5,000 troops to augment his forces. Scott's request stated, "You will put in movement for the mouth of the Rio Grande the following troops: About five hundred regular cavalry of the First and Second Regiments of Dragoons, including Lieutenant Kearny's troops."[6] For Scott to specifically request Kearny and his dragoons to join his forces speaks highly of his regard for Kearny and homage to his uncle, whom he also respected.

Initially Kearny and his dragoons took up assignment as a complement to General Scott's staff. Once Vera Cruz surrendered, Scott struck southwestward toward Mexico City via Puebla. In an interesting historical parallel, Scott took almost the exact route the Spanish, under Hernando Cortez, made their way in the early 1500s against the warlike Aztecs, who occupied the Valley of the Sun (Mexico City). Military history was not lost on Winfield Scott. He understood the land, and more importantly, he understood his adversary, Antonio Lopez de Santa Anna. General Winfield Scott, veteran of the War of 1812 and architect of Mexico's defeat, could be considered one of the greatest military minds of his age and father of the American Army.

Because of his assignment to Scott's party, Philip Kearny initially saw little action as the Americans moved across the Mexican lands. Kearny was exposed to the ingenuity of Scott's plan against Santa Anna's forces and probably made note that this was the way to manage a campaign. "That he profited by the lessons in strategy taught by that superlative commander, at the expense of the enemy, the future proved."[7] In December 1846, Philip Kearny was made captain of dragoons after the Battle of Cerro Gordo, and was soon serving under Colonel William S. Harney as the force made its way towards the Mexican capital. The influence of Winfield Scott was paramount for Philip Kearny. His direction of this army and its success was not lost on the young captain, and its influence would forever mold him.

The Mexican forces were now up against two American armies under Zachary Taylor and Winfield Scott. For President and General Antonio Lopez de Santa Anna, the Mexican situation looked grim as he rushed from one threatened sector to the other, trying to stem the movements of both U.S. armies. Having suffered defeat at the hands of Taylor at Buena Vista, he now faced off with Scott. Moving up from Vera Cruz, Scott was nearing Cerro Gordo on the road from Puebla to Mexico City. It was here, at Cerro Gordo, that Philip Kearny made a cavalry sortie against withdrawing elements of Santa Anna's forces. For Kearny the feeling of having his "blood up" was exhilarating.

There was little opposition against the Americans and Winfield Scott's army as they made their way towards Puebla. With scattered resistance

IV. Valley of the Sun

from Mexican cavalry "Santa Anna … evacuated Puebla and retired to Mexico City. General Scott remained at Puebla for three months, awaiting reinforcements."[8] It was while the American army was reinforcing and training during these three months that Captain Kearny was given the task of trying to gain the release of some Americans captured in previous actions. It all must have been exactly what Philip Kearny expected. This is what he had been waiting to do all his life, since his early years, participating in desperate combat against a seemingly well-trained European-style army.

In July 1847, General Scott decided to take some action on behalf of the Americans held prisoner by the Mexicans. "To Captain Philip Kearny was entrusted the proposals for an exchange, and he was sent forward with two companies of dragoons, under a flag of truce."[9] On July 12, Kearny moved out at the head of the dragoons. Thinking of his mission, Captain Philip Kearny marveled at the sublime scenery of the countryside. Looming before him were the chiseled volcanic mountains, "the Malinche," and the rich dark soil that was filled with greenery very much different from that of the American High Plains, but somewhat similar to what he had seen in the Atlas Mountains in North Africa during his experience there under the French.

Philip Kearny was confident in his mission. The Mexicans were less so, and not so inclined to accept the overtures of General Scott. In fact, the Mexican forces removed themselves at the sight of the American dragoons approaching San Martin on the Puebla road. This had been the site of General Portillo's command, and he eventually would meet with Kearny and his escort. "The next morning, 13th July, Kearny, with Semmes…, and one dragoon to carry the white flag, rode forward to meet General Portillo."[10] Portillo, whom Kearny found to be dour and unpleasant in manner, agreed to forward the request, but "refused permission for Kearny either to continue on to Mexico, or even to proceed any farther."[11] Once the dispatches from Scott were handed over Kearny, the dragoons headed back to Puebla.

The three months that General Winfield Scott's American army spent at Puebla, resting, training and reinforcing their forces, gave the Mexicans an opportunity to take the offensive. Santa Anna instead used this time to readjust his forces for the defense of the City of Mexico. He was more concerned about where General Scott might approach the city and where he, Santa Anna, could rapidly deploy reinforcements. By going to Puebla, Winfield Scott could now approach Mexico City by way of the Acapulco road, moving up in a southerly direction and cutting communication with the Pacific coast.

Major General Philip Kearny

General Winfield Scott and the Army of the South had already decided to remove itself from its line of communication at Vera Cruz and live off the land. By shattering paradigms, Winfield Scott was rewriting how to execute military strategy. This was a lesson that was not lost on Philip Kearny, who would well remember this technique in McClellan's advance up the Peninsula in 1862. On August 7, 1847, the Army of the South removed itself from Puebla and filed up the Acapulco road headed toward Mexico City.

Coming up from the Mexican town of Puebla, on August 10, 1847, General Scott's Army of the South entered the Valley of Mexico. "Scott had abandoned the idea of making a direct attack on Mexico from the east, and accomplished his remarkable movement, from the south."[12] As his forces moved up an increasingly mountainous terrain, the land gave off a spectacular appearance. "This remarkable interior basin, as is generally known, is absolutely closed on every side by a mountain barrier varying in height at different points from two hundred to over ten thousand feet above its bottom.... First to attract notice are the six lakes—Chalco, Xochimilco, Tezcuco, San Christobal, Xaltocan and Zumpango—stretching across the valley in an almost continuous line from north to south."[13] The Army of the South's first barrier as they moved up to the basin toward Mexico City was the Pedregal.

Six miles south of the city, as the Acapulco road enters Mexico City, looms the massive lava field named the Pedregal. Lying on either side of the Pedregal are the two villages of San Antonio and San Augustin. The army had to reduce the fortifications on the other side of these villages to engage the enemy. "While the engineers searched the lava bed for a crossing, their escort clashed with Mexican pickets. This implied the existence of a path."[14] Philip Kearny himself made his way across the Pedregal, and soon army engineers were hard at work creating a road across the black lava. The Mexicans took notice and engaged the Americans on the east side of the Pedregal at Contreras (San Augustin). The Battle for Mexico had begun.

Colonel Harney was in overall command of the cavalry, and under him was Captain Philip Kearny. Kearny was looking forward for some action, and it was not long in coming. Moving from the southern environs of the capital, the U.S. forces found that they had to move by narrow causeways in order to envelope the city and engage the enemy forces. The forces of Santa Anna arrayed themselves along the causeways leading into the city, at bastions called tete du pont. One of these fortified places was located along a tepid little stream, more like a canal, called Churubusco.

IV. Valley of the Sun

The Army of the South moved along in a two-pronged advance toward the center of the Valley of the Sun. The roads were to prove too narrow and were often flanked by shallow and stagnant water that was slowly being drained. It was here that the infantry of General Worth and Gideon Pillow, overtook a "hamlet of scattered houses ... a strong field-work (tete du pont) ... at the head of a bridge over which the road passes from San Antonia to the Capital."[15] Once the site of a church and monastery, Churubusco had now become a choke point bristling with mounted cannons and "swarming with troops, as well as the river banks to the right and left."[16] Having retreated for most of the day with nothing more than delaying actions, the Mexican forces would now make a stand.

General D. Antonio Lopez de Santa-Anna, president of the Republic of Mexico c. 1847, observed Kearny's charge on the Garita at Churubusco and called it heroic (Library of Congress Prints and Photographs Division, Washington, D.C.).

Previous to this time, Kearny was able to affect nothing. Moving over broken and flooded ground, he was joined by the 3rd Dragoons under Captain Alexander McReynolds. Working together, Kearny and McReynolds tried to turn the enemy's left flank without success; however, the Mexicans withdrew, making for the fortified gates near Churubusco. Here, coming up in support, was the rest of Harney's command in time to see the Mexican forces flee from a tete du pont down the causeway towards the San Antonio Gate. "Here, Col. Harney, with a small part of his brigade of cavalry, rapidly passed to the front, and charged the enemy up the nearest gate [San Antonio]."[17] The San Antonio Gate, the main gate to the heart of Mexico City, was heavily manned by soldados (infantry). These Mexican forces started a withering fire at friend and foe pressing toward the towers and gate. Just as the cavalry force was lunging forward, General Scott had decided to take pause of his assaults, and he signaled a recall. Kearny was

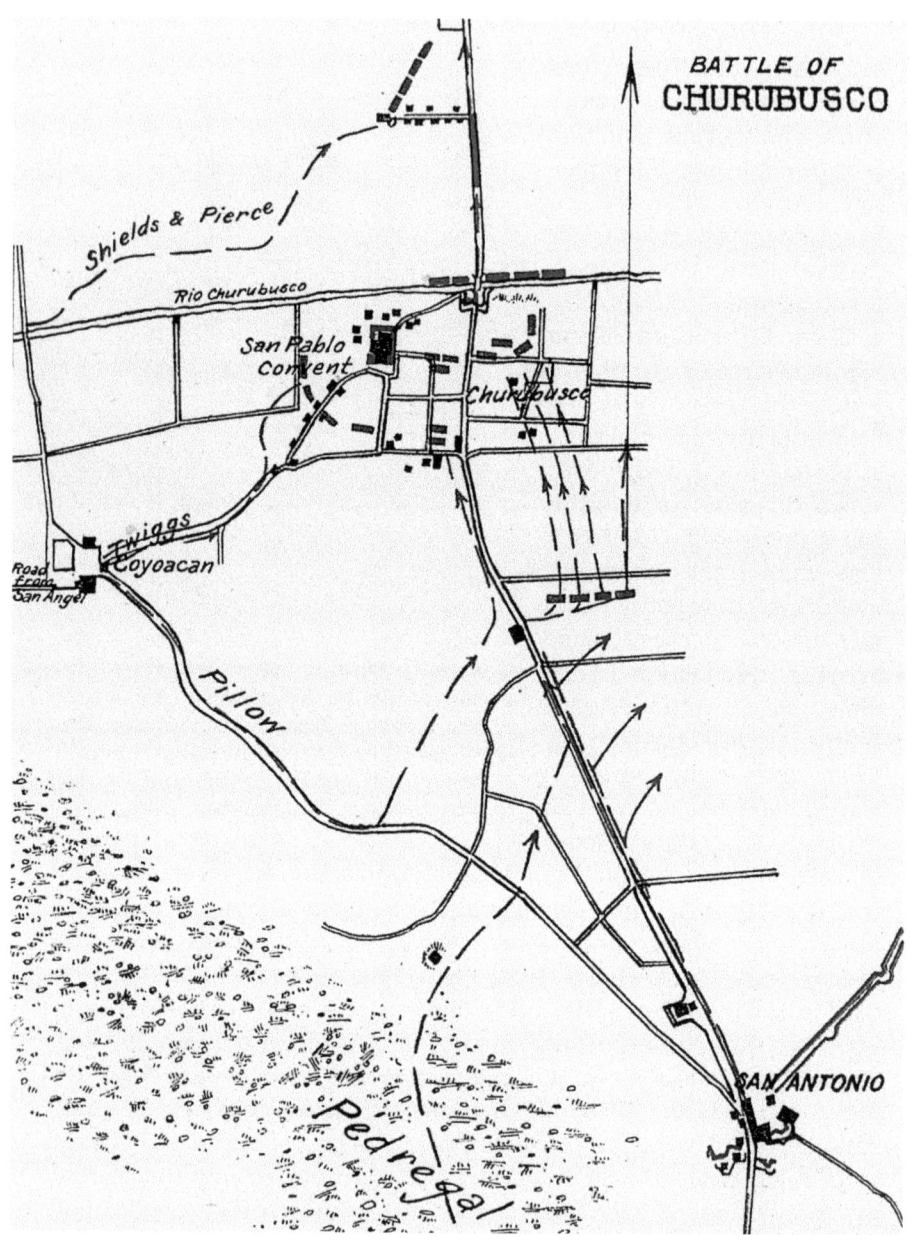

Battle of Churubusco, Mexico (Library of Congress Geography and Map Division, Washington, D.C.).

IV. Valley of the Sun

oblivious to the sound; he slipped the reins of his horse at a gallop, and with Company F, he disappeared in dust.

The infantry assault of Pillow and Worth was mostly spent; the road was littered with broken wagons and other debris everywhere. "The Dragoons had to make their way through the mass of obstacles which encumbered the causeway before they could operate or even form."[18] Not realizing that the recall had sounded, with cavalry aplomb Captain Philip Kearny saw opportunity. Moving forward with a small group of infantry, his dragoons were targeting the garita (guard house) of the San Antonio Gate. Encountering an earthen berm in front of this gate, these few men became embroiled in hand-to-hand fighting. "The cavalry charge was headed by Captain Kearny, of the 1st dragoons.... The gallant captain not hearing the recall, that had been sounded, dashed up to the San Antonio Gate, sabering in his way all that resisted."[19] The young captain's excitement was palpable as he could hear his heart beat faster as he rode in among the enemy. This is exactly what he wanted, facing his adversaries in desperate combat, and he fully expected to be victorious.

At the moment of the attack, General Antonio Lopez de Santa Anna made his way to the San Antonio gate and observed the American attack. He witnessed young Kearny and others, mixing in combat with his dragoons and soldados. In the confusion of this attack, in the midst of soldados and the limited space in which to maneuver, Kearny was hard pressed, and the previous momentum of the charge was slowed and blunted. Being seriously outnumbered, and with men and horses falling all around, the small unit began to remove itself rearward. Kearny mounted a horse and began to extricate himself from the melee. No sooner had he done this than a cannon unloosed a volley of grape and canister at his position, near the San Antonio Gate. Kearny felt the impact on his left arm, and it felt as if a hammer blow had fallen. In that moment the noise seemed to have died away and everything appeared to be in slow motion as Kearny tried to pick himself up off the road.

In the extracts garnished from the Mexican history of the war, the following notation was recorded: "At this moment an American officer, in a uniform of blue, penetrated through the low earthen rampart, mounted on his horse, sword in hand, dealing sabre-blows, and falling wounded on the esplanade. [The placement of this action inside the San Antonio Gate must be inferred from the Mexican account.] Many swords were drawn to kill him; but the others also hastened to defend him on seeing him fall. He rose crippled, radiant with valor, and smiling at the felicity of being at the Gates of the Capital. This officer was Philip Kearny."[20] In the initial impact of the shot, Kearny's left arm was literally shattered. Making his way down the causeway, he realized he had no use of his left arm, and it felt as if it was weighted down. Losing blood, he made his way to a group of American soldiers, where he collapsed. Making a makeshift litter out of a blanket, these soldiers took Kearny to the nearest aid station.

Somewhere down the road, the ragtag group of disheveled soldiers made their way to a makeshift aid station. Moving in and out of consciousness, Kearny recognized Dr. Deleon, who informed him the seriousness of the wound and the need for amputation. At the same time, a future U.S. president, General Franklin Pierce, was present, and offered assistance as needed to keep Kearny still while the surgeon did his grisly deed. With Pierce holding the young man still, the doctor sawed off Kearny's left arm at the shoulder. He then pinched off and cauterized the veins and arteries to prevent Kearny from bleeding to death, and cleaned the wound as best as possible to prevent infection. General Scott was made aware of Kearny's actions that day and heard of his serious wound. Scott, who was genuinely fond of Kearny, often referred to him as one of the bravest and most perfect soldiers he knew, but his service in Mexico was over. (See Appendix B: Extracts from Official Reports.)

As Kearny convalesced back in the States, the war with Mexico ended in 1848. In that same year, news came to the Kearnys of New York that their uncle, the indomitable Stephen Watts Kearny, had died of a fever while in service to the U.S. government. Though saddened at the death of his uncle, Philip Kearny successfully recovered from his amputation. He soon learned to ride a horse while swinging a sword and carrying a revolver in his right hand. To do this, he learned to keep the reins of his horse in his teeth even while in motion. He would not let a disability get in the way as he worked constantly to master horseback combat with just one hand.

By 1849, Kearny was progressing well in adjusting to his disability, and was soon getting back to work. Some of his activities after the war included recruiting in New York, and soon an opportunity would come to once again get back in the saddle and get into action. Unrest in the Pacific would give him his first opportunity since that fateful day in Mexico City. The U.S. War Department cut his orders and assigned him to the Pacific Northwest, where he would participate in putting down the Rogue River Indian uprising. He was promoted to major for the occasion. In 1850, Major Philip Kearny boarded a steamer and headed for the California port of San Francisco. At the time of his arrival, San Francisco had turned from a small port to a boom town due to the discovery of gold in the Sierra Mountains.

IV. Valley of the Sun

While in the Oregon country, Philip Kearny kept a diary of his experience there. Initially his assignment was originally to help remove United States soldiers, principally the mounted rifles stationed at Columbia Barracks and at Fort Vancouver. According to Kearny, the Oregon governor, Joseph Lane, had insisted on having the troops brought in, but thought better of it and instead insisted that these troops be removed. Kearny's mission soon resulted in the Rogue River Indian War, with the intention of clearing the trade routes from California to Oregon.

The situation of U.S. territories on the Pacific Ocean was complex. First, the presence of both British and Russian agents, and their continued influence on the local Indians, was still considered significant. The British still had considerable sway over much of the area, particularly over local native inhabitants in the Washington and Oregon areas. The Russian Empire had once had a presence on the California coast and held the area of Alaska and the myriad tangle of the Alexander Archipelago that stretched like multiple fingers south to near the mouth of Puget Sound, and its influence in the area still remained a concern. Finally, some of the local Indians, encouraged by British agents, had not entirely embraced the presence of U.S. authority, particularly in Oregon, and were reluctant to cooperate with U.S. government or local officials.

By April 1851, Kearny was on his way to Fort Vancouver on the Columbia River. Here Kearny would set out for the Rogue River with the intent of interdicting with the local Indian tribes and their opposition to U.S. control. On June 2, Kearny began his campaign. Governor Lane described the situation: "During the summer of 1851 Major Philip Kearny was informed of a recent attack of the Rogue River Indians ... killing a number of miners and doing other mischief. These Indians at that time [were] the most war like and formidable tribe on the Pacific Coast.... Major Kearny determined, if possible, to give them battle, and finally found them, three hundred Braves strong, in the occupation of an excellent position. He ordered an attack and after a sharp engagement succeeded in dislodging them."[21]

The experience that the young Kearny had in the Atlas Mountains in Algeria, and his service under his esteemed uncle at Fort Leavenworth, made Kearny the likely choice for the assignment to confront the Indians on the Rogue River. Major Kearny's orders were to proceed north to the border of California and Oregon. Here the Rogue River Indians had been unresponsive to U.S. government overtures and were attacking and harassing miners and settlers. "What rendered them more formidable was the fact that they occupied a district which intercepted all intercourse between Oregon and California; scattered along and across the direct road, north and south, on the banks of the Rogue River, which drains a rugged, mountainous wilderness, and flows as a general thing west and perpendicular to the coast, emptying into the Pacific, twenty miles south of Port Orford, and fifty miles north of Crescent City."[22]

For Major Kearny, the opportunity was at hand to implement and develop the precepts that he had expressed in his letter to Secretary of War Poinsett in July 1840. As he points out in his letter, his intent was to observe the tactics utilized by the French component in the Algerian campaign. He viewed the coming Oregon action as an opportunity not only to employ the tactics he had learned, but to show the utility of cavalry over difficult terrain, which may be of use in Indian wars. The only limitation on Kearny was that he would command a small force, but he would utilize it in a way that would be of note for operations by other commands in the future.

In his first engagement since losing his arm, Philip Kearny moved very well in the saddle, seeming to have no difficulties in handling his steed. Moving at a speed that surprised even the Indian force, Kearny moved his men through the mountains and the constant rainy weather to bring his force to bear on the pressed natives. At a place known to locals as Table Rock, Kearny caught up with the warring Rogue River Indians. With only two companies of dragoons, he dislodged the warriors from a prepared position and drove them across the Rogue River to Evans Creek. There Kearny attacked again, capturing forty, including the Great Chief's wife. In two engagements, Stuarts Creek and Evans Creek, Kearny decimated the tribe even after losing one of his lieutenants, Captain Stuart. With the pressure brought to bear on the tribe and the effectiveness of Kearny's forces, the hard-pressed Rogue River Indians asked for a peace.

The speed and positive results of the actions of Major Kearny greatly impressed the local officials, particularly Governor Joseph Lane. The governor had high praise and was extremely grateful. He said of Major Kearny, "I can with great truth and do with no less pleasure bear testimony to his gallantry as a soldier and his ability as an officer. I was then and still am sensible of the great good secured to Oregon by his achievements at that particular time."[23] It was all over in a few months, and Kearny was now beginning to examine his place and his position and whether to continue his service. It was soon, there in the Pacific Northwest, that Kearny tendered his resignation and decided that travel could help restore him in what may be the most difficult time of his life.

By the early 1850s, Kearny was becoming increasingly dissatisfied

IV. Valley of the Sun

with his domestic circumstances. He loved his children dearly, but was becoming more distant from his first wife, Diana Bullitt. At the time of his removal to Rogue River, his wife left him after the birth of their fourth child and took the children to her native Kentucky. Diana never fully accepted the military life and in many ways resented the constant interruptions of her domestic pursuits. She could no longer abide that kind of life, and the strain ended the marriage. Philip also experienced misgivings brought on by his failing marriage, the strain of his recovery from his wounds in the war in Mexico, and his continued frustration with his military career. It all finally culminated on the west coast, and Kearny decided to leave the United States for other adventures. By the time his service ended with the army expedition against the Rogue River Indian uprising, he had resigned his commission in November 1851, and it was too late to save his marriage.

Philip Kearny was now a civilian no longer in the service. He embarked from California for a world tour that first took him out in the Pacific. While in the port of San Francisco, Kearny's military connections put him in touch with officers in the U.S. Navy, one of whom offered passage to the Orient. "Kearny's next letter, dated 14th November, 1851, spoke of sailing the next day in the United States ship-of-war USS *Vincennes*, as a guest of the Commander, Captain Hudson, to the Sandwich Islands, from thence to proceed to China, Calcutta, Bombay, where he expected to arrive in April, 1852."[24] On a cold and foggy day in November, Philip Kearny boarded the USS *Vincennes* and headed out of San Francisco Bay, sailing for islands in the Pacific and watching the shore of the United States slip from view.

With obvious means to support him without relying on the pay of an officer in the service to the U.S. government, Kearny had decided to relocate to France by the spring of 1853. Philip Kearny, now citizen Kearny, arrived in Paris and took up residence at 15 Avenue Matignon. His fondness for France stemmed from his assignment there as a young officer in the 1840s. Now with homes in both France and in Bellgrove, New Jersey, Kearny was keeping an eye on the growing political contention involving the South and its disaffection with northern political directions.

While in Paris, he had caused a sensation in New York polite society, when he started dating a U.S. government customs employee's daughter in France. This ruffled some feathers in New York, and Kearny must have realized that it may cause political problems for him if war broke out between the states. Britain and France had serious financial interests in America, and closely watched the developments there as war clouds seemed to be gathering in the halls of Congress and the states. In April 1861, at Charleston, South Carolina, the federal installation at Fort Sumter was shelled. French newspaper headlines were replete with news of war between the citizens in the U.S. Living in Paris, Kearny was reading of the events in the U.S. and knew that he must return to the States and offer his service. He was in favor of restoring the Union, and was concerned that the nation his father and uncle had worked so hard to establish was now preparing break apart. Philip was hoping for an appointment from his native state of New York. This may have been too optimistic. Kearny had been gone for a while, and politics in the state and the federal government were not the same as when he had left.

When he returned from France in 1861, Kearny took up residence at Bellgrove, the family residence of the Kearny family near Newark, New Jersey; he had been involved in a contentious divorce from his first wife and was settling in with his new family. He had met and married a vivacious young woman in Paris named Agnes Maxwell. This did not sit well with most of the social elites in New York. Agnes's father was a U.S. Customs official from the New York Customs house. This institution was, at that time, the largest means by which the U.S. government obtained revenue for its coffers. Many a prominent American vied for the role as a customs official in service to the U.S. The future governor of Minnesota, Alexander Ramsey, was much more interested in becoming tariff collector of the port of Philadelphia than the governor of an undefined territory, and he accepted the post only after a number of others turned the governorship down. Lucrative as customs was, it was also heavily influenced by the corrupt political organization of New York's Tammany Hall. It had a great deal of influence on New York politics, which many in the New York elite accepted, but also turned a blind eye to.

Kearny's family association with a customs official probably displeased many of these people who had political influence in Albany, well-heeled influential families who wanted to see their sons gaining commissions in the new Union Regiments from New York. Of course, many of these people believed the war would be of short duration, and therefore hoped to gain political advantage for their offspring. Kearny, as opposed to most, had just come off the battlefields of the Piedmont in the Franco-Austrian War; he understood what this war could become and had no illusions of what the fight would entail. He was for restoring the Union, but he had friends who had served with him before the war who now were on the Confederate side. People like John Bankhead Magruder and Roberdau Wheat, trained soldiers who would now oppose him in the coming conflict. Kearny's experience and knowledge did not count for much with some in the state of New York.

When Kearny returned to the U.S. from France, he was not immediately considered by his native state for a commission. The well-heeled New York politicos seemed to ignore Philip Kearny's experience and sacrifice (he had even been awarded the Legion of Honor). His relation with the Maxwells probably did not help his cause, nor did his association with Agnes Maxwell and the ugly separation from his wife. Fortunately for Philip Kearny, this did not deter him. Just across from New York was the state of New Jersey, and New Jersey was in need of qualified officers. Kearny was a resident of that state, and the governor there was more than willing to offer a commission to Kearny. The State of New Jersey consented. It was here that Kearny was offered command of the First New Jersey Brigade of Infantry Volunteers.

V

Camp Seminary

The fact that Kearny had real military experience at home and abroad would lead one to believe that it would set him in good stead when war broke out between the states in 1861. The case for this argument can best be illustrated by his performance in Europe just three years before. He had been living in France since 1851, and putting aside his difficult personal life, Kearny decided to offer his military services to that country when in 1858 relations with the Austrians over the Italian Piedmont rose to a pitch. The rise of nationalism versus what had been recognized by the Congress of Vienna in 1815 came to a head with Italy's bid for unification. Lines were being drawn by the old guard, and the Austrians were set against Italy's being reunified.

For many years, Austria and France had been taking careful note of an Italian Peninsula that had been broken and susceptible to influence. The Piedmont in northwest Italy was vying for unification with the rest of the country. France, under Napoleon III, was in support of Italian unification and offered the Piedmont and King Victor Emmanuel support if Austria threatened. In 1859 war broke out between France and Austria. With Italian forces gathering to confront Austrian Armies on the march, France moved to support the Italians.

Philip Kearny was interested in getting back in the saddle and soon offered his service to the French authority. Initially Kearny believed that he may be able to regain the post he had held when he was there in 1840, with the Chausseurs d' Afrique. This was not to be. Instead the French military authorities, realizing Kearny's ability and knowing of his U.S. citizenship, decided to appoint him to the staff of General Morris. Kearny considered it a distinguished honor to serve under the general, since he had served with Morris in the Algerian campaign in 1840. "Dressed in uniform as a major of the First Regiment, U.S. Dragoons, Philip Kearny left Paris on May 12, 1859, the day after the departure of Napoleon III."[1] French élan was on full display as the French army moved on to the Piedmont of Italy.

V. Camp Seminary

The Franco-Austrian War was not the ordinary fare that the European continent was accustomed to. Even before the American Civil War began, this war would set an example as how brutal modern war would become. In the Battle of Solferino, the combined armies of France, Piedmont and Austria totaled more than 270,000 men. Kearny took part in a battle that consumed a total of nine hours. In that battle some interesting innovations in arms took place. The conical Minié ball, made for a rifled barrel, was used, as well as the novel tactic of communication by wire telegraph, and troops were actually transported, where possible, by rail.

The Battle of Solferino proved to be vicious, with little quarter given before it was over. The battle was considered basically a draw, with casualties lying all about the Italian countryside. Kearny remembered it this way: "I have roamed about everywhere, and in the day of Solferino, I was not only present with the line of our cavalry skirmishers, [but] as well in every charge that took place. That day I was mounted from six in the morning till eleven at night."[2] The night before the battle, some scouts had mistakenly sent Kearny toward some enemy pickets, and he remembered how he made a miraculous escape from those sentries in the darkness. This would become an all too often experience for Kearny and it seemed to beg ominously for the future.

Not long afterward, Austria acquiesced and the Franco-Austrian War ended. So did Philip Kearny's association with Europe's entanglements. His attention was increasingly focused on the newspapers from America and the growing tensions between the Southern states after the election of 1860. Kearny saw the crisis as the U.S. was now presented with secession. "Early in the spring of 1861, on receiving the first reliable intelligence of his country's imminent peril, Kearny broke up his luxurious establishment in Paris, took ship for the United States, and without the loss of an hour, as soon as he arrived in New York."[3] After all the difficulties with getting a commission, once Kearny had one he was prepared to make good use of it, even with the war underway.

Alexandria, Virginia, was awash with activity. The noise was tremendous just south of the city as the largest military operation in North America was underway. Philip Kearny stood on the dock looking at the huge undertaking before him; his concern was for getting his regiment on board safely. He was back in his native land and in the midst of an internecine strife which would pit him against many of his Southern friends whom he had known well before the war. Kearny understood that they would be just as interested in pressing the Union, and he knew what he had to do to press them even more, friends or not.

Before them was a host of ships with steam cranes loading supplies on side wheelers and schooners while barges were being loaded with wagons, horses and artillery pieces. "Nothing comparable to it would ever be seen again.... Vessels of every imaginable kind arrived by the hundreds at the wharves of the historic little brick town that had marked the head of the deep-water navigation on the Potomac since colonial days."[4] The Union Army of the Potomac was on the move. A campaign of monumental proportions was at hand, but where was it headed?

Kearny knew what it meant to have these forces in motion. Outside the secure confines of Washington's fortifications, a campaign was underway that had never before been attempted. He had waited a long time and truly wanted to be involved in the action. He already thought that he was a latecomer; the war was already a year long, and its progression was leading to a continuing stalemate. The commission he had so wanted came in July, just prior to the first Battle of Bull Run. It was not the ideal situation he had envisioned, but he could not sit by as the war continued; he had to make a decision as soon as he could.

The journey to this point of command was a tortuous one filled with political pitfalls. He was always confident in his military capabilities and was well respected by the French officer corps for his exploits in battles in Europe and Africa. He was highly regarded by his fellow American officers he had served with in the Mexican War, both North and South. He believed the value of his experience was unmistakable and he would immediately be offered substantial command. This was not immediately forthcoming from avenues he expected, but he did land the opportunity to command the First New Jersey Brigade, and he readily accepted.

In August 1861, Philip Kearny's commission came from the State of New Jersey, and he came to command the First, Second and Third New Jersey Regiments of volunteers. As a brigadier general, he found his regiments under the command of the division of William B. Franklin. Kearny's regiment was posted near Pohick Church in northeast Virginia, and settled into the camp routine of drill. When he arrived in August 1861, he found the regiments of the First, Second, Third and Fourth New Jersey poorly disciplined and lacking morale. The men possessed none of the soldierly qualities that Kearny would expect in all soldiers, no matter what their rank was. His troops had found little sign of the enemy, and he reported that he believed that at best there was "minimal confederate activity in his area." referring to the Confederate presence as a variable one.[5]

V. Camp Seminary

The Jersey unit had been held in reserve during the Battle of Bull Run, and by the time Kearny arrived, the initial jubilation of going off to war had lost its appeal to these New Jersey volunteers. Corporal Charles Hopkins admits that his comrades, considered a bunch of miscreants and malcontents, had been reduced to participating in nothing more than merriment and mischief. With Kearny's arrival, free time was over; close-order drill was the constant activity from morning to night, and weapons were cleaned in between. Even Corporal Hopkins admitted that by the end of summer the unit had become well-ordered and well-trained.[6] Soon all the New Jersey regiments became well acquainted with the intentions of their new commander Philip Kearny. Kearny made it known what was expected of them and what they could expect from their commanding officer. Kearny made sure his officers followed suit so that esprit de corps was maintained and discipline enforced.

By October 15, 1861, Kearny and his New Jersey regiments became part of the newly formed Army of the Potomac.[7] Shortly after the new army was formed, a stinging defeat of a part of that army occurred along the banks of the Potomac River near Leesburg, Virginia, at a place called Ball's Bluff. This disaster had a significant impact on the political influence that now was to permeate the ranks in the Union armies. The results of Bull Run and the disaster at Ball's Bluff resulted in the federal government's establishment of a committee to monitor military activity. The Congressional Committee on the Conduct of the War would lead to unfortunate results. When George Briton McClellan became commander of the Army of the Potomac, he was very aware of this committee, and it had some impact on his plans for attacking the Confederate States. The Congressional Committee would have a psychological effect on many an officer in the Union on how they executed their plans, and many, like McClellan, may have allowed it to influence their thinking.

The plan was for striking from the area around Fort Monroe up the Peninsula between the James and York rivers toward the Confederate capital of Richmond. Kearny believed in striking from the outskirts of Washington and had little confidence in McClellan's plan. He had already proved to his superiors in March 1862 that the forces outside the city were negligible.[8] General McClellan believed that to strike south on the Peninsula, where he believed the Confederate forces were light, could unhinge the enemy force and he could take Richmond. Little did McClellan know that General Joe Johnston had already moved much of the Confederate Army to Richmond.

Kearny and his New Jersey Brigade's first engagement was in spring of 1862. As part of Franklin's Division, his unit was sent out from Camp Seminary to the area near Fairfax Courthouse on the road leading to Centreville, Virginia. Kearny led his regiments forward with cavalry covering his movement: "[T]he Third Regiment New Jersey Volunteers has been so far in the advance, the Second supporting it Colonel Simpson holding Fairfax Station."[9] Kearny found that the Confederates had abandoned the area and reported that he could hear trains continually running in the direction of Manassas Junction.[10] "Sangster's Station, March 9th 1862: The First New York and First New Jersey Regiments—Kearny's ... present command—reconnoitering in large force over a wide area far in advance of the Federal Army, decided the Confederate Commander to close his decision to abandon Manassas. Kearny pursues; defeats Confederates at Sangster Station and occupy their stronghold. McClellan orders the Army to retreat."[11]

In his official report, Lieutenant Colonel Robert McAllister of the First New Jersey Infantry said, "Permit me to say that General Kearny deserves a great deal of credit by his bold push towards the enemy lines, and the energy and bravery thus displayed caused the enemy to leave in great haste, leaving many valuables behind them."[12] With river bridges blown in the area, Kearny took the initiative to occupy the surrounding area around Centreville, as he states, to "protect his flanks."[13] He believed there was opportunity here to move on the enemy, or as Clausewitz stated in *On War*, it was time for "reciprocal action." As it was, Kearny would have to remove from his position outside Centreville and relocate his command to the loading areas of the military wharfs at Alexandria, Virginia. The move on the Confederates would not be by land, as Kearny believed that it should be, but by sea transport for an operation down river along the Potomac.

As he peered out over the Potomac, watching the transports load his troops, Kearny could take some satisfaction that he had now been promoted to major general. In Special Order No. 75, Kearny was now assigned to command Edwin Sumner's Division. This order came from Commanding General of the Army of the Potomac George McClellan. We do not know if this was due to Kearny's action outside Centreville. The more obvious reason was probably the reorganization of the Army of the Potomac due to its move down the Potomac River to the Army garrison at Hampton Roads, Virginia.

As well-rounded a soldier as Kearny had become, one would think he would have welcomed this new command, but his feelings were mixed. He had become very fond of his Jersey Blues and insisted that he would accept this command as long as his Jersey Blues were part of his division. Kearny's

V. Camp Seminary

corps commander, William Franklin, did not believe that this would be possible and refused the request. Brigadier General Philip Kearny reiterated his request and then decided to decline the promotion.

The rank and file of the Jersey soldiers heard what their commander had done when he personally informed them. With that, a resounding cheer went up from those men.[14] On March 20, 1862, the legislature of New Jersey passed a resolution declaring "That New Jersey highly appreciates the disinterested fidelity of General PHILIP KEARNY, in declining pro-offered promotion."[15] It was probably a shrewd political decision and would work in favor in Kearny's future, as events would now develop. These events were now looming large for the Army of the Potomac. "The affairs of the Rivers," as Kearny referred to the operation, was off and sailing; by mid-March, Union forces were moving off the wharves at Alexandria. The destination was the strongly fortified bastion of Fort Monroe, Virginia, adjacent to Hampton Roads. It took weeks to ferry the troops and all the equipment necessary to move an army. It would prove to be a logistical challenge never before attempted and would be considered one of the greatest feats in military history.

Kearny and his brigade embarked on the steamer *Elm City* on April 16, 1862. From Alexandria the steamer made its way down the Potomac to the Chesapeake Bay into the Poquoson estuary near Ship Point north of Fort Monroe. Kearny recalled the journey as "cribbed, crammed and confined."[16] He was concerned that so many soldiers were allotted so little space, and believed that if they were kept there too long, it would lead to a number of problems. General Kearny was relieved when they disembarked to solid ground at Ship Point on April 30. It was at this time that Kearny learned that he had been ordered to a new command.

Acting Union Quartermaster General Brigadier General Stewart Van Vliet was in charge of establishing "a large depot for all kind of supplies at Shipping Point ... for the forwarding of stores up the Poquoson River."[17] With a myriad of offloading activities going on all around him as stores were being gathered, Kearny learned that Brigadier General Charles S. Hamilton was being replaced. The lateral command came from General McClellan in Special Order No. 129, dated April 30, 1862. "Brigadier General Philip Kearny is assigned to the Command of the Third Division of the Third Army Corps in place of Brigadier General C.S. Hamilton, relieved. By Order of Major General McClellan."[18] Since he was already listed as Hamilton's second in command it was natural that Philip Kearny was the logical choice to assume this command. Indeed, his acceptance of this command was understated, and he went to meet his new brigade commanders Brigadier General Charles Jameson, David Birney and Hiram Berry.

The promotion was a bittersweet opportunity for Kearny, for now he had to say goodbye to the Jersey soldiers he had trained into a cohesive unit. He did leave with a great deal of respect of those soldiers, and now he had the opportunity to march to the sound of gunfire, something he was anticipating. The opportunity was now at hand, opening the next phase of the generalship of Philip Kearny.

The logistical problem that Kearny and generals like him would face down on the James-York Peninsula would be unprecedented. Here was the situation of the U.S. Army at the beginning of the War Between the States. On January 1, 1861, the Regular Army of the United States consisted of 1,108 officers and 15,259 men organized into 19 regiments: 10 infantry, 5 mounted and 4 artillery. This was a wholly inadequate force to face any enemy, let alone a regular standing force like the Confederacy or even Mexico.

Spread over an extensive continent and a nation still in the growing stages, the U.S. Army was overextended, which made the logistical situation monumental. With the outbreak of war in 1861 and the call for 300,000 volunteers, the Army would have to adapt to a changing situation. "Both the passage of time and the new, strenuous, and urgent demands of the Civil War brought new men to the fore in the supply departments. Quartermaster General Thomas Sidney Jesup died in June 1860 after 48 years at his post. The next senior man in the department had been on duty since 1819 and was passed over in favor of Major Ebenezer S. Sibley. Sibley then served as Acting Quartermaster General until the appointment in May 1861 of Brigadier General Montgomery C. Meigs, who served as Quartermaster General for the remainder of the war."[19]

Kearny's division, like all others in the Union Army of the Potomac, would experience the vagaries of logistics in the Civil War. The rank-and-file soldier would be in need of these accouterments, as furnished by the federal government. The soldier's load consisted of about 45 pounds, including a rifle-musket and bayonet, 60 rounds of ammunition, three to eight days of "marching or short rations" carried in a haversack or knapsack, a canteen, and a blanket. This also included a shelter half which he would share with another comrade carrying another half in the field.

By and large the Union armies were well fed. Their sustenance in the field included: 20 oz. of salt or fresh beef, or 20 oz. of pork or bacon; 18 oz.

V. Camp Seminary

of flour or 20 oz. of corn meal; 1.6 oz. of rice, .64 oz. of beans, or 1.5 oz. of dried potatoes; 1.6 oz. of green coffee or .24 oz. of tea; 2.4 oz. of sugar, .54 oz. of salt, and .32 gill of vinegar. "Peas, hominy, or fresh potatoes could be substituted, and bread, either soft or hard [hardtack] was provided when possible in lieu of flour."[20] This was the main source of sustenance for the U.S. Armed Forces during the war, and was mainly consistent during the course of the war.

Of course, for transport the soldier in the ranks had simply to march from one point to the other. Other means for transport were available when needed. Water transport would prove to be crucial for this movement down the Potomac River to the Chesapeake and Hampton Roads. This was significant, for it proved that large armies were capable of dramatic maneuvers. "The most spectacular water movement of the Union army was the transportation by sea of the Army of the Potomac from Washington to Fort Monroe at the beginning of the Peninsula Campaign."[21] Planned in over five weeks, this was a rapid and surprisingly successful movement which incurred very few losses in matériel.

Moving by sea would prove easier than movement by land. The men responsible for this task were well qualified. The army that made its way to the Peninsula in the spring of 1862 was the largest in American military history to that point. The force that was sent in the Mexican War did not exceed 41,000 troops and moved independently in two columns under different commands. The Army of the Potomac on the Peninsula would number no fewer than 100,000 effectives. The largest logistical operation the army was responsible for before this was the Mormon Campaign in 1857, and that operation was less than successful from a military operation standpoint.

It would be entirely problematical for the Peninsula operation to be successful. The men responsible for this logistical operation understood completely what was required. Brigadier General Stewart Van Vliet was the chief quartermaster for the Army of the Potomac and would travel with the army's headquarters. His lieutenants would be Lieutenant Colonel Rufus Ingalls and Captain Charles Sawtelle; all three came as West Point graduates. Moving the stores by sea was probably much easier than what the quartermaster would face on land. Still, none of them expected the woefully inadequate maps that McClellan was relying on. What faced the army was a peninsula that consisted of small, poorly drained roads ill-suited to the size of the force that would traverse them.

The bay and the York River would become a valuable asset for Van Vliet. He established two depots on the York River, one at Ships Point,

Major General Philip Kearny

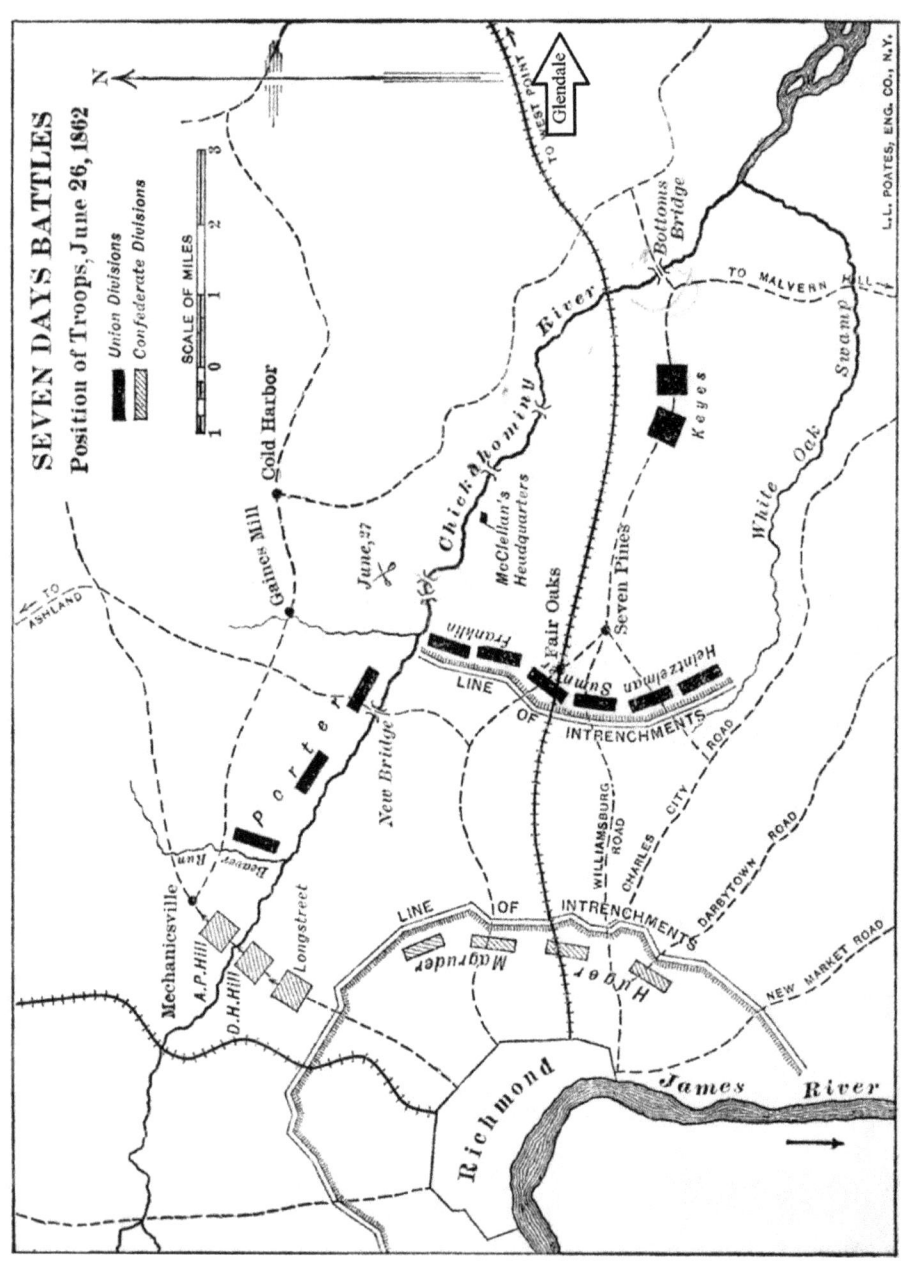

Campaigns of the American Civil War (Library of Congress Geography and Map Division, Washington, D.C.).

V. Camp Seminary

where Kearny disembarked, and a larger one at Cheeseman's Creek. When the Confederates abandoned their river batteries near Yorktown, this allowed the Army of the Potomac to augment movement of supplies. Again, the one problem would be the roads and the wagons that would ply them. To help move material somewhat more easily, the army engineers cut down the abundant trees in the area and corduroyed the roads.

Once the Confederates were gone from Williamsburg and Yorktown, the Army of the Potomac moved on White House Landing and was in possession of the Richmond and the York River Railroad. The possession of this rail line allowed resupply of McClellan's forces in a much more efficient manner, but still did not make up for the deficiency in the road transport, which was still the main source for most of the individual units' supplies. This problem would be exacerbated when and if McClellan would have to abandon White House Landing and change his base. The army of the Potomac would have to move briskly over a low and wet geographical region, heavily wooded with little upland and wide wetlands. It was soon found out by the corps and division commanders that, as Kearny put it, the army would take the pace of a Virginia creeper.

VI

Williamsburg

Now operating in what could be considered enemy territory, the Army of the Potomac was making slow progress. The logistical situation was less than ideal, and many of the men took the skeptical view that the operation was folly, even though President Lincoln approved it. He believed, and Kearny recognized this, that the enemy could just as well be fought outside Washington. Lincoln wrote to McClellan:

> I suppose the whole force which has gone forward for you is with you by this time, and, if so, I think it is the precise time for to strike a blow. By delay the enemy will relatively gain upon you—that is, he will gain faster by fortifications and re-enforcements than you can by re-enforcements alone. And once more let me tell you it is indispensable to you that you strike a blow. I am powerless to help this. You do the injustice to remember I always insisted that going down the bay in search of a field, instead of fighting at or near Manassas, was only shifting and not surmounting a difficulty; that we would find the same enemy and the same for equal entrenchments at either place. The country will not fail to note, is now noting, that the present hesitation to move upon an entrenching enemy is but the story of Manassas repeated. I beg to assure you that I have never written you or spoken to you in greater kindness of feeling than now, nor with a fuller purpose to sustain you, so far as, in my most anxious judgement, I consistently can. But you must act. Yours Truly, A. LINCOLN[1]

With this urgency and the reminder of Washington's concern for forces that may be nearby, McClellan now found his army before an entrenched and fortified Confederate force inside Yorktown.

Moving an army of this size was problematic and became increasingly so as the days moved on. The terrain on which the Army of the Potomac found itself was poorly mapped and ill-suited for maneuver, and when it started to rain, the problems only became magnified. The life of the army would increasingly be in the hands of the logistical command of the Army of the Potomac. This command would provide a valuable service in the face of all of the said problems and more. Under the command of Van Vliet, the Army of the Potomac would move like a leviathan as it crawled onto the tidewater shores of Virginia.

VI. Williamsburg

Logistics would become vital in these conditions. As previously indicated, the army had an excellent logistical expert in Van Vliet. To prepare depots on the peninsula, most stores would have to be supplied by ship and moved forward by railroad where available. Kearny's division of nearly 12,000 men would need the following:

3 wagons for division staff...
9 wagons for brigade staff,
1 wagon for division artillery,
80 wagons for regiments,
10 wagons for artillery ammunition,
10 for entrenching tools tents commissary etc.[2]

It was not a surprise that the army was slow to move in order for the campaign to begin.

When Kearny took command of Hamilton's Division, it had already made its way to its present encampment before Yorktown by way of the road to New Bridge and Big Bethel. Upon his arrival in April, Kearny found out that his good friend John Magruder (whom he knew well before the war) was believed to be in command of the forces opposite him. The earthen ramparts the Confederate forces were behind were described as "lines of entrenchments and mounds of redoubts ... like a chain across a field."[3] On Saturday, May 3, 1862, Kearny's official first day of command, the adjutant general had his force of over 8,900 facing these enemy works.

The weather had begun to deteriorate since April. This did not help McClellan bring up his siege guns, which he expected to use on Yorktown, so Kearny and his men waited outside the Confederate works. When the weather did clear, the opportunity presented itself to launch some observation balloons that had been brought to the peninsula by Thaddeus Lowe. When the Confederates ceased artillery fire, the balloons went aloft, and the Union spotters reported back that the Confederates could not be seen anywhere.

At 6:00 a.m. Sunday, May 4, Kearny allowed General Jameson to feel out the enemy positions. He soon reported back that his skirmishers had found the enemy absent, leaving empty tents and unattended campfires. Kearny soon had his division moving toward a defensive work called the Red Redoubt. The 38th New York (Scotts Light Guard) and the 40th New York (Mozart) Regiments soon occupied those works without having fired a shot. General Kearny reported to his superior General Heintzelman, who soon reported to his superior General McClellan that the enemy indeed was gone. On the same day, Kearny received orders for the first Division

Major General Philip Kearny

VI. Williamsburg

to be ready to pursue those forces down the Williamsburg road or have his "division ready to move at once."[4] Kearny had now been in command for only five days.

Having replaced General Hamilton (see Appendix F), General Kearny may or may not have known that more politics was involved in his promotion than was thought. General McClellan and President Lincoln continued to spar over McClellan's progress up the Peninsula. Lincoln had written McClellan on Hamilton's dismissal that he had "lost the confidence of at least one of your best friends in the senate."[5] If Kearny knew about this, it did not faze him, and he continued on his duty and responsibility, which was to strike at the enemy. He was not a proponent of this operation, but he had an opportunity and he certainly was going to make the best of it. As he relished the thought of action, Philip Kearny was in good spirits. His cousin John Watts De Peyster was serving with Kearny as a volunteer aide and liaison with McClellan's staff. His childhood friend and companion now had the opportunity to see real action.

McClellan had in mind to occupy the head of navigation of the York River at a strategically important place called White House. From here an army could use the Richmond and York Railroad to supply its movement toward Richmond; McClellan said as much to the commandant of Fort Monroe, John Wool. Wool would work to facilitate water transportation up to that point on the peninsula; but to do this, the Army of the Potomac would have to get past Confederate forces at Williamsburg. Wool knew that his position was well placed in the largest, most heavily defended fortification in America and an important Union base for the campaign. Basically, Fort Monroe would be there no matter what the outcome.

Williamsburg is approximately twelve miles from Yorktown. Two roads converged there, the Yorktown Road and the Lee's Mill/Hampton Road. Located almost exactly in the middle of the James Peninsula, Williamsburg was once the capital of colonial Virginia and is the longtime home of William and Mary College. Halfway between Richmond and Hampton Roads and directly in the path of the oncoming Federal Army, it was ideally located to impede the advance of McClellan's Army of the Potomac. It was vital to the Union army to eliminate any force there in order to take advantage of the new supply base at White House, near the York River.

Opposite: **Part of Kearny's division, the Mozart (40th N.Y.) and the Scott Life Guard (38th N.Y.), taking possession of the Red Redoubt at Yorktown, Virginia. Sketch by Alfred Waud (Library of Congress Prints and Photographs Division, Washington, D.C.).**

Major General Philip Kearny

Major General George B. McClellan was confident in his own abilities and became a constant frustration to President Lincoln and Maj. General Kearny. McClellan is on the left and Prince de Joinville is on the far right, standing next to the Comte de Paris (Library of Congress Prints and Photographs Division, Washington, D.C.).

VI. Williamsburg

Kearny saw the task before him hindered by the fact the rain just kept coming in torrents. At approximately 4:00 a.m. May 4, 1862, he wired assistant adjutant General Williams that "under a misconstruction of the orders of General Heintzelman I have advanced to a point on the Williamsburg road 3 miles beyond Yorktown, where I am encamped and awaiting orders from General Heintzelman."[6] Kearny now found that he had to make up time and make a forced march in muddy weather. Even General McClellan noted that it was "raining hard now and most of the night; roads consequently infamous."[7] The Union forces, like the rain, did not let up and moved forward.

It was still dark in the early hours of May 5 when Philip Kearny grabbed hold of the pommel of his saddle with his one hand and swung himself into the saddle. Once he was in the saddle, he tugged at his left shoulder with his right hand, as was his wont to do, and turned his horse toward his staff; he then ordered them to bring the division forward. The rain came down steadily as dark forms of massed troops began to stir and move forward to commands of regiment sergeants and officers. Kearny, with his reins in his hand, move back and forth along his lines as he encouraged his units forward.

Covered by his riding cloak and riding at the head of his command, General Kearny moved his men through the pelting rain. He moved his force down along the Cheesecake Church road toward Lee's Mill road in the direction of Williamsburg. Even with the dawn, the day still felt like the night with the overcast and raining skies. Kearny's columns now caught up with other federal units who had become bogged down, with stuck wagons and abandoned stores littering the sides of the roads. Kearny railed to those in his way to move aside and he forcibly pushed his way through the muddy scenes.

There was now to be heard gunfire to Kearny's front, and it was at this moment that an urgent request of orders came from both General Sumner and corps commander General Heintzelman to proceed as quickly as possible. General Joseph Hooker's command was being hard pressed outside of Williamsburg by Confederate forces under the command of General James Longstreet. These Confederates were posted on either side of Fort Magruder, an earthen redoubt strategically placed, guarding the eastern approaches to Williamsburg's roads.

Hooker had responded to George Stoneman's Union cavalry earlier that day and had come into contact with and was soon engaged by the Confederates. Stoneman was being hard pressed and outnumbered and he soon had to ask for assistance. Hooker, who was leading up the road, soon moved off the Yorktown road to a connecting road to Lee's Mill. There had engaged the Confederates on their right flank, commencing his attack around 7:30 a.m.[8]

The movement of men and matériel was going badly for the Union forces. Knee-deep muddy roads were thick with broken-down wagons and baggage strewn along the way. With very few openings and pine forest covering in every direction, troops had to be funneled along the roads, no matter how clogged they were. This was to become problematic, and the extended lines of blue-clad soldiers had to push and shove their way forward to the sound of increasing gunfire. Before them they faced multiple redoubts, all anchored on Ft. Magruder.

The Union army was making its way over a wilderness that had not been anticipated by the Army's higher command. The Union forces would be deployed in a piecemeal fashion that would benefit the defending Confederate forces ensconced in their formidable redoubts overlooking the cleared fields before them. The weather was abysmal, and the Union forces would contend with advancing in pouring rains over difficult terrain. It was a perfect storm.

General Kearny and his forces rested at a place called Cheesecake Church. This was the same place in which General Hooker had made his detour to reach Lee's Mill road. It had been a difficult morning for his division, stumbling along in the rain almost single file. Now he received urgent messages from his corps commander to come up quickly in order to support a hard-pressed General Hooker. Hooker's unit was now being pressed by rifle and artillery fire from the Confederates as he closed in on Williamsburg. This was a moment that Kearny now relished: the enemy was at hand, and he had the opportunity to strike him. He passed the order along his ranks to leave their packs and kits. He was a little more than three miles from the scene when he took the vanguard of his troops and led them forward.[9] At this moment the heavens decided to let loose a driving rain with the sound of thunder echoing overhead. This presented an eerie, ghostly scene as Kearny's Division moved along.

Since early morning the engagement had continued unabated. Hooker's line was giving way on his left flank, near the Lee's Mill road, threatening his artillery support. Even with the unrelenting rain, the sound of battle could not be mistaken as the military figures started to appear out of the daytime darkness. With all available field officers engaged, experience would now prove invaluable, and as John Watts De Peyster had said, "Phil Kearny was the general most experienced in war on the field."[10] This experience would soon be evident, for at around 2:30 p.m., Joseph Hooker

VI. Williamsburg

Kearny's division coming to the relief of Joe Hooker's brigades at the Battle of Williamsburg. Sketch by Alfred Waud (Library of Congress Prints and Photographs Division, Washington, D.C.).

was glad to see Kearny coming up in his rain-drenched cloak leading his division.

Passing through Hooker's beleaguered men, Kearny rode forward quickly with his staff to reconnoiter the situation, continually tugging at the shoulder of his missing left arm as his excitement began to rise.[11] He found few open areas except near the road-fronting abatis put up by the Confederates before their many redoubts. Kearny understood only one premise in war, and that was to pressure the enemy and attack him. And this is what he was going to do. Kearny deployed his men, barking orders to his lieutenants, all the while leading his forces from the front.

Being not really that familiar with Philip Kearny, who was barely a week in his command, General Heintzelman was concerned with what Kearny might be up against. Heintzelman rode forward to briefly confer with Kearny. "General Heintzelman asked him if he had not better let General Hooker aid him, as he was a stranger to his command."[12] Kearny, probably amused at the question, indicated that he was now engaging the

Major General Philip Kearny

enemy and said to Heintzelman, "I can make men follow me to hell."[13] With sword in hand and the bridle of his horse in his teeth, he galloped from one side of the road to the other as the bullets whizzed past him, to encourage his officers and men. It seemed as if Kearny himself was not afraid of Hell.

As the division deployed, two of his staff officers were shot from their horses, but Kearny seemed unfazed and kept his men moving. He seemed to have a disregard for personal injury as he exhorted his officers and men. He personally made the example as he took charge of the beleaguered 2nd Michigan regiment and led them into action, saying to those who could hear, "Don't flinch, boys, they're shooting at me, not at you!"[14] At other times he could be heard saying, "I am a one-armed son of gun, follow me." He did this time and time again, always making sure to be seen by his troops.

General Hiram Berry and his brigade were the first to be posted. The rain had now become more like a drizzle as his men came forward. As Berry moved off the road, he was minus a couple of regiments that had been detailed to other Union forces farther to Berry's left. Like Kearny, he did not let this deter him from his mission to get in contact with the Confederates. Soldiers were making their way forward as bullets cut through the rain and men now began to fall to enemy fire. The battle unfolded in an eerie way as the pounding rain muffled the sound of the rifle fire. General Kearny lost two of his aides. G. James Wilson was fatally shot in the head, and Lieutenant Phineas Barnard, while riding to give orders, was shot in the stomach. Unfortunately, Barnard later died from his wounds after reaching an aid station.

It was at this point that General Kearny noticed a gap that had presented itself in his line. He had General David Bell Birney coming up behind General Berry, and Kearny escorted Birney's men to the point where the gap was, exhorting Berry's men along the way, all the while exposing himself to the same gunfire that they were exposed to. General Birney saw the situation developing and led the 38th (Life Scots Guard) and the 40th (Mozart Regiment) to the right of Lee's Mill road. James Laughton, standard bearer of the 38th New York regiment, was uneasy at first, but his training was soon to come into play, and he soon began to overcome the uneasiness.[15] The discipline that Kearny had instilled in his men helped to alleviate the initial jitters all soldiers feel in action.

The Confederates were deployed before their redoubts, thinking that they could now blunt the oncoming Yankees. The 38th and the 40th New York came up on the double-quick, filed into line, and commenced

VI. Williamsburg

a deadly accurate fire that soon staggered the force before them. As the Union troops fired into the Confederate flank, the enemy was completely caught by surprise and began to give ground to the advancing Yankees. The battle being joined, Kearny kept up the assault, giving more pressure and giving the Confederates a scare. In his eventual official report, Kearny simply stated that his troops "charged up to the open space ... and gaining the enemy's rear caused him to relinquish his cover."[16] The Confederates had no answer for Kearny's assault. It was now getting late and the Confederates reluctantly gave even more ground. Kearny had reconnoitered the ground before him and realized that the enemy was withdrawing behind their redoubts. Because of the lateness of the day and the lack of forces attached to other Union units, Kearny's assault soon ended. Soon only sporadic musketry fire and the rain-muffled ping of the artillery could be heard, as darkness was descending.

Kearny's appearance helped save the Union left flank, and Hooker was thankful for his actions. He rallied Hooker's depleted force and bolstered it with his regiments. In his official report, Kearny gives credit to his brigade commanders Birney and Berry, and goes on to acknowledge Colonels Hobart Ward of the 38th New York and Riley of the 40th. In his report Kearny states, "I have to mark out for high commendation of the Generals-in-chief, Generals Jameson, Birney and Berry, whose soldierly judgement was alone equaled by their distinguished courage."[17] It would be a mark of Kearny's qualities (caught in Waud's sketch) as he led his division through the rain undaunted to grip the enemy.

Kearny would also commend others in his rank and file. He praised one of his junior officers, Colonel Poe of the 2nd Michigan Volunteer Regiment, for his immediate response to General Kearny's direction in the initial phase of the attack. It was one of the few times Poe would act with decision. It may be this need for direction that was Poe's weakness. Kearny may have not realized this at the time, but Poe lacked what Kearny instinctively always possessed, to take initiative as needed. This would come back to cause grief and cost Philip Kearny much.

In his report on the battle, Maj Gen George McClellan, who came late to the action, praised the Union forces under Winfield Scott Hancock. He did not immediately praise the forces under Kearny. Kearny was not amused over the slight, and it was soon brought to McClellan's attention what the division under Kearny had done that day. McClellan later corrected his report and gave the 3rd Division its due, as well as Hooker's, but it was something that Kearny would not forget. Kearny was not a fan of this peninsula operation in the first place, and for this seeming slight to occur only cemented his growing dissatisfaction with the Army commander.

May 6 dawned mostly cloudy. Kearny's Division found the day quiet of enemy activity, with David Birney's Brigade leading in the van. He soon moved into the Confederate works and found the enemy gone. The move toward Richmond continued. For all intents and purposes, the Confederates seemed to have staged only a delaying action in front of Williamsburg. The march of McClellan's army, and he believed it was his army, would go on to Richmond, the Confederate capital, now less than 50 miles up the Williamsburg road from the Union Army.

The Army of the Potomac now had its supply base established at West Point Landing, but would the army be able to move quickly to take Richmond? The Confederates had bluffed Union forces for a time at Yorktown, and then presented some Confederate ire at Williamsburg. At some point, as Kearny rode along with his troops, he probably thought that there would be a reckoning battle somewhere down the line. How could the Confederates continue to allow the Union forces to proceed up the peninsula without an all-out attack on McClellan's strung-out forces? Kearny anticipated that there would be a fight, and he hoped that his division would be in the thick of it.

Kearny was not only astute in his military reports and singling out others for commendation, he was also astute in recognizing his state units and their association with his division. Possibly thinking of the missed recognition by the Army of the Potomac's commander, Kearny made a point of sending a letter to the governor of Pennsylvania. To Governor Curtin he wrote: "Sir:—As the commanding officer of this division, of which three regiments, the Fifty-seventh, Sixty-third, and the One-hundred-and-fifth Pennsylvania volunteers form a portion, I cannot refrain from calling to your notice the important part performed by them at the battle of Williamsburg.... I have to bring to your notice and to the people of the State, that the second brigade of my division was commanded by a Pennsylvanian, General Birney. This officer displayed coolness and courage .... He has proved himself a good colonel—his brigade is the model of good discipline."[18] The use of politics was not a foreign concept to General Kearny.

VII

Seven Pines

The movement from Yorktown to Williamsburg was lightning-fast compared with the movement from Williamsburg to the outskirts of Richmond. McClellan could not think about moving very far from his base of supplies and his dependence on U.S. Navy support. He had the idea of advancing along a broad front with his entire force while keeping his railroad supply open for moving up his siege guns. Philip Kearny believed that quick action was the only way to victory over the Confederates. He did not subscribe to McClellan's approach, and he constantly referred to his commander as a slow-moving creature in the form of a Virginia creeper.

It didn't help that the weather remained inclement and that the roads became atrocious even in dry weather, once the rain stopped. Kearny's soldiers recalled how "after two or three days of hot sun the roads would dry and turn thick as powdery dust."[1] By May 8, Union forces began making movement down the roads toward the Confederate capital. Kearny's movement brought him, by May 13, to the vicinity of the Diascond road, where he left for a moment one of his brigades at Ropers Church.

All the instruments for the defeat of the Confederate forces were in place. The Army of the Potomac had initiated what military theoretician Carl von Clausewitz called first reciprocal action. But could it maintain that contact, since the action had now gone from a single point to one distributed in breadth and depth?[2] There was at least one Union officer who believed that the initiative had been surrendered to the Confederates. Philip Kearny had just participated in a sharp action that forced the enemy to fall back on his means of supply and communication. The Union forces must, if the momentum were to survive, take the initiative. McClellan, instead of attacking, decided on what siege operation he would take against the Confederate capital. Kearny was not entirely in favor of this approach.

The Union Army now moved in stages. On May 12, Union forces moved by way of New Kent Courthouse toward Bottoms Bridge. Kearny and his 3rd Division would move from here toward the Chickahominy

River in line with the rest of 3rd Corps. It rained almost continuously, tying up roads and slowing traffic. Kearny and his force reached the Cumberland area on May 15, covering eight miles in three days and eventually bivouacking near Ropers Church on a road leading to Bottoms Bridge on the Chickahominy. The terrain was becoming problematic for the drainage of the roads. Continuously flat and heavily forested, the peninsula of the York and James rivers proved to be no ally of the Union Army.

By May 19, the Army of the Potomac was in place, precariously straddling the northwest to southeast flowing Chickahominy River through White Oak Swamp. This area consisted of broad, poorly drained flats that were heavily wooded. The Richmond and York Railroad paralleled the river for a short distance where a number of water and refueling stops were located. It was this railroad and many of the stops where some of the Union forces now concentrated. One of these stops was at Savage Station, and just down the road, in the direction of Richmond, was the small station stop at a place called Fair Oaks.

Fair Oaks intersects with Nine Mile Road and the Richmond and York River Railroad. One mile south of that intersection is the road junction referred to by the local people as Seven Pines; this is the intersection of Nine Mile Road and the Williamsburg–Richmond Road. This was one of the few open-ground areas in the otherwise forested flats in the poorly drained surroundings. It was mainly farmland, and this farmland centered on the two twin farmhouses of the Kuhn family, just off the Williamsburg Road to the south. This localized farmstead now soon found itself surrounded with units from the Union Army's IV and III Corps.

Directly east, about two miles down the line, was Savage Station, and just beyond there was Bottoms Bridge. General McClellan was satisfied with the army's progress; he reported that all his corps had advanced and that all was going well.[3] South of Seven Pines stretched a desultory small stream of undetermined width called White Oak Swamp, poorly drained and practically impenetrable, which would have to be bridged in select areas just to be crossed. Corps Commander Samuel Heintzelman remarked how low and heavily wooded the area was with the ground constantly wet and swampy, as the Union forces soon began building abatis and a redoubt near the Williamsburg Road.[4]

Under command of Lt. General Joseph E. Johnston, the Confederates were not idle and were massing for a strike at McClellan's Union forces. The Army of the Potomac was exposed, with two corps on the south side of the Chickahominy River. The Confederate command believed these units could be isolated and destroyed. General Joe Johnston had given

VII. Seven Pines

up his positions outside Washington and Manassas in April. It was there, near Manassas, that Brigadier General Kearny had driven the small force of Confederates at Sangster Station and could hear the Confederate trains leaving at Manassas Junction, probably heading towards Richmond.

The Army of the Peninsula under Lt. Gen. Joe Johnston was positioning itself to strike the Army of the Potomac under the less than watchful eye of Lt. Gen. George McClellan. Spread out on the eastern outskirts of Richmond, Virginia, two corps of that army found themselves somewhat isolated south of the Chickahominy River. General Johnston was planning a three-pronged assault along three separate roads leading out of Richmond, south of the Chickahominy. On May 30, Brig. Gen. Daniel Harvey Hill reported to Johnston that Union forces were now near the crossroads at Seven Pines.

For the Confederates, it was now time to act. Confederate Commander General Joseph E. Johnston could no longer prevent the inevitable; he would have to commit his forces. "Johnston's aim in the battle of May 31st, 1862, was to overwhelm the IV Federal Corps at Seven Pines before it could be reinforced. His concentration and deployment were based on the direction of the three highways that led to the enemy's position."[5] The Williamsburg Road led directly to the Seven Pines crossroads and Fair Oaks Station. This was the center of the Confederate line, and it was here that the blow was struck. Johnston was a proponent of the tactics of Emperor Frederick the Great of Prussia. In his time the Prussians used something called the oblique attack, and at Seven Pines (Fair Oaks), this type of attack was to be employed.

At Casey's Redoubt, a small opening in the Virginia Pines and close by Seven Pines, D.H. Hill sent in his forces full tilt. At 1 o'clock, Hill ordered the signal gun to fire, starting the attack. Moving through mud and water that could reach waist-deep in some places, the Confederates found the ground before the federal abatis and redoubt more suitable for a rush. The Rebel yell echoed through the flats, and soon the Yanks were being hard pressed and driven. Robert Emmett Rodes's Confederate brigade had the Federals retreating. It was near this moment when Kearny's Division arrived and found fighting all along the line.

Kearny and his men found themselves, by May 30, encamped at and defending Bottoms Bridge. The rest of 3rd Corps had advanced forward and were encamped near 4th Corps at Seven Pines. Both these corps were south of the Chickahominy, separated from the rest of the Army of the Potomac. Well north of here, the Confederate Army, on May 27, began to probe Union Army forces at a place called Hanover Court House. With this attack, the Confederates would soon take action. On Saturday, May 30, a terrific rainstorm broke over the area and drenched the Union army, which would now advance no farther.

Sunday, May 31, was overcast and threatening rain. In the distance could be heard the far-off church bells of the city of Richmond. Forces of the Army of the Potomac began to dig in, and soldiers of Casey's Division of General Erasmus Keyes's Corps were busy cutting down trees and clearing an area around a redoubt named for their commander. The Williamsburg Road ran just to the north of the redoubt and near the two Kuhn houses. The ground was extremely wet from the previous day's rain. It seemed unlikely that the Confederates would attack in these conditions. Even General Kearny reluctantly began to believe that the siege McClellan was implementing may be the best way to envelope the city, considering the weather; events would now change everything.[6]

The situation on that Sunday had Casey's Division occupying ground that was approximately two miles long by one-half mile wide. This was open ground centered on the redoubt just completed. Around this area was a dense tangle of forest and wetlands. To the north of the road was positioned Neglee's Brigade and to the south was Palmer's, centered on Casey's Redoubt. These units occupied the very front of the IV and III Corps that was forward of the Chickahominy River. The troops went about their routines, not expecting any action from the enemy, and the pickets began to relax in their isolation.

Around one o'clock on May 31, 1862, the Union pickets in the brush were startled by an advance of Confederates headed en masse toward their splendid isolation. Now tumbling back toward the main camps, they indicated a force of butternut uniforms converging on their front that were coming in force of numbers. Earlier that morning, General Kearny had decided to move forward two of his brigades to Savage Station. From here they could move rapidly to support Keyes's Corps. This would become important, as the Confederates came through and out of the forest in earnest.

This was no probing attack by the Confederate Army. This was a mass of screaming banshees storming over the wet and muddy ground, eagerly seeking to engage anyone in their way. This was an absolute shock to the Union forces facing this onslaught. Keyes's forces had not yet been baptized by combat, and the sight of muddied men moving over wet ground was somewhat intimidating. Most of Casey's regiments were positioned on the north side of Williamsburg road. Wessel's Division, south of the road, occupied the area around the redoubt, and this was the focus of the enemy attack.

VII. Seven Pines

The artillerymen could barely get to their guns and get off shot and canister before the Confederates' red banners were moving over and into the redoubt. Here muzzle flashes exploded all around and rifle butts came down on heads as the Confederates swarmed over the abatis and drove the Union troops out. Soldiers slipped and fell on the wet and muddy ground as they fired and struggled bayonet to bayonet. Absolute confusion reigned inside the redoubt as Union soldiers broke and fled and Confederates swarmed all around. The whiz of bullets filled the air in every direction, and even Confederate officers were not spared, as Colonel Robert E. Rodes found out as he stumbled when he was struck by a bullet.

Northern troops were fleeing in panic. Only Naglee's Brigade stood the onslaught north of the road. A flood of butternut and gray came slogging through the wet ground, stopping at intervals to concentrate musket fire toward the Union line. The 104th Pennsylvania Volunteer Regiment matched volley with volley as the firing intensified. With his flanks now becoming overlapped by Confederates, Naglee's force soon began to give way, but they stood their ground long enough for the 7th New York Light Artillery to limber their pieces. Union forces moved back toward the Nine Mile road.

The Union Army had been surprised and was now being pressed. Unsure of the strength of the force before them, General Heintzelman was looking for support across the Chickahominy. It was not until 3:00 p.m. that he received word from Heintzelman, but Kearny was already on the move. He was already down the Williamsburg road with his staff at about 2:00 p.m. when they heard the gunfire in the distance. Picking up his pace, Kearny moved forward.

Kearny reined in his horse and ordered his staff to inform Generals Berry and Jameson to bring up their forces. Kearny rode forward to assess the situation and rally the retreating Union force as a trickle of them began to move past. At the Seven Pines crossroad he beheld a tattered and beleaguered Union force. Kearny remembered, "Captain Hunt … made me aware of the discomfiture of most of Casey's Division as the retiring wagons and a dense stream of disorganized fugitives arrived nearly simultaneously."[7] Units now blended with other units; these were the remnants of Casey's force.

It was nearing 4:00 p.m. and Kearny was rallying what Union forces he could when General Berry's regiments came up. Kearny remarked to his commander to "set forward without delay" and lead these regiments forward in person.[8] At the same time, he sent orders for Jameson to come up as quickly as possible. With these forces moving into position, Kearny

Major General Philip Kearny

had but one regiment, the 3rd Michigan, when he met Casey, who urged him to move quickly. He now moved with the 3rd Michigan into the line to the right of the Confederate force and soon engaged the enemy personally.

With General Berry moving up with the 37th New York to support this movement, General Kearny faced the forces of Confederate General Robert Rodes, now in the abatis. It was here that a devastating fire was poured into both ranks. General Kearny engaged some Confederates and slashed his way through with his sword in his one hand and with the reins of his horse in his teeth. To the surprise of the Confederate soldiers, here was a Union officer seemingly oblivious to danger, fighting and hacking at the rank and file as if he may be the devil.

The impetus of the Confederate attack was now blunted by the arrival of Kearny's Division. Even Corps Commander General Heintzelman took part in the battle: coming up, he directed one of Jameson's regiments to the north of the Williamsburg Road. Jameson relates: "With the remaining two regiments (63rd Pennsylvania Volunteers and 150th Pennsylvania) I filed off through the woods to the left of the Richmond road. I there met General Kearny."[9] Kearny had now just come from his encounter and was his blood was up. With sword in hand and his left shoulder moving back and forth in excitement, he exclaimed to Jameson and the men within ear shot, "There's the devil's own fun, boys ... along the whole line."[10] Another officer asked, "Where shall I go in? Through the clearing or pine?" Kearny answered, "Oh anywhere: forward! 'Tis all

Major General Samuel P. Heintzelman was an irascible and prickly III Corps commander, which resulted in tense interactions with Kearny and almost everyone else (Library of Congress Prints and Photographs Division, Washington, D.C.).

VII. Seven Pines

the same, Colonel, you will find lovely fighting along the whole line."[11] This was vintage Kearny, and his men who heard it loved it.

It was getting later in the day when Jameson came up to support Berry's left. Acrid smoke filled the soggy air as the two armies grappled with each other and muzzle flashes shone like fireflies in the haze. The resultant appearance and fire from the two Union regiments halted the Confederate force. The colonel of the 105th Pennsylvania remembered the action: "The firing was quite animated and told fearfully on the enemy, so much so that we succeeded in drawing them back from their position."[12] Unfortunately there was no more support for Kearny and his men as they slowly withdrew back up toward the York and Richmond Railway. Casey's Division was spent, and the determined fire of the Confederates continued unabated. Attrition, the melting of forces, was taking affect. "Lieutenant Cummings of Company D, had his head blown off by a cannonball while gallantly leading his men."[13] General Kearny rode from one point to another, holding the line, and he later remembered that "the dead lay in clumps in the dwarf pine."[14]

With the loss of Casey's and Darius Couch's forces on his right, Kearny, Berry and Jameson were now cut off from the Richmond–Williamsburg road. The only line of withdrawal was toward the White Oak Swamp, and there were only a limited number of roads to take. General Kearny made a cursory reconnaissance of the roads and, making his way through the tangled growth, found a little-used logging road that made its way to a sawmill. This road could be used to re-route his command to the main Union base at Savage Station.

With stragglers from other units and his remaining regiments, Kearny moved his force down and across White Oak Swamp. Jameson remembered Kearny's move along that old mill road: "By order of General Kearny I moved back through the woods to a road leading to a steam saw-mill (Anderson's, I believe) which road I followed to said mill, thence to a position now occupied by my brigade."[15] Between 6:30 and 8:00 p.m., Kearny concentrated his forces back across the Richmond and York River Railroad line, near Savage Station.

The Confederate forces had pushed the Union Army back from Seven Pines. General Kearny had helped stem the tide. His constant presence on the line bolstered morale and kept his soldiers from a panic as bullets whizzed past his head as his men did their duty. His other brigade commander, David Birney, had been detailed elsewhere and was advancing along the railroad. Birney had received conflicting orders. Initially occupying rifle pits near Savage Station, he was soon ordered to advance down the

Major General Philip Kearny

rail line to support General Couch. His official report related that he "had been ordered to support by the railroad side, not to attack."[16] It was General Heintzelman, who was at that time in overall command, who eventually ordered Birney up the railroad to support the flank of General Keyes's Corps.

With the 38th and 40th New York Volunteer Regiments and the 3rd Maine and 57th Pennsylvania, Birney advance toward the Nine Mile road. He soon encountered numerous frightened soldiers fleeing rearward. These troops were some of the remnants of Couch's forces fleeing in advance of the oncoming Confederates, after the disastrous defense around Casey's Redoubt. Birney's appearance slowed their progress as he implored the men to stand and do their duty.

General Kearny had by this time made his way back from their re-route from White Oak Swamp and the mill road, up to the railroad near Birney's position. As rain began to fall again, General Kearny's Division took its post up behind the Richmond and York River Railroad as the daylight was waning and gunfire slackened off. It had been an exhilarating day for the general, and he anticipated a continuing fight on the morrow. The night now settled in as campfires were lit along the rail line around Fair Oaks.

On the morning of June 1, 1862, the Confederates resumed their attack. Situated on the Union line was Kearny, with his right flank resting on General Richardson's left flank, and what was left of Couch's forces forming his right flank on Kearny's left. General David Birney's Brigade, which had seen somewhat limited action the day before, found that they would soon participate in the upcoming action, but Birney would not be here on this day. He had been summoned to General Kearny's tent and was informed that he would have to report to General Heintzelman's headquarters. Kearny then informed General Birney that he should not be too concerned, and that he would have General Kearny's support.

Headquarters Third Division, Third Corps, June 2, 1862

Sir: - I am positive that General Birney has never disobeyed orders, intentionally, nor by any want of either courage or intelligence. I look on him as a superior officer. I am positive that if you would accord him a hearing, or enable him to answer any categorical demands, it would be perfectly satisfactory to you. In a wooded country orders apparently conflict. In fact of his saving Couch's division seems a proof of his affecting what was intended. As for myself, with Berry's brigade, I retook Casey's lost ground, and the consequence was, that my troops were completely cut off from the enemy, forcing in other troops of Keyes' corps. I take the liberty of bringing this to your notice, knowing your kindness, as well as generosity of disposition towards all under your command.

Most, respectfully, P. KEARNY,
Brigadier-general, commanding Third Division.[17]

VII. Seven Pines

Major General David B. Birney, similar to Philip Kearny, had no formal military training and learned much while serving with his commander, which he did to the end (Library of Congress Prints and Photographs Division, Washington, D.C.).

Birney had been summoned to General Heintzelman's headquarters to answer questions about his activity on the day before. Command of his brigade fell to the capable hands of Colonel Hobart Ward, of the 38th New York. He describes the action of that day: "New fire was opened to my right.... I gave the order to fire and immediately thereafter to charge. The units of Richardson, Kearny and Hooker advanced and drove Confederates back across Nine Mile and Williamsburg roads and at 11:30 a.m. the action was over ... the rout was complete."[18] General Birney satisfied General Heintzelman's questions of the day before and presently returned to his unit. Kearny had insisted to his superiors his unquestioned confidence of Birney's ability.

It was at this moment that General Kearny decided that, in order to improve identification and keep up morale, a patch should be worn by the troops. John Watts de Peyster, a staff officer and a relative of Philip Kearny, recalled: "According to officers of the Third Corps on the Peninsula, Kearny, about the time of the battle of Fair Oaks, directed his officers to wear a red patch or diamond as a distinguishing mark. As there were no red goods on hand for this purpose, Kearny gave up his own red blanket as material for these patches."[19] Initially only Kearny's officers wore the patch, but the rank and file would eventually follow suit.

This was done, as previously said, to distinguish his officers from other officers and staff of other units. In the heat of battle, the confusion

Major General Philip Kearny

and smoke from the action left units separated and intermingled, as was the case at Seven Pines. It was a successful attempt to instill esprit de corps and the spirit of élan in his division, singling out the men in his command as distinct from the rest of the Army of the Potomac. Eventually it would soon be recognized as the Kearny Patch.

VIII

Pivot at Gaines' Mill

The success at Seven Pines in blunting the Confederate attack convinced General George McClellan that if he could hold his line, particularly his flanks, he could bring up his siege guns and shell Richmond. McClellan had one of his favorite lieutenants, Maj. Gen. Fitz John Porter, holding his far right. All McClellan had to do was just get a little closer via the Williamsburg road toward Oak Grove, just another two miles. One more push forward would be the ideal. What McClellan had failed to anticipate was that the newly constituted Confederate Army of Northern Virginia, under the new command of Robert E. Lee, had other designs.

The results of the Battle of Seven Pines (Fair Oaks) were to change the makeup of George McClellan's opponents. With the wounding of Joseph E. Johnston, command of the Confederate Army, reorganized as the Army of Northern Virginia, now fell to the capable hands of Robert E. Lee. General Lee spent the next three weeks planning to strike George McClellan's Army of the Potomac as he observed its slow move astride the Chickahominy River. General Lee sized up the fact that General McClellan was heavily dependent on his extended supply line, and decided that to relieve the Confederate capital, he needed to strike the Union Army and move it off its base from the landing at West Point.

What would presently be called the Seven Days began on June 25, 1862. On the Williamsburg Road, near a place called King's School House or Oak Grove, McClellan decided to move his lines closer to the city of Richmond. Kearny's division occupied the ground south of the road, and Lieutenant-Colonel George. D. Wells, commanding the 26th Pennsylvania, was just across on the north side. In the misty light of the morning, the federals began to rustle forward when they soon came into contact with the enemy coming up from the woods. Col. Wells recalled:

> I received from General Hooker an order to push the line forward on the Williamsburg road.... I found that it needed only two companies to establish a sufficient line between Blaisdell's left and Kearny's right, and I held the five companies remaining as a support to hold a wood road in which my left rested.... The attack

was made, however, upon Kearny's line, farther to the left. The enemy broke through, and we heard them sweeping by our left flank and to our rear. The Seventh New Jersey coming, we formed a strong line of battle, and with them and the Sixty-third Pennsylvania Reserve I waited. General Kearny soon appeared on the left with re-enforcements, driving the enemy before him, and we held the line until relieved."[1]

Believing that a strong Confederate force was facing the III Corps, the Union attacks were not pressed. The attack of the Union force at Oak Grove on the 25th was only the opening of what would become a Confederate offensive that was completely unexpected by most of McClellan's command. With his forces astride the Chickahominy River, McClellan's V Corps was seemingly isolated from the rest of the Army of the Potomac. As Kearny looked out over the fields of the previous day's battle from the redan he occupied, little did he know that the enemy was planning a massive attack just north of the Chickahominy. The holding operation in the Confederate center and the bluff that went with it was enough to signal the next day's assault on Union forces at Mechanicsville (Beaver Dam Creek), and the even more intense battle at Gaines' Mill.

General George McClellan had his V Corps of General Fitz John Porter north of the Chickahominy River at a right angle, fronting the river and covering Beaver Dam Creek at Mechanicsville with the option of falling back onto Boatswain's Swamp near Gaines' Mill. To dislodge the Federals, the Confederates under General Lee decided to strike the V Corps of Porter. Moving into position, Brig. Gen. Charles Field, of A.P. Hill's Light Division, reported:

> I have the honor to report that on the 26th ultimo I was directed to cross from my camp at Meadow Bridge to the north side of the Chickahominy as soon as General Branch's brigade, which was to cross higher up the stream, should appear opposite to me. It was designed that his movements should take place early on the 26th. Certain causes having delayed its execution, it was 3 p.m. on the 26th when Major General A.P. Hill, commanding the division, directed me to wait no longer, but to cross and attack the enemy at Mechanicsville. The enemy made no opposition to my passage of the Chickahominy, but, posting skirmishers in a thick wood about a mile beyond, fired on the advance.... From this point to Mechanicsville the road was open, but as I approached that place a heavy fire from several batteries on my left and front and from sharpshooters, all behind entrenchments, was opened.... Meanwhile an active and vigorous fire was opened on us from the batteries situated on the north side of Beaver Dam Creek.[2]

Holding in place on the 26th, General Kearny could only watch and wait as the Confederates now took the initiative by attacking north of the Chickahominy. Moving easily across the Chickahominy at Meadow

VIII. Pivot at Gaines' Mill

Bridge, A.P. Hill's Division launched the attack on Union forces arrayed across Beaver Dam Creek (Mechanicsville). Occupying the high ground above the creek, the Union forces pummeled the Confederates with cannon and rifle fire. All that day the Confederates pressed the attack, but could not dislodge their enemy.

> The battle now raged furiously along my whole line. The artillery fire from the enemy was terrific. Their position along Beaver Dam Creek was too strong to be carried by a direct attack without heavy loss, and expecting every moment to hear Jackson's guns on my left and in rear of the enemy, I forbore to order the storming of their lines. General Branch, having come up, was ordered forward as a support to the brigades already engaged, and Johnson's battery took position near McIntosh and Braxton. Gregg was held in reserve near Mechanicsville. The Thirty-eighth North Carolina, Colonel [William J.] Hoke, and the Thirty-fourth North Carolina, Colonel [Richmond H.] Riddick, of Pender's brigade made a gallant but abortive attempt to force a crossing."[3]

It was a bloody affair for the Confederates, and as night fell, they had made little progress against their foe. By 9:00 p.m. the firing ceased, and quiet descended over the battlefield. General Porter's men had stood their ground and he was taking stock of the situation with the commanding general of the Army of the Potomac. General George McClellan had arrived on the grounds and was meeting with Porter to decide what next, if anything.

> All was made ready for a renewal of the contest on the old ground, or an advance toward Richmond via the bridges which the enemy had crossed, should our success warrant it. During the night, however, as the commanding general (who had joined me at an early hour in the afternoon and remained until about 10 o'clock at night) is aware, numerous and unvarying accounts came in from our outposts and scouts toward the Pamunkey which tended to corroborate the previously received intelligence of the advance of the whole of Jackson's force from the direction of Gordonsville, whereby our right was to be effectually flanked.[4]

It was then decided to give up the ground at Beaver Dam Creek and move back to ground above Boatswain's Swamp near Gaines' Mill.

It must have been on General Kearny's mind that now was the time to move on the Confederate capital. Just miles away, the Union army had the position, but General McClellan had no design of an assault on the capital until he could bring his big guns to bear on the defenses. George McClellan was more concerned with his base of supply, and this influenced his decisions from the beginning. McClellan's opponent, General Robert E. Lee, understood this about McClellan and had already decided to take the initiative and strike. Here is how Lee presented his plan to

Major General Philip Kearny

his officers: Richmond could not survive a siege, so it was necessary to take the offensive. The offensive could not be a direct assault due to the inexperience of the Confederate troops; therefore, Lee had decided on a turning movement against the Federals. Additionally, Lee pointed out that because McClellan had part of his army astride the Chickahominy, that portion of the Union army would be the point of the turning movement. This would go to the point Lee was stressing: that McClellan would always fall back if his lines of communications were threatened. Concentrate and strike the Union army north of the Chickahominy, and McClellan would be forced to change his base toward the James River.[5]

Holding the line at Oak Grove near Seven Pines, Heintzelman's III Corps Divisions, including Kearny, waited for the Union heavy artillery slowly making its way over the heavily saturated ground to bring Richmond under fire. Events would soon prove that this would not come to pass. North of the Chickahominy, the enemy was moving to bring McClellan's plans for Richmond to an end. Philip Kearny stood near the precipice of the redan, his force occupied outside Richmond, and shook his head as he contemplated that now was the time to strike the Confederate forces, just east of his position. This idea would always be in Kearny's mind, and it would eventually cause him to vent his frustration as events continued to develop.

Friday, June 27, 1862, would be a pivotal day for both Northern and Southern armies. Sitting on his horse, Colonel Maxcy Gregg was moving his South Carolina regiments across Beaver Dam Creek as they headed south toward Powhite Creek. General A.P. Hill had expected his Light Division to come up against a strong Union position, but to his surprise, he found the area above Powhite Creek unoccupied by the enemy. "It was soon found that the enemy had retired from his lines along Beaver Dam Creek, two companies from Gregg's brigade having handsomely dashed across and cleared the pits of the few men left as a blind. The evidences of precipitate retreat were palpable all along the route. Arriving at the creek upon which Gaines' Mill is located, half a mile from Cold Harbor, the enemy were discovered upon the opposite bank."[6] This initial elation of the enemy's withdrawal was short-lived as the Confederates moved down from Powhite Creek.

Confederate General Ambrose Powell Hill was correct: the Union Army had taken up a much more defensible position on the plateau above the stagnant waters of Boatswain's Swamp. The Confederates were not intimidated by this, and Maxcy Gregg did not lose a step as he pushed his units forward. "Gregg's brigade was at once thrown in line of battle, and

VIII. Pivot at Gaines' Mill

skirmishers directed to affect a lodgment. Andrews' battery was brought up and the woods opposite vigorously shelled. The skirmishers rushing forward cleared the crossing and Gregg immediately filed his brigade across, forming line successively as each regiment crossed. His whole brigade being over, he made the handsomest charge in line I have seen during the war. The enemy was pressed, and the general soon sent me word that he had brought the enemy to bay, and that they were in force in his front, and requested permission to attack."[7]

At that moment, Gregg's South Carolinians were brought to a halt as A.P. Hill waited for supporting forces of the Army of Northern Virginia to come up. At Watt House, just above the slope of Boatswain's Swamp, Union Major General Fitz John Porter looked out over the well-defended terrain around him and was satisfied that any attack by the Confederates could be easily turned back. "About 2 o'clock p.m. they began with their skirmishers to feel for the weakest point of our position, and soon large bodies of infantry, supported by a warm fire of artillery, engaged our whole line. Repulsed in every direction, a few hours of ominous silence ensued, indicating that their troops were being massed for an overwhelming attack. Our infantry and artillery were drawn in toward the center and posted to meet the avalanche. Re-enforcements were again asked for, and all available troops were sent forward by the major-general commanding."[8] For hours the slopes around Boatswain's Swamp were covered with dense smoke and writhing bodies as waves of Confederates advanced on the V Corps' center.

General George McClellan was informed of the Confederate attack and was making his way towards Porter's Headquarters at Watt House. The general had already made up his mind to change his base of communications and supply even before General Lee initiated his attack at Gaines' Mill. Word now filtered into III Corps headquarters that the enemy had moved on Porter. General Kearny looked over his position, arrayed around earthen forts. Kearny grinned as he suddenly realized that an attack on his front was unlikely. Kearny now fully understood General Lee's plan. He knew that his prewar friend and former fellow officer John Bankhead Magruder's force, which he faced, was nothing more than a holding force. Kearny pulled nervously at his left shoulder as he thought. Soon Kearny realized that now was the time to send the III Corps and his division rushing forward to force the Confederates to fall back into the city of Richmond; it would shatter a paradigm.

The fact that the Chickahominy River divided the Union army only invited attack, and McClellan's failure to understand the situation alone proved fatal for any move on Richmond. The most experienced officer in the Union army, Philip Kearny, was the only soldier who might have had the ability to do otherwise. Even before the attack on the Union lines at Gaines' Mill, George McClellan had determined that he was going to withdraw his lines from Richmond, or as he put it, change his base. Before that change of base could be done, it fell upon Major General Fitz John Porter's V Corps to blunt any attack that would occur in his sector above the Chickahominy River. "The commanding general, however, left me with the intention of deciding on information he should receive on arrival at his own headquarters, whether I should remain where I was and hold Beaver Creek, or retire to a position selected by General Barnard near Gaines' Mill. General Barnard remained with me to conduct my command to the new position, if decided upon to withdraw from Mechanicsville."[9]

By early afternoon of June 27, the Confederates under Maxcy Gregg made their way over the abandoned ground of the Union army. Making for Boatswain's Swamp, these forces soon engaged federal pickets, and as they drove them back, they came under the thunderous volleys from Union artillery cresting the banks. A.P. Hill reported: "Arriving at the creek upon which Gaines' Mill is located; half a mile from Cold Harbor, the enemy was discovered upon the opposite bank. Gregg's brigade was at once thrown in line of battle, and skirmishers directed to affect a lodgment."[10] With James Longstreet holding on the right and Thomas Jackson coming up on the Confederate far left flank, A.P. Hill's Corps moved on the Union center. After some three hours of disjointed assaults, the Confederates, under the direction of General Lee, made a coordinated assault that sent the Union V Corps in sudden retreat.

It was going on late in the evening as General Porter looked out over his lines near the Watt House and was satisfied that they remained steady. He believed he could retain the ground that the enemy had been continuously assaulting all afternoon. Cannon and rifle fire continued all along the lines as the fight remained unrelenting. Before long the signature sound of the rebel yell started to rise along the Confederate lines in the gathering darkness. It was the final push of the Confederates, and it bore down along the Union lines. General Porter witnessed: "As if for a final effort, just as darkness was covering everything from view, the enemy massed his fresh regiments on the right and left and threw them with overpowering force against our thinned and wearied battalions. In anticipation of this our artillery, which till now had been well engaged at favorable points of the field in dealing destruction upon the enemy or held in reserve, was now thrown to the front to cover the withdrawal of our retiring troops."[11]

VIII. Pivot at Gaines' Mill

The Union front now collapsed as desperate Union artillerymen tried to extradite their guns among the surging Confederate infantry. A futile and desperate cavalry charge by the Union force did little to stem the onslaught, and General Porter ordered a withdrawal, eventually moving across the Chickahominy. The attack by the Confederates looked very much like the oblique attack that General Joe Johnston had envisioned at Seven Pines (Fair Oaks). Here, however, there was no holding action on the part of one wing of the army. Instead, it was an all-frontal attack in which General Daniel Harvey Hill's Division moved in the oblique and sent Porter's right wing fleeing across the Union rear area. It was a Confederate victory, but it was a costly one, as nearly 8,000 killed and wounded Confederates were strewn all over the grounds near the Watt farm.

Sitting in place, III Corps commander Major General Samuel Heintzelman continued to listen to the loud crash of cannon and rifle fire coming in from the north of his lines, over the Chickahominy River. Holding his line, General Philip Kearny looked out over the area as he too listened to the sounds of battle coming from across the marshy Chickahominy. From time to time his men had to engage an enemy sortie as their skirmishers came forward to test the Yankee lines. Later that day, a flurry of messengers rode into Heintzelman's headquarters with news of what was occurring. General George McClellan had decided to make an ordered withdrawal covering his move south of the Chickahominy River. "On the night of the 28th of June I received orders to withdraw the troops of my corps from the advanced position they had taken on the 25th of June, and to occupy the entrenched lines about a mile in rear. A map was sent me showing the positions General Sumner's and General Franklin's corps would occupy. About sunrise the next day our troops slowly fell back to the new position, cautiously followed by the enemy, taking possession of our camps as soon as we left them."[12] Confederate General Lee now had the measure of Union General George McClellan.

Here was the idea that General R.E. Lee had in mind: with Union forces pushed south of the Chickahominy, the Confederates would continue to drive and push them out of the peninsula, with Lee all the while hoping he could somehow corner and destroy some or all of that force. All the gains that had been made by the Union Army since May were on the verge of being surrendered, including the well-provisioned supply depots at Savage Station and at Golding's Farm, both of which were south of the Chickahominy. Geographically, the Garnett and Golding Farms were well placed and well drained in this swampy ground, holding a strategic advantage for the Union force for a move on Richmond. Union troops had fortified and made the Golding Farm a principle lynchpin for McClellan's strategy. It was very much on the mind of offensive driven generals like Philip Kearny that the farm could very well be the jumping-off point for a drive by his division and Heintzelman's III Corps toward the city.

On the night of the 28th, orders arrived stating something that would probably irritate General Philip Kearny when he was informed. Heintzelman recalled his orders: "The night of the 27th of June I was sent for to general headquarters, and was there informed of the determination to change our base of operations of James River."[13] After informing his division commanders, he determined that Kearny's Division would be part of the rear guard of the Army of the Potomac; as the force made its way towards the Charles City Road, General Heintzelman stated in part in his report that General Kearny was indeed in a favorable position for a strike on Richmond. Whether General Heintzelman forwarded to General McClellan this idea of the favorable position Kearny held is uncertain. It was now to become a contest of posts as McClellan and Lee moved to counter to one another.

The initiative shown by Lee and his lieutenants at Gaines' Mill, though costly, had put in motion the removal of Union forces at Golding's Farm through Savage Station. "Lee waited for further news…. Soon after sunrise on June 29, he received a message of great import from two engineers who had been sent by Longstreet to attempt a reconnaissance…. Their report sent a thrill through the army; the great frowning works around Golding's Farm were empty!"[14] This key position south of the Chickahominy River, now abandoned by McClellan, proved that the Union Army was moving to the James, just as the Confederate command had believed it would.

General Kearny truly believed that the Union Army had lost an opportunity as he prepared his men to move in ranks toward the roads through White Oak Swamp. He would have been even more dismayed had he learned of a letter written by McClellan to President Lincoln through Secretary of War Stanton and later filed in his official report.

> On the 28th I sent the following to the Secretary of War: Hon. E.M. Stanton. I now know the full history of the day. On this side of the river we repulsed several strong attacks. On the left bank our men did all that soldiers could accomplish, but they were overwhelmed by vastly superior numbers, even after I brought my last reserves into action…. Had I 20,000 or even 10,000 fresh troops to use to-morrow I could take Richmond, but I have not a man in reserve…. I have lost this battle because my force was too small…. I again repeat that I am not responsible for this, and I say it with earnestness of a general who feels in his heart the loss of every brave man who was needlessly sacrificed today. I still hope to retrieve our fortunes, but to do this the Government must view the matter in the same earnest light that I do.[15]

VIII. Pivot at Gaines' Mill

The differences between Philip Kearny and George McClellan could not be more evident than in the remarks made in this letter to the U.S. Command in Washington, D.C. Three things stand out. First, McClellan takes no responsibility and blames a lack of numbers, which actually had nothing to do with the loss at Gaines' Mill. Second, General McClellan seemed to have no intention of attacking the Confederate force anywhere at any time. Third, unlike Philip Kearny, McClellan did not understand the numbers and the need to make the sacrifice of sending troops into battle as a matter of course. General Kearny finally came to the realization that the Union command did not have the will, particularly after the contest at Malvern Hill, and called it correctly as nothing less than cowardice. It is possible that his remarks, although seemingly insubordinate, may have filtered through the ranks to the offices of the War Department in Washington, D.C., and if they did, they made him a choice in some circles as possible commander of the Army of the Potomac.

IX

Glendale

Before there was a pivot at Gaines' Mill, the activity of the III Corps and Kearny's Division had been basically to hold in place for three weeks prior. Three miles just outside Richmond, III Corps of the Army of the Potomac waited. The Battle of Seven Pines took place on May 31 and June 1. With June at hand, this wing of that army remained on the same ground recently vacated by the Confederates. Kearny listened as the rain pelted his tent; he now believed that this army had lost the initiative as McClellan planned to move up large siege guns. He believed in action and thought the terrain now occupied by the army would allow it, even in this wet weather, to move on the Confederate capital. Even with the Chickahominy flooded and the bridges threatened, the enemy could easily be taken by surprise.[1] At least Kearny believed this.

Even with these bad conditions, Kearny believed hesitation would prove costly. He and Heintzelman were in agreement, and their belief was based on what John Watts De Peyster described as swinging in on the left of the Confederates.[2] To General Kearny the left was the point of vantage.[3] There were, however, other plans; Philip Kearny read the Special Orders from General McClellan and was probably incredulous as he read it. In part it stated: "In order to secure uniformity of action among the Corps.... The general positions occupied by the Corps will be those held at the close of yesterday's battle.... The general purpose is to hold the positions now occupied by the Second, Third and Fourth Corps."[4] The whole idea of maintaining the initiative was slipping away.

In a position along the Richmond and York River Railroad, Kearny held the 3rd Division. On June 3, his division received orders from General Edwin Sumner, overall commander of Union forces south of the Chickahominy. These were the directions: "From information I have received I have reason to expect a formidable attack ... come directly up the railroad, so as to arrive at Fair Oaks Station by daylight."[5] Kearny in turn sent out instructions to General Jameson and Colonel Hobart Ward, acting

IX. Glendale

commander of David Birney's Brigade. These units were to "be ready to move up the railroad and attack the enemy in flank toward Fair Oaks Station."[6] The concern over this attack was based on misinformation; no attack materialized, and Kearny's forces settled into a lull that would last for 12 days.

This lull in the action brought about some changes to the 3rd Division. On June 12, General Jameson received instructions to turn over his command to executive commander Brigadier General John Robinson. Jameson had already been reassigned and he took command elsewhere. The 3rd Division now consisted of Brigadier Generals Berry, Birney and Robinson. Lack of intelligence over the enemy's intentions would allow for the enemy to implement what military theorist Karl von Clausewitz described as Second Reciprocal Action: "As long as the enemy is not defeated, I have to apprehend that he may defeat me, then I shall be no longer my own master, but he will dictate the law to me." General Kearny, from his training with the French, was probably well aware of Clausewitz's notions and was going to make sure his men were prepared. He circulated General Order No. 15: "Brave Regiments of the division ... after two battles ... you may be counted as veterans.... I appeal then to your experiences ... it will enable you to conquer with more certainty."[7] Kearny was still thinking in terms of an offensive and not of a siege.

Union army commander George McClellan was still thinking more along the lines of moving closer to Richmond to emplace his siege guns. With this in mind, he directed Heintzelman to advance his corps up the Richmond and York River Railroad to near a place that was referred to as Oak Grove, just east of Nine Mile Road near King's School House. While his Army was now divided by the swamp of the Chickahominy River, McClellan believed that the Confederates had sacrificed too much in the Battle of Seven Pines to resume an offensive. Little did the Union command realize that the Confederate army had real designs on striking the Union forces and sending them pell-mell through the swamps around the Chickahominy.

General Kearny would help lead the attack and cover the left flank of the Army Corps. General Robinson would move his brigade forward while Berry was held in reserve and General Birney covered their flank. On the morning of June 25, the operation was put in motion.

General Robinson's troops advanced east over swampy ground, south of the Richmond-Williamsburg road. Advancing toward King's School House, the Brigade soon encountered Confederate forces, pushing them back and exchanging heavy gunfire. General Berry was covering the approaches toward the Charles City Road on the left, and he too was covering the division's flank and exchanging fire with the enemy.

The Confederates tried to mount a turning action against Berry's brigade, but were checked by supporting artillery fire. Berry reported the intense action in this way: "At 3:00 p.m. the firing was heavy for a time. The two pieces of artillery of Beam's battery were now at work. The enemy seemed to be arranging for something. I judged it to be to make a dash for the road in rear of the field pieces."[8] Berry's brigade effectively checked this attempt and stalled the Confederates. This was not a determined effort to drive the Confederates, and they seemed to eventually realize that if they could deceive the federals concerning their numbers, they could bluff long enough for what was coming across the river the next day.

The Union lines advanced a little less than a mile, but General McClellan thought it enough for bringing up the heavier guns and initiating the siege. In his official report, General Kearny reported little of the action, showing his disappointment. As usual, he took a very active role in the limited engagement and was in constant contact with his division commanders. He praised the 20th Indiana and the 63rd Pennsylvania, who led the advance forces. These men had forced the Confederate pickets and covering forces back, but only into another tree line at Oak Grove.

"The Affair of the Peach Orchard," as General Heintzelman referred to it, was described by him in this way: "General Robinson, after he had been re-enforced ... recovered the little ground he had lost and drove the enemy back ... and seem to be in considerable force."[9] General Kearny understood full well to now hold his position. He was ordered by Army Headquarters that if withdrawal was necessary, he should not mask his artillery so as to give full play to his front. It was soon to play out that events would change his position and that Kearny was well aware that "[a]s long as the enemy is not defeated ... he will dictate the law."[10]

The initiative for the Army of the Potomac may have ended on May 27, 1862. Remaining in their works around Seven Pines, north of White Oak swamp, III Corps stood idle. Meanwhile, north of the Chickahominy River, Confederate forces assailed McClellan's right at a place called Beaver Dam Creek. It did not stop there. On the following day, Union forces were again assaulted at Gaines' Mill, initiating a bloody hammer blow. The Army's supply line from White House and the Pamunkey River was now in danger of being cut off. McClellan now determined that a change of base would become necessary if he could not hold. This would mean that the ground gained at Oak Grove to emplace those heavy siege guns was meaningless.

IX. Glendale

As for Kearny and his division, his thoughts were for advancing, not withdrawing, and striking the enemy in his front. He was only a few miles from Richmond, and if this new Army of Northern Virginia attacked elsewhere, it would relieve his front of any real opposition. Catching this army in transit and moving on its flank would definitely catch it on its heels. Instead of moving on the Oak Grove front, the III Corps was ordered by the federal command to maintain their position and possibly prepare to move back to the supply area at Savage Station. Kearny could now do nothing except keep his three brigades together and hope for an opportunity that the Army of the Potomac would regain the initiative and strike.

The change of base maneuver would expose the 3rd Division to attack, and Heintzelman had to refuse his line in order to repel an attack by the Confederates at Golding's Farm. As Heintzelman fell back, the Confederate forces in his front moved units forward to determine the weaknesses in the Union lines. This holding action occurred at a time when Kearny's forces were in transit. Holding a line near the farms, Colonel Hobart Ward was in need of relief on his line and reported to General Kearny his situation. "About 1 O'clock a.m. I received a communication from General Kearny, directing me to state to General Hooker that unless the regiments were relieved in an hour, he (Kearny) would relieve them."[11] Kearny pressed this message and Ward was able to move off in good order.

It was on this date, June 27, that it was decided to remove the entire Union force to a new base on the James River. Heintzelman informed his divisions, and General Kearny stated that "on the 28th of June, at midnight, I received orders to prepare to retire from Fair Oaks."[12] Repulsing the probing Confederate forces, the Union forces released from the refused position moved over ground at Seven Pines, making their way to Savage Station. This movement by Union forces would not stop the Confederates. The army had settled into holding actions against the advancing Confederates and at Savage Station, a large union depot. The position would soon be flanked, and this large Union supply base would be the next to be abandoned.

This supply base on the Richmond and York River Railroad was festooned with every possible supply needed by an armed force. The situation for the Northern forces was becoming untenable, at least for General McClellan. It was at this moment, with the Confederate Army bearing down, that General Heintzelman, in charge of the base, was given orders that all those provisions and supplies were to be destroyed: "To give the necessary orders for the destruction of the railroad cars, ammunition and provisions still remaining on the ground."[13] Some of the supplies were quickly loaded onto army wagons that were moving through and heading southeast, but most of them were set on fire and abandoned. A hospital treating the Union forces was also abandoned, along with a number of Union wounded. The men simply could not be transported, and it was decided by the high command that they would be left to be cared for by the Confederates.

Third reciprocal action was now in the hands of the Confederates, who were applying the theorem of utmost exertion of powers. The Confederate Army was moving in pursuit, advancing as opposed to withdrawing. With orders to withdraw, General Kearny was now basically on his own for deciding a route to extradite his men. He had a good insight on the local terrain and immediately decided to reconnoiter a route for crossing White Oak Swamp. He found three crossings that would do; these were Jordan's, Fisher's, and Brackett's Fords. Kearny initially sent David Birney and his brigade across Jordan's Ford. Here Birney encountered a force of Confederates: "My advance skirmishers were fired into by the enemy and we had soon unmistakable evidence of a superior force."[14] With the enemy now on Kearny's left, he withdrew Birney from Jordan's Ford and redirected his force to cross at Fisher's and Brackett's Fords, a little more to his right, where he could navigate southeast. Little did Kearny know that the Confederates to his left where just as concerned with Kearny's whereabouts as he was with theirs.

Successfully extraditing his division across these fords, Kearny was to work his way toward the southeast along the Charles City road. Kearny's force was on the mind of the Confederates, who were unaware of his whereabouts and were concerned he would get in their rear. Confederate General William Mahone reported, "It was anticipated that by this White Oak Swamp road Kearny's division, which had been more immediately confronting our lines, would attempt its retreat, crossing the swamp either at this point or at Fisher's Crossing, where another division of the enemy was known to have been fortified, or at White Oak Bridge, where he was also known to have been in large force formidably fortified."[15]

Author Douglas S. Freeman relates in his book *Lee's Lieutenants* that General Mahone "believed that Kearny's Brigade ... had gone northward—and he thought his adversary ... might wait in the swamp and get in rear of the Confederates after they had passed down the road."[16] Kearny was already down the road, but not in the way the Confederates feared, and would rendezvous with the rest of the army at a place the locals referred to as Glendale Crossroads, or Frayser's Farm. The irony is striking that

IX. Glendale

the offensive that General Kearny was so in favor of was actually dictating Confederate actions, when in fact Kearny was withdrawing as ordered.

The Confederates looked over their shoulders and listened in the dark for any signs that the one-armed devil, as the Confederates referred to Kearny, might be lurking in the swamp, ready to strike along the Charles City Road. Kearny's Division and Birney and Robinson's brigades crossed at Brackett's Ford, and Berry, having found Fisher's Ford uncontested, crossed there. With General Kearny in the van of his force, the men moved silently in the darkness, with only the clatter of canteens making any sound. Moving toward and along the Charles City road, Kearny's troops took the night just short of the Glendale Crossroads. What Kearny had unwittingly done was slow the Confederate advance along his front and had helped prepare the Union force for what was to become a hot contest near a place called Glendale Crossroads.

Glendale (Frazier's Farm) was the key crossroads for moving the supply trains and the soldiers of the Army of the Potomac. It was well known to locals and the Confederate command as a serious choke point where a rumbling wagon train could easily back up. With McClellan's change of base, the Union trains were headed to Harrison's Landing on the James River, and the trains had to pass by the crossroads to get there. Here at the former home of William H. Harrison, of "Tippecanoe and Tyler Too" fame and former president of the United States, would be McClellan's new base for operations. To get to Harrison's Landing, the Charles City road, Long Bridge and Willis Church road all converged at Glendale, and it had to be defended.

At around 10:00 p.m. on June 29, 1862, General Kearny reported that his force was encamped along the Charles City road just short of the crossroads of Glendale. Charles Marks, in his memoir about the Peninsula Campaign, remembered that night "was a march in the gloomy forest where nothing could be seen but the flash of a firefly."[17] All that night and all the next day, the wagons of the Army of the Potomac steadily clanked down the adjoining roads in an unending column that stretched for miles, snaking their way across Glendale Crossroads aiming for the James River shore.

With so much matériel and soldiers converging on Glendale, a bottleneck, as expected, was now ensuing, and it created an excellent opportunity for an enemy force to strike and cut this force in two. Kearny had selected an advantageous position that would allow him to pivot towards the Confederate capital. Corps commander Heintzelman decided that Kearny's division should remove from there, admitting in his official report that he held a "strong position very favorable for an advance on Richmond, but much too forward for the object we had in view."[18] That object was Harrison's Landing, in the opposite direction from Richmond.

June 30 came with expectancy of action in the air. The eventual line of battle would look see Henry Slocum's division covering the Charles City road and Kearny resting on Slocum's left. McCall's division, of Sedgwick's II Corps, rested on Kearny's left. General Robinson and David Birney's brigades would form front on the west side of the Charles City road, with General Berry forming in reserve on the east side of the road. Kearny's 3rd Division would be supported by six pieces of artillery consisting of Battery G, 2nd U.S. Artillery under the command of Captain James Thompson. Kearny remembered that he came into contact with the Confederates at about 4:00 p.m. as they moved up a slope through the heavily forested area. Thompson's battery, located on General Robinson's left, immediately opened fire.

The roar of the cannon was soon followed by the distinct sound of the crack of rifled musketry as the Confederates made a determined effort to penetrate the Union line. The red battle flag of the Confederacy fluttered in and out of sight on the increasingly smoke-filled slope. Artillery Captain Thompson remembered the moment when "they advanced in line, stooping down and firing and we continued firing."[19] Spherical case shot tore through the sky and exploded with tremendous fury, cutting down scores of attackers, but still the butternut and red plaid soldiers came on. The spectacle was of thousands of Confederate soldiers moving over open ground over a mile down the slope, making their way in line toward the Union lines.

Kearny was impressed with the courage of the individual Confederate soldiers and understood the magnitude of this attack. His observation was that this was "a determination and vigor and in such masses as I had never witnessed."[20] It was at this moment that Kearny recognized that the well-positioned battery was in danger of being flanked and cut off. Kearny looked for infantry support and found the 63rd Pennsylvania under the command of Colonel Hays. He brought them up to reinforce the artillery. Kearny was the right man in the right place as the battle turned critical.

It is very possible that no one in the Union command realized the opportunity that was transpiring for the Confederacy at this moment. The Confederates were in a position to cut the Union Army of the Potomac in half and deal them a death blow, reducing them piecemeal. General Kearny's left flank had become exposed due to the fierce attack on McCall's Division and its collapse. All that was needed for the enemy was to

IX. Glendale

immediately take up the ground lost by the Union force. What the Confederates could do was recognize the opportunity. Under the command of General James Longstreet and A.P. Hill, troops were now directed to move up against the heavy smoke and take the Glendale Crossroads.

General Kearny realized something was wrong as he rode forward of his line, which he was known to do, to get the bigger picture. He did not realize how close the enemy really was. "He rode out ... and Kearny dashed directly into a body of deployed troops ... he was in the midst of the rebels."[21] With the battle smoke obscuring almost everything, Kearny coolly realized the danger. A Confederate officer actually came up to Kearny and to Kearny's surprise, asked him what course of action was he to make next. Kearny quickly eyed the man, admonished him for asking, and confidently rode off. It was a cool bluff that worked in this instance, but it was a revealing mistake that the general was unwittingly to make more often than not.

The Confederates were now pressing in on the Union force. The situation that Brigadier General John C. Robinson found himself in was that

This drawing of fighting in the woods shows Kearny's division repulsing the enemy on Monday June 30, 1862. Sketch by Alfred Waud (Library of Congress).

Major General Philip Kearny

McCall's division had practically disintegrated. McCall himself had just been captured and his division was leaderless. With his left exposed on open ground, Robinson was barely a few hundred yards from the Charles City Road. As he had always done, Kearny was moving from one part of the field to the other. He knew he had to shore up the space. Even Heintzelman realized the danger: "The whole open space, 200 paces wide, was filled with the enemy."[22] Kearny had to find units to fill the threatened gap; it was a critical moment that probably would decide the outcome of this contest.

On Kearny's right, Brigadier General Birney was holding his own against the Confederate forces of Maxcy Gregg's South Carolinians, who had problems and made little progress. He had considerable support from Berry's Brigade who had to also support Robinson's right. With this in mind, General Kearny looked elsewhere for units to bring up in order to keep his line functional. The hour was now getting later in the day, and it was nearing eight o'clock when Kearny found the forces needed. The situation was critical for the Union line. A gap now presented itself for the Confederates to exploit. It was a decisive moment for both armies as this was a point in time where the fortune of war could have turned in favor of the Confederacy. There was one factor that the Confederates could not escape, and that was Brigadier General Philip Kearny.

With the battlefield heavy with smoke from musket fire, Kearny could still make out the gap that was developing where McCall's force once occupied. At this critical point, Kearny now led a regiment to the point where McCall had once been and recalled, "It was at this conjuncture that I arrived at my right and found McCall's position abandoned.... I placed in it the First New Jersey Brigade ... the enemy were abusing my entire front."[23] This was the entire force of General Taylor, consisting of the 1st, 2nd, 3rd and 4th New Jersey Regiments (Kearny's old command). The Confederate force, consisting of much of General A.P. Hill's Division, were slow to arrive before the gap in the Union's smoke-filled line, but were also making up time once they realized that the enemy had slackened his fire at that point in the Union line.

The Union New Jersey boys had appeared just in time. The six pieces of Captain Thompson's artillery had expended their ammunition, including solid shot that they directed at the tree line. Battery G, 2nd U.S. Artillery was now limbering up and moving away. General McCall was not to be found, and General Kearny believed him to be dead. The Confederates' advance to this point had been a little tardy because of the previous day's movements, when they had believed that Kearny had actually been

IX. Glendale

in their rear. This gave the Union time to cover their line, but just barely. The one-armed devil had stifled the Confederates once more.

Kearny now took the lead role for the forces arrayed around him and kept up a staccato gunfire exchange with the Confederate force, as it tried to close in. General Kearny realized that this exchange of gunfire would now go on to nightfall. The reality of this engagement might have been lost on others, but it was not lost on Kearny's Division. The continuation of holding the line was at the peril of the Army of the Potomac. Kearny would not have the opportunity for attack as long as the supply trains filed past him on the Long Bridge Road. He had to remain where he was, at least until the trains had passed.

The shadows were now growing longer as daylight gave way to night on the Charles City Road. Intermittent firing continued along the line until about 9:30 p.m., by which time General Kearny had been everywhere along his line. He constantly would be seen by the soldiers, rallying them to hold the line. His military instincts were such that he sensed how important this engagement had become and said so in his report. "In concluding my report of this battle, one of the most desperate of the war, the one most fatal if lost,"[24] etc. He also praised his regiments and singled out the 1st New Jersey Regiment for coming to fill the ground lost by McCall. This was one of the regiments in his Jersey Blues, his original command just months earlier.

The American Civil War almost ended at Glendale. An Army in transition from one point to another was in grave danger of being cut in half. If General McClellan was concerned, it did not outwardly show. His adversary General Lee and his officers did understand the relevance. General Longstreet and A.P. Hill, had they been part of a better coordinated attack, as designed, could well have dislodged the Federals. Longstreet's artillery commander, Edward Porter Alexander, said as much: "The plan offered Lee's army a chance to be within reach of military success so great we might have hoped to end the war with our independence." He went on to point out that the chance for victory on June 30 was probably their best one of all. Kearny and his division's performance had a lot to do with that lost opportunity.

At about midnight, Kearny met with Corps Commander Heintzelman, who had been in charge of all units during the battle, and received his orders to remove his command towards Malvern Hill and disengage from the enemy. It was now dark, and the procession of men, horses and wagons continued their monotonous slog from the intersection of Glendale on echelon down the Willis Church road towards Malvern Hill. Located about two miles south of Glendale intersection, Malvern Hill was a low rise commanding the approaches overlooking the heights above the landings along the James River.

Kearny's Division made its way in the dark past Willis Church and the parsonage, across a tepid stream, and up the undulating slope that is Malvern Hill. The orders from General Heintzelman were these: "It was now 12 o'clock and I could wait no longer ... having heard that General Franklin was leaving. We arranged for his division [General Slocum] to leave immediately, to be followed by General Kearny and then by General Sumner."[25] By daylight on July 1, 1862, Kearny had reached his ordered destination. Setting up camp on a slope in an open field, Kearny sipped on coffee as he contemplated what would the day bring after contributing to saving the Union Army from what could have been an absolute disaster.

Riding with the Union Army command was Prince de Joinville, a French observer. He was primarily attached with the staff of General Fitz John Porter and the Army of the Potomac's commander George McClellan, and had pointed out the importance of the Glendale Crossroads. The Prince also was a keen observer and took note of division commander Philip Kearny. "Kearny, left alone on the battlefield, electrified the men by his intrepidity."[26] It is possible that Kearny had known the Frenchman socially; Kearny may have crossed paths with Prince de Joinville while in France in 1850s. Whether they knew one another or not, it probably had little influence on the Prince's view as he began to take a critical look at the role McClellan had on this army.

X

Malvern Hill

By July 1, 1862, the weather had become increasingly warm and sultry. But the sky continued to be overcast and seemed to threaten rain. The Union forces arrayed themselves on a strong position near the Crew and West farmsteads, which occupied the roads converging toward the James River. A severe engagement is what Glendale had been. It provided the opportunity to show the firepower of the large force that was the Army of the Potomac, particularly the Union artillery. The full force of that army was now arrayed before the Confederate forces still in pursuit and looking to gain on the withdrawing Union force. Malvern Hill would be the next contest for the two opposing armies.

General Kearny may have realized just how important Glendale had been, and he was thinking on the offense. A few days before the Glendale engagement, a soldier of Kearny's division had been captured en route. When questioned in front of Confederate General Stonewall Jackson, the man was asked who might be his commander. The young man answered. "'Kearny, a brave a man as ever drew a sword; do you know him, general?' 'Oh yes, well; you are led by a good officer.'"[1] Kearny's reputation was continuing to be well earned among the Confederates. Kearny had become the single general the Confederates recognized as one of the Union's best, which may have reinforced the belief among some in the Confederate ranks that he was the one to watch in the future.

Kearny had known a number of Confederate officers before the American Civil War broke out, and there was some mutual respect, but not enough to not want him out of the way. From Williamsburg to Seven Pines, Kearny's reputation as a leader from the front marked him as an ideal target among those soldiers who took the brunt of Union musket fire. In fact, it is believed that Kearny was being closely watched by his Confederate antagonists, who were looking for an opportunity to deal with the one-armed devil in whatever manner necessary. The fear that Kearny generated in close order, slashing with his one good arm and with

Major General Philip Kearny

the reins of his horse in his teeth, must have painted a fearful picture to the rank and file Confederate soldier.

Falling back toward the James River and Harrison's Landing, the Army of the Potomac concentrated on the strategically important height of land that was referred to as Malvern Hill. Giving up approximately 20 and 25 miles of front along Richmond, the army's retreat had not, as feared, turned into a rout. Situated some eight miles northwest of Harrison's Landing, Malvern Hill was described this way by Lieutenant General George McClellan: "Malvern Hill is an elevated plateau about a mile by three fourths of a mile in area, well cleared of timber."[2] This clearing presented an excellent open field of fire, especially for Union artillery, which had at this point performed very well in the face of the enemy.

The hill resembled an iron wedge, with the wide part of the wedge forming the highest elevation. The edges were flanked by two swampy streams: Turkey Run on the west, and Western Run or Turkey Island Bend on the east side. The iron plateau would be the forge that would help hammer, at considerable cost, both armies into battle-hardened troops. The southern end of the height of land was soon festooned from one side to the other with Federal batteries of artillery backed by a phalanx of infantry. A contingent of some sixty to seventy guns now looked down the modest slope where it was believed the Confederates would try to ascend. It resembled a flattened hook with the flanks refused and anchored along its physical features.

After receiving his preemptory orders to fall back to Malvern Hill, Kearny's division arrived just before morning light on July 1. Corps commander Heintzelman was not present when Kearny arrived, so he had to confer with other officers for positioning his troops. It was General Humphreys who would confer and help General Kearny position his forces. He decided to position them to the right of Darius Couch's men, on the Army of the Potomac's right flank. Humphreys knew Kearny and had the utmost respect for his fighting qualities. It would be from this point on the right of center that Kearny would take part in the anticipated upcoming battle. With artillery units in place, Kearny took position behind them. Just before the enemy engaged the Union position, Kearny encountered an officer, pale in appearance, who rode up to him. "An officer rode up to Kearny just before Malvern Hill and asked to be relieved on account of illness. 'Sir,' said Kearny, 'this is no time for well men to get sick; these are the times, for sick men to get well, sir.'"[3]

A poem from the *Georgetown Courier* described the contest at Malvern Hill like this:

X. Malvern Hill

> The morning kiss'd each sleeping flow'r
> And woo'd each sparkling rill,
> And rose the sun in haughty power
> On fated Malvern Hill.

The battle would prove to be a pounding artillery assault of haughty power that was fought over five hours as the Confederates tried to mount a coordinated attack. The Confederates set up their support artillery about one mile away from the Union lines; according to one Confederate officer, the plunging fire of their guns would crisscross the field and give the troops cover. The action was joined when those cannon opened fire on the positioned Northern army. This Confederate fire brought Kearny's division under grapeshot that exploded overhead, raining steel pellets and scattering his command as they sought cover.

The troops took cover as best they could on exposed ground with little to hide behind. This call to action was immediately responded to; the return fire from the massed Union guns was a ground-shaking, thunderous roar. Soon the air was filled with acrid smoke as the skies resounded with fire and the ground seemed to tremble with concussions. The nearly one hundred guns of the Union line belched forth a murderous roar of shot and steel. The Confederate artillery could not match the massive Union fire. To maintain their position would be folly as Union ordnance soon began to tell, upending carriages and forcing the Confederates to limber many guns and move away.

With Kearny's division was Company G, 2nd United States Artillery, commanded by Captain Thompson, along with Company E, 1st Rhode Island Artillery of Captain Randolph's Battery. Captain Thompson's artillery was made up of six 12-pounder Napoleons that could lob a shell 1,600 yards at 5-degree elevation. The Union command had determined to combine various artillery of the Army of the Potomac and mass those guns so they could to be relieved by one another and thus keep up a continuing fire, never having to have to pause, but only to limber and unlimber their guns.

Another one of those many artillery sections was Captain Randolph's Battery, consisting of six 10-pounder Parrotts that could lob a shell 2,000 yards at 5-degree elevation. Easily bringing the Confederate force within range, General Heintzelman recorded, "Captain Randolph with his Parrott guns persecuted all that attacked him, silencing several times batteries that were sweeping our front."[4] For the Confederate force it was becoming a withering and deadly fire. As the Confederate rank and file came up, it seemed as if time was moving in slow motion. Not only did the

Major General Philip Kearny

Confederate Infantry face the hail of artillery, they soon encountered the fire of whizzing musket balls as well.

Early in the battle, dressed in their prominent green uniforms, Berdan's Union sharpshooters had moved forward to act as pickets and to look for targets of opportunity. This would mean that some officers and enlisted men started to fall as they moved forward toward the Union line. Confederate General D.R. Jones put it this way: "We commenced ascending a hill in front of the enemy … the grape and bombs falling and bursting just above our heads, taking off a great many and cutting some in half."[5] With all this firing going on, the battle smoke was getting heavy on both sides, and the Confederate troops had little to fire at as they sought to hug the ground. The flashes of enemy gunfire started to look like flicks of light off in the distance.

With musket fire whizzing by, General Kearny decided to get a closer view. Mounted on a light gray horse, Kearny moved his way toward the West house. Located on the Union center, the West and Crewe houses became the focus of the attack and the main line of defense for the Union. Here the Federal artillery pounded down the slope at the massed Confederates. Kearny moved along the line of artillery, pausing every now and then to peer out into the haze to see what the progress of the enemy might be. Kearny was interested in the action and was probably curious as to how well the artillery would perform in keeping infantry at bay. He managed to make his way to the West house and found some officers of the 5th Corps taking in the action. One 5th Corps officer remembered seeing Kearny and promptly warned him of his exposed presence. "All was quiet on his end of the line and he had come to see how things were managed by the 5th Corps."[6] The whistle of Confederate sharpshooter bullets could plainly be heard and when one Union officer warned Kearny of his exposed position sitting on a horse, Kearny merely laughed it off. The whistle of bullets was not unfamiliar to the "one-armed devil," and he was at ease as he made his way back to his units' positions the same way he had come.

By the time he returned, the action in his sector had picked up. Cannon were now blazing away and units in his division would soon see some action. Off to the right front of his division was a ravine that descended toward what was called Western Run. The Confederates were now starting to move toward that depression in order to engage General Couch's far right flank. Kearny decided to support Couch by moving the 4th Maine to cover the area. Brigadier General Birney in his action report says, "We held the front line during a furious cannonade and entrenched our entire front. The Fourth [Maine] and four companies of the Third Maine held

X. Malvern Hill

the wooded ravine in front of Kearny's line.... Couch's right was in danger of being driven back ... my command gallantly aided him in driving the enemy back."[7]

With smoke now covering the field of fire in all directions, only the cannon fire in the immediate front could be heard and seen, and only at a close distance. General Kearny remembered that Generals Berry and Robinson, held in reserve, "were constantly sent forward in support as the tide of battle swerved to and fro on our left."[8] The Confederates had the harder time of it. They failed to reach the ravine and fell short of their goals across the entire field by at least hundreds of yards, and they paid the price as they soon had to fall back, keeping as close to the ground as they could. By 9:00 p.m. cannon fire began to subside, and the only sound heard was the melancholy moans of wounded and dying soldiers. Kearny's division remained in their reserve position until well after midnight.

Writing in his official report after the battle, Kearny simply reports that sometime after midnight he received orders to "move in retreat and tired as were all our command, it was again executed with much regularity."[9] Moving off in the darkness, the units of the First Division made for the landing on the James River. Many an officer and soldier believed that the day had been theirs, and they could not understand the reasons for leaving the ground already won. By the time they reached Harrison's Landing at 10:00 a.m. the next day, rain had again started fall in buckets, making for a miserable bivouac at this site. Kearny's division made camp on the edge of the plantation grounds with much of the Army of the Potomac all around for miles.

Incensed by the thought that again the army had fallen back and not turned to attack what was probably a spent enemy, Kearny finally vented his personal feelings. Chaplin Marks, part of the 3rd Division, recalled Kearny's ire at a moment with his staff. "I Philip Kearny, an old soldier, enter my solemn protest against this order to retreat."[10] As with all great captains of war, Kearny sent his men into combat as a matter of course; he recognized that the numbers favored the Union army and that this was moment to strike the enemy. Kearny truly believed the enemy must be spent and vulnerable after the disastrous assault at Malvern Hill. This was a moment for attack. The senior officer in command, General George McClellan, thought otherwise.

He was not alone in his protest. General Fitz John Porter, a McClellan supporter and confidant, could not understand giving up the strong position the army had held on Malvern Hill and was reluctant to move off. Kearny went on to remark, as recalled by Chaplin Marks, that such an order seemed to border on cowardice. Kearny never used McClellan's name in that remark, and there is no indication it was directed at the general, although it is probable that Kearny thought it. It was rather a frustration, on the part of Kearny and others, that giving up ground to a defeated enemy was historically abhorrent in Kearny's experience.

Kearny believed that the way to Richmond was now open and driving the Confederate forces was theirs for the taking. As right as Kearny probably was, McClellan had made up his mind, and the army was not going anywhere except the campgrounds around the old Berkeley Plantation at Harrison's Landing. It was raining heavily as troops filed in at Harrison's Landing. The grounds around the plantation spread out gently along a three-mile stretch of the James River. It is here that a significant historical home of a colonial family important to the founding of the United States once lived. The Harrisons had now left the Berkeley Plantation, and it had become the headquarters of the Army of the Potomac.

Now the place had become the crowded center for an army of more than 100,000 men with all their accouterments of war. George McClellan decided on it in this way: "I selected Harrison's bar as the new position of the army. The exhaustion of our supplies of food, forage and ammunition made it imperative to reach the transports immediately."[11] Ironically, McClellan had blown up and abandoned considerable supplies at Savage Station that he could have used to turn on the offensive, as Kearny had wanted him to do, and Kearny had railed against giving them up.

Heintzelman reported that all his forces had arrived and had started to bivouac near the army's northern edge. On July 3, Confederate forces began to take watch of their activities. Finding an opportunity to make some mischief, the Confederates started to shell some Union positions. They took range of Kearny's position, and corps commander Heintzelman later reported, "Captain Reno has just returned from a reconnaissance on the Charles city road. He went almost one and one half mile from the mill ... when he found the enemy."[12] Heintzelman recalled that it was reported that the enemy had but two guns and that they were driven off by Union cavalry videttes. No damage was reported by Kearny and there was no loss of life.

In Washington, the consternation was just as great as General Kearny's. It was early July when President Lincoln decided to visit his forces in the tidewater. The president's concern was now for defending Washington, D.C., and he needed some of McClellan's now idle forces. General John Pope had been given command of a force called the Army of Virginia, and he needed more men to launch an attack. McClellan had

X. Malvern Hill

failed to attack in unison with General Pope's Army of Virginia as Pope had hoped, and Lincoln was not pleased. It was therefore decided to detach units from McClellan and move them by steamer back to the Northern Virginia area. Many in Washington feared that the capital was now in danger.

Kearny and his troops were allotted to move to join Pope's Army of Virginia, as soon as could be expedited. By mid–August, Kearny was moving through Williamsburg in the opposite direction of the way that he had come. For a general like Kearny, this was not the direction that he would have anticipated. In fact, he protested at the time of Malvern Hill that the time was ripe to strike at Lee's forces and Richmond, but now the reverse was occurring. He soon followed Fitz John Porter onto transports at Hampton Roads and was moving up the tide toward Washington. The general in charge of logistics (probably Van Vliet) reported everything was moving successfully.[13] The Northern Virginia Campaign was beginning as Northern infantrymen slowly moved their way up ramps to board the steamers and barges that would make their way back up the Potomac.

XI

A Long Roll of Thunder

A swirl of activity was taking place around John Pope's headquarters, located just behind the Rapidan and Rappahannock rivers. His assignment, as directed by Army Chief of Staff General Henry Halleck, was now to bring to bear the Union Army of Virginia and reduce the enemy, as George McClellan had not. The victor of Island No. 10 and New Madrid, Missouri, in April 1862, John Pope now set his eyes on the task of defeating Robert E. Lee's Army of Northern Virginia, if not actually destroying it. Here was the problem: Pope would now command a combined army that was by no means united. In fact, Kearny observed, "How do they expect Pope … to beat, with a very inferior force, the veterans of Ewell and Jackson? Get me and my fighting division with Pope."[1] This statement leads one to believe that General Kearny actually looked forward to another fight, even if it was alongside General Pope, but it also reveals some skepticism as to the ability of Pope's force.

That fight was to become a certainty as a portion of Pope's army came across Stonewall Jackson's Division, which was moving toward the Orange County Courthouse near the Rapidan River. A number of scenarios presented themselves to the Union Army Command. Lincoln, to his disappointment, had General McClellan ensconced with the Army of the Potomac along the James River at Harrison's Landing. Major General John Pope had his Army of Virginia spread along the Rappahannock and Rapidan rivers in northern Virginia, looking to cooperate with the Army of the Potomac and bringing to bear two armies against Lee's Army of Northern Virginia between them.

The Confederate forces were confident in that they were free to move anywhere in Western Virginia. Thomas J. Jackson's Army of the Valley had cleared the adjacent Shenandoah Valley earlier that year, by repelling three different Federal armies that were supposed to act in concert against him. The bold moves of Jackson that spring shocked the Federal command and the politicians in Washington, D.C., and caused consternation as to

XI. A Long Roll of Thunder

where would Jackson appear next. General Jackson had the freedom of movement that Phil Kearny could only hope to have. The principles were simple: Jackson believed in isolating and striking a portion or segment of the enemy forces and possibly destroying it. The other principle was to get between an enemy and his lines of supply and communications, and so disrupt them as to cause the enemy to act in a manner that could be easily manipulated. This is exactly what Stonewall Jackson had in mind as he moved his division toward Cedar Mountain (Slaughter Mountain).

Pope was delighted that the enemy was now being encountered. Pope was less delighted that cooperation between his Army of Virginia and McClellan's Army of the Potomac was not acting in concert. The best he could expect was a slow repatriation of some of the Army of the Potomac's units to his command by way of steamship and rail. One of the Army of the Potomac units was Philip Kearny's Division of Heintzelman's III Corps. On August 9, Jackson struck at Cedar Mountain, and Pope reported: "The action of August 9 at Cedar Mountain with the forces under Jackson, which compelled his retreat across the Rapidan, made necessary still further re-enforcements of the enemy from Richmond.... I remained at Cedar Mountain and still threatened to cross the Rapidan until August 17, by which time General Robert E. Lee had assembled in my front and within 3 miles nearly the whole of the rebel army. As soon as I ascertained this fact, and knew that the Army of the Potomac was no longer in danger, I drew back my whole force."[2]

What Pope failed to realize was that the Confederate force arrayed against him had ascertained his intentions and now prepared to act boldly against the Army of Virginia. The Army of the Potomac was never in danger, because by now it was moving its units back toward Washington's defenses, and Pope was not its deliverer as he thought. Two federal armies were trying to combine with one another; it was a difficult and confusing order. Meanwhile, shortly after the Cedar Mountain contact, it was decided in a conference of Confederate Generals Lee, Jackson and Stuart that Jackson would separate from the Confederate main column and make a sweeping movement to get behind General Pope and attack Union supply lines to keep the Union command off balance. It was a gamble, but the rewards could be great.

Curiously, General Pope seemed to believe that the enemy's movements were as one. Even more revealing, Pope had doubts about his own command. On August 25, Pope recorded:

> The column of the enemy alluded to in my dispatch of 12.30 p.m. to-day passed Gaines' Cross-Roads, and when last seen, near sunset, was passing to the north-

> east, under the east base of Buck Mountain, in the direction of Salem and Rectortown. I am inclined to believe that this column is only covering the flank of the main body, which is moving toward Front Royal and Thornton's Gap, though of this I am not certain.... McDowell's is the only corps that is at all reliable that I have. Sigel, as you know, is perfectly unreliable, and I suggest that some officer of superior rank be sent to command his army corps. His conduct to-day has occasioned me great dissatisfaction. Banks' corps is very weak, not amounting to more than 5,000 men, and much demoralized.... Kearny's division is the only one that has yet reached me from Alexandria. I shall at all events push McDowell's corps and Kearny's division upon the enemy's rear, if I find my suspicions confirmed in the morning.[3]

Due to lack of intelligence, Pope seemed to believe he was taking on the entire Army of Northern Virginia. The Armies of Virginia and Northern Virginia now began to waltz with one another across the Northern Virginia countryside, as they maneuvered for position.

As these two opponents faced off across the Rappahannock River, General Lee decided to send Jackson's Corps around the flank of Pope's Army by way of the Blue Ridge and Bull Run Mountains. Lee had come to believe that at this point General Pope's Army was spread too thin, and that to get at him he needed a bold move before General McClellan's forces could move in and support him. At an impromptu meeting, Lee decided to send Jackson's entire corps around the enemy's right flank, using the western mountains as a screen, and then get behind Pope while the rest of the Army of Northern Virginia would come up and surprise the enemy. As previously related, it was a bold plan in the face of a combining Union Army.

In a report written after the Battle of Second Manassas, Pope seemed to try to cover up the fact that Lee and Jackson had indeed outmaneuvered him due to McClellan's slow response:

> Mean time my force had been much diminished by actual loss in battle and by fatigue and exposure, so that, although I had been joined by a detachment under General Reno and the other division of McDowell's corps, my force barely numbered 40,000 men.... The movement of Jackson toward White Plains and in the direction of Thoroughfare Gap while the main body of the enemy confronted me at Sulphur Springs and Waterloo Bridge was well known to me, but I relied confidently upon the forces which I had been assured would be sent from Alexandria, and one strong division of which I had ordered to take post in the works at Manassas Junction. I was entirely under the belief that these would be there, and it was not until I found my communications intercepted that I was undeceived. I knew that this movement was no raid, and that it was made by not less than 25,000 men under Jackson.[4]

Pope had the luxury of hindsight and more than likely was completely unaware of Jackson's move until Jackson was in Manassas Junction.

XI. A Long Roll of Thunder

Scrambling to keep up, Pope began to move some of his forces from Warrenton toward Gainesville. The supporting force from the Peninsula and McClellan's Army were arriving. Major General Joseph Hooker's Division had made its way to Bristoe Station, and Philip Kearny had also detrained and had made his way outside Warrenton Junction, but the lack of creditable intelligence began to take hold. These units alone had now bolstered Pope's forces, taking away his claim of a diminished force. The attachment of these Army of the Potomac divisions from the Peninsula should have strengthened Pope's hand; instead, it seemed to only add to a confusing field. As it would soon become clear, Jackson's Confederate forces were already in the Union rear.

On August 27, things began to get underway when Jackson's force took action against the Union supply chain. Attacking Pope's supplies at Manassas Junction, Jackson raided and then set afire all of the Federal supplies and munitions, not to mention destroying rail cars and engines for good measure. Pope's response was,

> I reached Manassas Junction with Kearny's division and Reno's corps about 12 o'clock in the day of the 28th, less than an hour after Jackson in person had retired. I immediately pushed forward Hooker, Kearny, and Reno upon Centreville.... I also wrote to McDowell, and stated the facts, so far as we were then able to ascertain them, and directed him to call back the whole of his force that had come in the direction of Manassas Junction and to move forward upon Centreville.... Late on the afternoon of the 28th Kearny drove the enemy's rear guard out of Centreville, and occupied that town, with his advance beyond it, about dark.[5]

The Union Command was now back at Centreville, just as they had been when McClellan had begun his Peninsula Campaign four months before, fighting a battle that probably could have been fought there then.

It had become obvious that Jackson withdrew his force somewhere west or north of Manassas Junction, and Pope was determined to bring him to bay. In accordance with Pope's orders, it was decided to move General McDowell's Corps of King, Sigel and Reynolds through Gainesville down the Warrenton Pike east, and Pope would move with III Corps of Heintzelman, Reno and Porter's V Corps to meet up at Centreville from Manassas Junction. To Pope's consternation, General McDowell, who had sparred with the Confederates at First Manassas, thought it prudent to send some of Rickett's force to cover Thoroughfare Gap. McDowell's instincts were correct, and he realized that the Confederates had indeed set a trap. Pope thought otherwise: "He had, however, without my knowledge, detached Rickett's division in the direction of Thoroughfare Gap, and that division was no longer available in his movement toward Centreville."[6]

Major General Philip Kearny

McDowell was certain that he faced only a portion of the Confederate Army; Pope was certain he had it all before him, and for some reason, he actually believed that this force was in retreat.

General Pope later reported that he was certain that Jackson was making good his escape toward Thoroughfare Gap, and that he was going to stop him. This notion, that Jackson was actually retreating, would never leave Pope's head. All of the actions of the next three days by the Union Army were predicated on the belief of the Union commander that Jackson might make good his escape and that the opportunity was there to destroy his command. This belief was probably reinforced when, on August 27, Joe Hooker's division dueled with the Confederate command of Richard Ewell. "The action commenced about 4 miles west of Bristoe Station. Ewell was driven back along the railroad, but still confronted Hooker at dark ... immediately in front of Bristoe Station, at which point I arrived."[7] Believing that he had Jackson trapped, Pope was actually grasping for Jackson's whereabouts as he sent McDowell and Heintzelman down the roads towards Centreville, possibly thinking he could trap this force. It would be elements in McDowell's command that would be singled out by the Confederate force for immediate attention as it moved unknowingly towards his guns.

It was going on evening of August 28 as the sun began its long, slow set, giving off a very red hue as it neared the western horizon. The blue soldiers were set off by the rays of the sun as they moved east along the Centreville road. General Rufus King, who commanded the First Division of McDowell's Third Army Corps, was having another one of his bouts with dizziness and was feeling ill (it is believed he suffered from epilepsy) as he led his division down the Centreville Road. He had commanded the future Iron Brigade of mostly Wisconsin men when it had arrived in Washington, D.C., in 1861. Now, luckily, he had Brig. Gen. John Gibbon in command of that unit, the Fourth Brigade. Gibbon was the consummate soldier and a West Point graduate who had drilled the Wisconsin regiments of that brigade into a sharp unit. Comprising the 2nd, 6th, and 7th Wisconsin and 19th Indiana, the Fourth Brigade (Western Brigade) was about to enter an intense fight and was soon to win its first laurels as the late afternoon sun turned toward evening.

Confederate General Thomas Jackson had his command of A.P. Hill and Richard Ewell hidden in a wood line along an unfinished rail bed near Sudley Spring to just past the Brawner Farmstead that stood some distance above the Warrenton/Centreville Pike that the Union Army now came along. Jackson and his command had now laid the trap that he was about to spring on the Union army. Mounted on his horse with binoculars

XI. A Long Roll of Thunder

in one hand and the reins of his horse in the other, Jackson trotted out just past the wood line near the farmhouse. Back and forth Jackson rode up and down the ridge by the woods as he watched the long roll of Yankees who seemed to be completely unaware of the lone rider's presence. Stonewall Jackson could not believe his luck as he calmly rode back to his officers and staff and turned to Generals Ewell and Taliaferro quietly saying, "Bring up your men, gentlemen."[8]

Plodding along the road, the Union men had spent most of the day marching from Bristoe Station to Gainesville and now towards Centreville, and many thought only of bivouacking for the evening. Some in the Western Brigade may have even noticed that a lone rider was watching their slow movement as they came forward along the road. No one could have guessed that it was one of their greatest opponents getting ready to call out his men against them. J.H. Brunemer related that they were "passing along through a fine body of oak timber. The sun was just sinking from sight in the west and everything seemed lovely and serene. We were very tired and not feeling very buoyant of spirit.... I do know that if any were indulging in day dreams of home ... such dreams were suddenly swept aside by the boom of cannon a short distance to our left."[9] As a blood-red sun was setting to their rear, the sudden flashes of artillery filled the air like lightning. Men looked up to their left to the sound of the guns; Gibbon's men now found themselves engaged.

King's Division was now in the thick of it. Stumbling into an artillery barrage, the units took cover on both sides of the road. The trees above them seem to explode as shot and shell rained in. As the opposing line drew up on the ridge above them, Gibbon understood what he had to do. The order was given that first the 2nd Wisconsin would move north to engage. Then the order was given to Colonel Robinson to bring his unit to the right of the 2nd Wisconsin and engage. Colonel William Robinson responded immediately, and the bearded New Englander who had fought in the war with Mexico soon had his men moving off the road.

The 2nd Wisconsin was outflanked and needed support. The 19th Indiana moved to the left and the 7th Wisconsin moved to the right on Robinson's orders. The command was "Left into line wheel." By that time, it was nearing 7:00 p.m. The fire of rifled muskets was by now intense. Before them, in the long shadows of the twilight, came the red, white and blue of the Cross of St. Andrew. Now fire seemed to belch in a line in front of them. Clutching their muskets and waiting for the order to fire, the left wing of the regiment had somehow overlapped with the 2nd. It didn't seem to matter, as a dense drifting smoke descended on all.

Major General Philip Kearny

From colonel to major, from captain to lieutenant, the order came down the line to fire at will. The regiment before them staggered at the first volley, but soon recovered and returned fire. Fire from both sides became commonplace. Colonel Gibbon remembered, "It was a regular stand up fight during which neither side yielded a foot. My command exhibited in the highest degree the effects of discipline and drill, officers and men standing up to their work like old soldiers."[10] There, within 100 yards of one another, the 7th began to exchange murderous fire with the Confederates.

This was the first engagement for Colonel Robinson's regiments. Mild confusion reigned as the 7th and 2nd tried to untangle from one another, and the fighting continued. It was soon realized that even the 7th was dangerously outflanked, or "in the air" with no cover, and Gibbon looked to fill the gap. Gibbon expected other units to come up and was incredulous when he realized that he was practically in the fight on his own. Gibbon was basically the only command engaging the enemy and he would continue the fight whether he could get support or not. Gibbon knew he would have taken action on his own. Never one to shy away from action, Gibbon deployed his men and at the same time went to find the reinforcing units he needed as the shells began to fill the air around him.

As the Brigade Commander went to look for support, the units of the Fourth Brigade continued to blaze at the opposing Confederates, who returned fire in kind. As one participant remembered the affair, "[T]here we stood one hour men falling all around."[11] J.H. Brunemen of Company H, 7th Wisconsin, found himself in a slow-moving dance of smoke and flashes as he saw two of his friends, Lucius Eastman and Luther Schnee, killed while holding their ground amid bullets flying everywhere.[12] Colonel Robinson, commanding the 7th Wisconsin, was seriously wounded, in his leg, and had to be carried off the field. Many other officers of the 7th were wounded that day while directing the men and bracing them against the heavy fire.

Gibbon looked for help to shore up his right. Colonel Marsena Patrick found that he could not support him at this time, as he moved down the Centreville road. Furious over Marsena's noncommittal, Gibbon hurried to Abner Doubleday and asked that he put two New York regiments on his right flank, which Doubleday did. By the time this was done, the darkness of the evening was upon them; it was now near 8:00 p.m., and the firing on both sides slackened and stopped. The Confederates were beginning to disengage and seemed to disappear behind the trees. Officers in the 7th and Gibbon himself must have wondered why they would engage at such an hour, only to break off. Surely the enemy was up to something.

XI. A Long Roll of Thunder

Pvt. Ludolf Longhenry of Company C, 7th Wisconsin Regiment describes what occurred after disengaging from the Confederates: "We retreated. The rebels retained the battlefield. I was among the last to leave the battleground ... as I was leaving I came across one of our wounded, a Captain Walter who was shot through the lungs. I gave the last drink of water from my canteen. But I could do no more. There was still a heavy rain of shells."[13]

The opening shots of Second Manassas were over, or as some called it, the Battle of Groveton. Even with the disengagement, John Gibbon's blood was up, and he thought that the field that had just been paid for by his troops should not be given up. In an impromptu meeting with General King, Gibbon said he thought that the division should remain, but it was decided to withdraw. When Pope subsequently learned of King's withdrawal, Pope ordered his command to meet up with the rest of the Army of Virginia in Centreville. "The disposition of troops on the west of Jackson having failed through Rickett's movement toward Thoroughfare Gap and the consequent withdrawal of King, an immediate change in the disposition and proposed movements of the troops for the succeeding day became necessary.... I immediately sent a joint order to Generals McDowell and Porter, directing them, with their two corps, to march with all speed toward Gainesville on the direct road from Manassas Junction."[14]

Earlier in the day of Thursday, August 28, the command of Major General Philip Kearny was making its way north toward the town of Centreville, Virginia. General Pope was making his way to Centreville with the ultimate aim of concentrating his now growing force in order to make an attempt to destroy Jackson's command. "About noon General Kearny reached the Junction. Our railroad trains fired by the enemy were still burning. We here learned that he had retreated on Centreville.... The pursuit was continued. The advance of General Kearny's division found but one regiment of rebel cavalry at Centreville which fell back at his approach."[15] Seeing the enemy falling back down the Warrenton Turnpike, General John Pope expected to find the Confederates somewhere nearby.

Curiously, the situation of that day, August 28, was one of differing realities. General John Pope believed he now had Confederate General Thomas Jackson isolated. As Ricketts and King were engaged along the Centreville road, Kearny had made his way up from Manassas Junction to Centreville. General Pope believed that King's division now cut off Jackson's retreat toward Thoroughfare Gap, and that he could now concentrate the rest of his army at Centreville to move on Jackson as he retreated. What Pope did not know at that time is that King and Ricketts had moved south towards Manassas Junction, away from Jackson. The reality was that

Major General Philip Kearny

Pope's army was not concentrated; Fitz John Porter's Corp was still on the move and was not yet near to be deployed. Heintzelman was ordered that evening to move on Jackson early the next morning, and he so directed Kearny and Hooker. First Corps, Army of Virginia, on the night of the 28th camped around the intersection of Sudley Springs road and Centreville road with orders to engage the enemy early the next day. Major General Franz Sigel, who was the nearest Union force to Bull Run, expected the rest of the combined Union army to be there in the morning. Sigel prepared to attack.

Thomas J. Jackson proved to be one of the most formidable adversaries to face the Union Armies and was one of Kearny's biggest admirers. Jackson and Kearny were both proponents of swift action against an enemy (Library of Congress Prints and Photographs Division, Washington, D.C.).

XII

Manassas, August 29: Pope Engages

Strategic initiative is a fickle child in war. When McClellan's army was ordered back up the Potomac, its initial embarkation at Fort Monroe gave Lee a signal to turn. Lee surmised that the Union would now direct operations from northern Virginia, but he needed more to verify his suspicions. His additional intelligence would come from a singularly reliable source in the efficient cavalry commander John Singleton Mosby, who would eventually win the sobriquet the Gray Ghost of the Confederacy. Mosby was a recently exchanged cavalry officer who watched and observed the Union movements while detained and reported to Lee's headquarters. There he informed the commander of the Army of Northern Virginia that a large Union force was gathering at Hampton and was preparing to leave by transports.

The die was now truly cast as Third Corps commander Major General Samuel Heintzelman received his orders to move his divisions. "On the 14th of August, at 9 O'clock p.m. I received orders to retreat from Harrison's Bar, on the James River."[1] Philip Kearny was probably none too happy to receive such an order, but he signaled to his three division officers to break camp and prepare the men to form ranks. It was Friday, August 15, when Kearny's forces began to move in the direction of the Chickahominy River, headed toward Hampton. General Birney's Brigade was to provide for the cover of the main body of the division as it now headed toward Williamsburg on the 17th, arriving on that date.

By August 18, elements of III Corps and Kearny's First Division arrived for transport at Hampton Roads. The plumes of smoke from the stacks of steamers rose skyward as the troops made their way to the gangplanks and one by one moved on board. Steamers, barges and warships of every description were everywhere in the vast expanse of water that was the roads. Once Kearny was there, he took his favorite gray horse, Baby, up to the transport barge and led him into the stall. His horse did not like the arrangement and kicked at the stall. Kearny's new orderly, Gustave Schurmann, was with him and remarked about the horse's manner: "I have known that same horse to kick at him as he went into the gate."[2] Neither rider nor horse were amused at this venture.

On Wednesday, August 20, the steamers slipped their moors and headed across Hampton Roads for the Chesapeake Bay, heading north for the Potomac and Washington. Initially the transports were to head for Aquia Landing, just south of the city of Alexandria. But new orders came from Army Chief of Staff Henry Halleck directing Kearny's forces elsewhere, "diverting McClellan's troops to Alexandria because of inadequate berthing facilities at Aquia."[3] Heintzelman remembered arriving at a more appropriate venue on the 22nd. "On our arrival from the peninsula at Alexandria we were hurried forward, without artillery or wagons, and many of the field officers without horses."[4] Waiting just off the wharfs were the military railcars of the Orange and Alexandria Railroad. The officers and men of Heintzelman's corps now loaded onto those railcars. General Kearny would have to wait for his mounts, like his horse Baby, at another time as he watched the hurried loading of troops and the weapons they carried with them onto those cars.

Philip Kearny and Heintzelman's III Corps of the Army of the Potomac were now attached to units of the Army of Virginia under the command of Major General John Pope, who initially was to operate in coordination with that Army. The wharfs of Alexandria had become exceedingly busy as troops disembarked and then immediately loaded onto railcars. The situation had become increasingly fluid as movement of the enemy closed in toward Washington. The Union forces initially headed southwest toward Warrenton Junction, but it was soon learned that the enemy, too, had changed operations. From Warrenton Junction, Kearny's forces were soon moving towards the northeast, marching in that direction from August 26 to the 28th, finally moving into position near Centreville, Virginia, the site of his first engagement with the Confederates.

While en route, Kearny observed the smoke rising from Manassas Junction and marveled at the enemy's audacity to run circles around the Union army. He rode with his staff and called on them to keep the men moving and close up the ranks. Curiously, General Heintzelman wanted his corps to move as rapidly as possible toward Centreville, and Kearny received this order from Commanding General Pope: "At the early blush of dawn push forward ... with all speed to this place.... I want you here at day-dawn, if possible and we shall bag the whole crowd."[5] It was clear that engagement was anticipated at or near the old battleground at Bull Run (Manassas).

XII. Manassas, August 29: Pope Engages

Major General John Pope did not endear himself to the local populace of the Confederacy while in search of Jackson's force. He issued a threatening circular in General Order No. 7, warning the locals that it was deemed offensive action for partisans and guerrillas to sabotage telegraph lines, railroads, and wagons. The latter statement was directed at Confederates like John Mosby. "Citizens living within 5 miles of the spot shall be turned in mass to repair the damage."[6] Pope further stated, since he had the power to implement martial law, that any locals who fired on soldiers would have their property forfeit and destroyed.[7] The heavy-handed manner in which this message was directed found its way to the Confederate command, and Lee himself now took notice. This directive by Pope would make for a very unfriendly response when soldiers of Kearny and other Union commands made their way through this part of Northern Virginia. The local populace seemed to disappear as soldiers passed empty farms and homes. A good example of this was the Matthews' Stone House, which was left basically empty after the First Manassas Battle (Bull Run) in 1861.

If Brigadier General Kearny was dismayed with General McClellan, and his performance on the James and York Peninsula, he was absolutely uncertain about General Pope's lieutenants. General Kearny did not have faith in the lieutenants that had been assigned to Pope's Army of Virginia after his initial response that he could work with him. His doubts of the ability of that force would manifest itself openly in the days to come. The signals and communications between the varied elements of a combined force hampered the ability of Pope's intelligence apparatus. Pope actually had a spy within the Army of Northern Virginia, and this spy soon eluded the Confederate lines and informed Pope of Lee's whereabouts.

It should be noted that General Pope kept Lee and his Confederate army at grips until after the action at Cedar Mountain. From that point on, Pope began to lose the ability to dictate events. The command of the Army of Northern Virginia now decided on the bold move of dividing the army and sending Stonewall Jackson's forces to move around the enemy and get in his rear. This surprising move took Pope off guard, threw him off balance, and led to the concentration of the dispirited elements of the Army of Virginia at or near Centreville, Virginia.

On arrival in Alexandria, Kearny's Division had been forced to travel from there to Warrenton Junction, and then were ordered back north to Centreville. Pope and his lieutenants were groping for the whereabouts of the enemy. But Kearny was willing to give Pope a chance, even if he thought he might be chasing the tail of the dog. Kearny's command now

Major General Philip Kearny

consisted of Brigadier General John C. Robinson of the First Brigade, Brigadier General David Birney of the Second Brigade, and Colonel Orlando Poe, commanding the Third Brigade after the departure of Hiram Berry on August 20, 1862. Once he reached the old Manassas battlefield, General Kearny was somewhat concerned about the situation. He thought that the Confederates had possibly laid a trap, but he also was ready for combat. He was excited that an opportunity was now presenting itself, even though he preferred to attack on his terms when he was ready.

Arriving at Centreville on the 28th, Kearny had received orders from Pope that the opportunity was now at hand to bag the whole crowd. There was no time to catch their breath when the need to expedite a march was ordered. General Pope had found the enemy, and he was soon to come to grips with the Confederate General Thomas Jackson. Pope believed he now had the enemy in retreat just beyond a railroad grade, and was determined to bring his forces up. Pope never expected that he actually was losing control of the situation; however, one observer remarked that "he had lost command of the situation once the armies were at close grips."[8] The rest of his army was not as sure, and it is explained in this way. "The march during the previous night had been confused and fatiguing due to changes in Pope's orders, which caused countermarching."[9]

General Kearny actions on that day, August 29, have come under scrutiny by some as not exactly his best; he even questioned Pope for his order to move up to Manassas on the Centreville Road with vague instructions to cover the Army of Virginia's right. Kearny may well have believed that he was blindly leading his force to a field with little intelligence as to what to expect. "The content of his orders [Pope's] indicate clearly that when he had formulated them he had neither correct knowledge of the activities of his own forces nor those of Longstreet."[10] He knew the general whereabouts of Jackson's forces, but not the rest of the Confederate army, including Lee and General Longstreet. Kearny was moving toward a confusing field, briefly believing, per Pope's orders, that he was pursuing a fleeing enemy.

Kearny prepared his brigades as soon as he thought necessary in order to advance toward Bull Run. Kearny had neither the correct knowledge of the activities of Pope's forces, nor those of the enemy. For Kearny was now assigned the task of positioning on the Union right flank and was to cover any possible turn of the enemy on that flank. Kearny did not know what he might face as John Pope fixated on striking Stonewall Jackson along an unfinished railroad grade. Pope thought Jackson's force was now retreating toward Thoroughfare Gap on the evening of the 28th.[11]

XII. Manassas, August 29: Pope Engages

Pope wanted to attack as soon as he could bring his force to bear on the Confederates in his front early the next day, and he relayed that information to Corps Commanders Heintzelman and Sigel.

On the evening of the 28th, Kearny's troops were bunking down for the night at Centreville. Exhausted, his forces had marched for days and had encountered no Confederates of consequence. Only the destruction of the Union supply system was observed as the 3rd Division made its way back towards Centreville. When Kearny received instructions to proceed to Bull Run quickly, he reacted with disdain. Kearny seemed to be unsure of Pope's orders and refused to immediately comply, instead waiting until the morning, knowing that the Confederates were not far off.[12] Kearny had engaged the enemy on the peninsula, and it is possible that Kearny understood the Confederates better than Pope had realized. Jackson's force was not withdrawing, but was waiting for a fight. Kearny may have been informed that Jackson had already engaged Union forces that very night on the 28th.

Major General John Pope served as the Commander of the Army of Virginia in late August 1862. The victor of Island No 10 and New Madrid believed that he could defeat Lee, and then developed an obsession that led to his own defeat (Library of Congress Prints and Photographs Division, Washington, D.C.).

Friday, August 29, dawned warm and muggy as the soldiers of Kearny's division moved into formation to begin the march toward the Bull Run Bridge on the Warrenton Turnpike. He had received orders from General Heintzelman the previous night to move out at 1:00 a.m., an order he could not immediately comply with. He finally complied at around 5:00 a.m. and directed the troops down toward the stone bridge. Heintzelman maintained that he had ordered Kearny to move earlier and could not

Major General Philip Kearny

explain Kearny's delay in action.[13] The mystery of Kearny's actions can best be explained by the fact that his force was moving on tired legs and that rest and some food were decidedly more important, since Jackson was going nowhere.

By the time Kearny's division arrived on the field of battle, Franz Sigel's divisions were already engaging the Confederates. These units were made up of mostly German immigrants and many spoke little or no English. General Franz Sigel had what one might consider a mixed service record. Sigel was a German immigrant who had fled to the U.S. after the abortive uprisings in Europe in 1848. His unsuccessful experience with revolutionary forces had put him at odds with imperial forces supported by Prussia and Russian Czar Nicholas, who had helped his neighbors in the region. At the beginning of the American Civil War, Sigel volunteered his services in the state of Missouri and commanded some pro–Union German troops there.

Early in the war, in Missouri, Sigel was in command of the wing that had fallen short in support of General Lyon at Wilson's Creek, and was, if anything, serendipitous in his actions at Pea Ridge. Now he was in command of an even larger force at Manassas, under Major General John Pope. Being unable to reconnoiter the field, Kearny had to rely on Sigel's report of the situation. This did not sit well with the experienced field commander, who would rather have been on the field first to observe what had been happening well beforehand. As it was, General Kearny had to rely on Sigel's command for information, and this he seemed unwilling to countenance. He was aware of Sigel's performance out west and had some misgivings about his ability and the difficulty in communicating with the varied German-speaking units under Sigel's command. Sigel knew of Kearny's service in the French army, and may have believed that, because of his own experience in the revolutions of 1848, he himself could better command his and Kearny's troops, whom he believed should come to his support in an attack.

Kearny reported, "On my arrival, I was assigned to the holding of the right wing on the turnpike. I posted Colonel Poe with Berry's brigade in my first line; General Robinson with the first on his right partly in line and partly in support, and kept Birney's most disciplined regiments reserved and ready for emergencies."[14] He was less than confident in the ability of the German troops on his left, and was concerned when General Sigel asked him for immediate support. Kearny's concern when he reached the field was to position his three brigades on the right of the Union line. Army of Virginia 1st Corps Commander Franz Sigel reported that he sent

XII. Manassas, August 29: Pope Engages

a request to General Kearny to move on the enemy forces, which he believed threatened his right flank. This confirms Kearny's initial concerns about positioning his forces. He was blind to the exact location of the enemy and was not prepared to support another command without positioning his. To General Kearny's disappointment, General Pope was sending in the Union forces piecemeal, with no timetable for deployment.

Initially Kearny's forces arrived by mid-morning, around 9:00 a.m. Kearny had had little time to reconnoiter the battlefield when he received word from Sigel, who needed his support. Sigel had already committed his force when he learned of Kearny's coming on the field. "In order to defend out right I sent a letter to General Kearny, saying that Longstreet was not able to

Franz Sigel fled to the U.S. after a failed revolution in Germany and had mixed success in the Union army. Sigel seemed to have a communications failure with Kearny at Manassas (Library of Congress Prints and Photographs Division, Washington, D.C.).

bring his troops in line of battle that day, and requesting him [Kearny] to change his front to the left, and to advance, if possible against the enemy's left flank."[15] Kearny was familiar with the area around Centreville from his actions from the previous March, but he was not entirely familiar with Manassas and may have been unaware that Sigel had already committed. It appears that the two generals simply corresponded with notes and not person-to-person, which in hindsight might have had better results.

With the sounds of gunfire off in the distance, Kearny brought his command down and around the Stone House Tavern and moved north up

Major General Philip Kearny

the Sudley Church road as part of his division moved over the hills behind. Moving up past Buck Hill (Pope's eventual command location), he started to deploy his brigades up over Matthews Hill. Initially Kearny deployed Orlando Poe's brigade to advance over Matthews Hill toward the Bull Run fords. Positioned slightly to Poe's right was Robinson's brigade. General David Birney's arrival coincided with Sigel's command to engage.

Initially David Bell Birney had his division positioned on the east side of the Sudley Springs Road. The arrival that morning brought Birney within range of Confederate guns. Kearny was not yet ready to commit all his units as he struggled with where to send his regiments. General Birney seemed to have arrived at a point where Sigel's command had created a gap. General Carl Schurz's division was moving in action, and Birney saw a gap developing between two of his regiments. Birney ordered the 1st New York Regiment to provide support and filled the gap. "During the first hours of the combat, as tired regiments in the centre fell back, General Birney, of his own accord, rapidly pushed across to give them a hand to stimulate them to a renewed fight."[16] The 1st New York now joined the attack on the Confederates in the railroad grade. It was a well-contested assault as the Confederates fended off the attacks and pushed the Union blue back off their positions along the rail bed.

With Kearny's Division now on the field, it brought some reassurance to General Sigel's command. However, Kearny's units advanced northward, somewhat away from the field of action: "Our advance was continued until our skirmishers had crossed Bull Run some 400 or 500 yards, and three regiments in support had also crossed."[17] Seeing that General Robinson had moved to the right of Colonel Poe, Kearny relayed the order for Robinson to file his regiments to the left of Poe. In doing so, Kearny was now positioning support for the Army of Virginia. By noon, Robinson's force was coming to the aid of General Carl Schurz's hotly contested division.

The scene of action was beginning to develop. Cannon shells started to fly overhead as the Union troops moved toward the Confederate lines. Smoke rose over the treetops as the staccato of gunfire was heard in the distance. Kearny needed to relay orders to move his forces closer to the point of enemy contact, and while the gunfire and shells screamed overhead, he dismounted from his horse. He would often bend on one knee and write a communique in response to or sending commands. In order to do this, since he had only one good arm, he required someone to stand next to him and hold a corner of the paper.

With Kearny on this day was the young Gustave Schurmann, his new

XII. Manassas, August 29: Pope Engages

orderly. Barely a teenager, the young man was responsible to be with the general and to assist him in his duty of command. He remembered the habit of the general of writing orders on one knee: "At the second battle of Bull Run ... the General had occasion to write orders ... which I steadied with my fingers."[18] With artillery shells screaming overhead, Kearny noticed that the young man was trembling, and he asked him what the matter was. Gustave looked at the general and said he was a little frightened. Kearny looked at young Gustave with his battle face, and Gustave remembered that he said to him "I must never get frightened at anything."[19] It is a classic look at the way Kearny would rise to the occasion at a difficult moment and display a keen insight in the face of difficult odds or situations.

Moving down toward Sudley Church and the road that fronted it, Kearny had given orders for General Robinson's brigade to move on it. Facing Kearny's troops was the Confederate brigade of Maxcy Gregg's South Carolinians, the same force that they had briefly faced at Glendale down on the Peninsula. Now in broken clearings flanked by forest, Robinson's men would soon come across an unfinished railroad grade near a slight rise that would become known as the rocky knoll. This is where the Confederates under Gregg expected to be attacked, and they were equal to the task.

John Pope arrived on the field at around noon. The early morning encounter of Sigel's corps had staggered but not dislodged the Confederates. The piecemeal attacks proved to be just too uncoordinated as Sigel and Schurz waited for Kearny's division to arrive. In late morning of August 29, Kearny's division arrived near the Stone House and moved slowly past it as the division marched around and up the hills that surrounded it. Pope had Heintzelman move Kearny's forces to the Union right, and Kearny was busy moving Robinson from his foray towards Bull Run. Poe and his brigade remained near the Bull Run crossings while his 3rd Michigan Regiment was detailed by General Kearny to move with Robinson's brigade. If Kearny was bothered by the confusion of Pope's orders, he seemed to parry it as he wanted to secure his right flank on the placid creek.

With two of his brigades positioned, Kearny rode to see how David Birney's troops were faring. It would be Birney who would initially see action. Moving down from Matthews Hill and crossing Sudley Springs Road, Birney would lead his brigade toward the railroad grade some 300 yards distant. Forces were moving up and along Dogan's Ridge, and Birney witnessed the activity as he moved his brigade toward the chosen point in the federal line. This chosen point would be in support of Schurz's division, already engaged.

Major General Philip Kearny

Battlefield of Bull Run (Manassas), Stone house on Warrenton Pike, 1862. Kearny's division passed in front and over the hill in back of this house toward Sudley Springs Road and Church (Library of Congress Prints and Photographs Division, Washington, D.C.).

On his left were the hard-pressed elements of Schurz's division. Finding he had a gap of some distance, General Birney ordered his regiments to move by the left to close ranks. He soon realized that he faced a very determined enemy and ordered Colonel Ward to support him. Ward recalled, "I remained a short distance in rear as reserve, the remaining portion of the brigade advancing. About 12 p.m. received orders from Lieutenant Philips, aide-de-camp, to advance to a position occupied by General Birney."[20] Colonel Ward moved in earnest to support General Birney, but the enemy had made good his defense and pushed the Union back from the grade.

The situation of the units Birney moved to support was untenable. Birney realized that he was outflanked and began to withdraw back towards Sudley Road. General Kearny later reported what transpired: "During the first hours of the conflict General Birney on tired regiments in the center falling back (supporting Schurz) of his own accord rapidly pushed across to give them a hand."[21] Moving to support his brigade, Colonel

XII. Manassas, August 29: Pope Engages

Ward soon came into contact with the surging Confederates and found that he might be overrun. "I found the regiment surrounded on three sides by a large force ... from the roads in front and a cornfield on my right and rear. I immediately moved by the left flank to the road and from thence to the woods ... enemy not following."[22] Evidently the Confederates were spent and were ordered not to give chase, and instead remained ensconced along the unfinished railroad grade to hold their line.

Poor coordination, bad communication, and the late arrival of the Army commander contributed too much of the confusion that day, not to mention a tenacious enemy. By 2:00 p.m., General Kearny was starting to come to life. He was now eager to hammer Maxcy Gregg's South Carolinians. Hobart Ward's observation of the enemy's not following was not an aberration; it was by design. The Confederates were determined to engage in a holding action as they waited for the entire concentration of the Army of Northern Virginia.

General Kearny may have realized this fact, and he decided to engage the Confederate left flank and maybe roll it up, thereby giving the Army of Virginia the initiative. Kearny started his movement shortly after 2:00 p.m. when he started General Robinson's brigade forward toward the railroad grade. The Manassas Gap Railroad was begun sometime before the war broke out in 1861, to provide farmers in the Shenandoah Valley a way to move their goods to the eastern markets. Sometime before the war, the project had been halted, but the rail cuts and fills still remained, and they provided an excellent place to

Brigadier General John C. Robinson replaced Charles D. Jameson as brigade commander. His action was considered commendable at Manassas, but less so at Chantilly, a.k.a Ox Hill (Library of Congress Prints and Photographs Division, Washington, D.C.).

defend against a superior foe. The railroad cut and grade ran northeast to southwest across Sudley Road. In looking over the ground, Kearny decided to place Poe's regiment on his right, protecting the crossings flanking Bull Run.

By midafternoon, General Pope sent orders to General Kearny "to send a pretty strong force diagonally to the front to relieve the center."[23] Kearny was already in that process with General Robinson's troops. His brigade consisted of the 63rd Pennsylvania, 105th Pennsylvania and 20th Indiana Regiment of Volunteers, along with the 3rd Michigan marksmen, detached from Poe's brigade. When Robinson's brigade arrived at the railroad grade, he found brigades of General Hooker engaged in the fight. Kearny and Robinson reported that he deployed the 63rd and 105th Pennsylvania along the railroad to the right of those forces engaged.[24] Robinson placed the 3rd Michigan toward his right flank and immediately sent out his skirmishers.

Just as Robinson was getting into position, he noticed that the troops of Hooker were beginning to give ground, potentially exposing his flank. General Robinson acted immediately, moving his regiments by file left, and was immediately beset by heavy musketry fire from Gregg's South Carolinians. General Kearny recognized the situation and dramatically rode forward quickly to the railroad grade to rally his troops.[25] He had the 3rd Michigan and 20th Indiana Regiments file across the railroad grade and wheel to their left to fire concentrated musketry into the exposed ranks of the forward-moving Confederates.

Sudley Hollow burst with the crack of rifle fire, and the air was filled with flame as case shot exploded overhead. Confederate artillery, located just beyond Sudley Church, had found its range. Soldiers of both ranks began to fall as the contest became hotly engaged. Kearny now understood the need to press the Confederate left flank and was pursuing such action. The pressure of Robinson's force now began to bend the regiments of Maxcy Gregg up around the railroad grade. With this happening, the Confederates' line was in peril of being enfiladed by the Federals, as a gap of more than one hundred yards developed between Gregg's Brigade and the next defending line.[26]

An opportunity had now presented itself, to Kearny's disappointment: just as the battle was developing, the regiments assigned to Hooker began to falter and withdraw. General Robinson recalled, "Soon after taking this position the regiments on my left gave way and passed rapidly to the rear ... leaving my left flank entirely exposed."[27] This exposure forced General Robinson to move by his left flank to close the gap that now pre-

XII. Manassas, August 29: Pope Engages

sented itself before him and the enemy. When Philip Kearny witnessed the withdrawal that exposed his command's left, he immediately rode forward onto the railroad grade, exposing himself to enemy fire. Raising his sword with his one hand, he exhorted the men around him that he would make generals of them if they would continue the attack. As Kearny moved forward, he had just sent a message to General Birney to move his regiments up to support General Robinson.

The situation on the field had become fluid as the clock moved toward 5:00 p.m. Robinson's men now moved over the railroad bed and found the opportunity to fire their muskets down the Confederate line. The raking fire took a toll on a number of the enemy, including officers directing their troops to refuse their line. This was a moment that seemed to favor the bold, and this is what Kearny expected as he urged his officers to keep up the pressure. It was now that the rifle fire was heavy and intense as bullets flew equally between the lines, hissing like fire as they went.

General Kearny had the Confederates constricted on three sides as he brought Birney forward on Robinson's left, closing the enemy in a vise-like grip. Lieutenant Colonel Nelson Gesner, in charge of the 101st New York Infantry, along with the 40th New York, recalled the action: "We were then ordered to march forward and attack the enemy ... the order was given 'forward' and the regiment went on in in splendid order through a heavy fire, at a double-quick."[28] The pressure was short-lived, and with no other units available, General Kearny's maneuvers had stalled. Shortly before, as his men surged forward, Kearny was in the mix and exhorted his men to continue to move on the enemy.

The Confederates were bent but not broken as their line continued to pour fire into the Federals. With the lateness of the day, and with no more coordinated support from the Union command, Kearny and his forces began to break off contact as the crackle of gunfire started to die off. The Confederates still remained behind the railroad grade. It had been an excellent contest between Maxcy Gregg's Carolinians and Kearny's troops. Holding their ground, Gregg's men had performed a desperate defense that was remarkable for their numbers. In a moment of pressure on his line, Maxcy Gregg drew his grandfather's Revolutionary War sword, swinging it about his men in exhortation. The effect was as electric as Kearny's promise that he would make all his men generals.

General Kearny was one to never second-guess himself and was of the belief that the day could have been theirs had he had the numbers of a combined Union army. He probably believed that this was a holding action on the part of the enemy. In his follow-up report, Kearny stated that he had "the enemy rolled up on his own right."[29] Oddly, he did not commit Colonel Poe, who remained across Sudley Church road and was not, as far as is known, ordered to cross. If this was the case, and Poe was responsible for holding the Union far right, he may not have had the authority to move his unit and come to the aid of the brigade. In the continuing darkness, only sporadic firing now remained. Opportunity now may have been lost, although Pope again began to believe that the Confederates were withdrawing.

It is unclear why Poe could not have taken initiative, or even send one regiment for support as Birney had done earlier, on his own accord, but in his defense, he was covering the northern reaches of Bull Run and the crossings there. One should recall that Kearny's initial order was to hold the Union right, and this may have been his thinking. It should be remembered that Kearny advanced to a confused field with little information as to the whereabouts of the enemy. That night, the rest of the brigade remained in position on the other side of the Sudley Church and Matthews Hill. Curiously, Kearny was remembered by one officer as stating, "Had Pope supported my flank attack by a vigorous charge on the enemy's front, we must have overwhelmed Jackson's inferior force. It is too bad, for I lost many fine fellows in gaining the ground we can now never recover." This was not Pope's fault, however, though it seemed to be so at the time. The blame lay with those who did not execute Pope's orders or work together to carry out his plans.[30]

There are some who believe that Kearny had not acted as early as he could have in supporting Sigel at Sigel's request, and to the disappointment of Carl Schurz, who blamed Kearny for not acting sooner. Kearny seemed to believe that other officers in Pope's command did not act to concentrate the Union Army, and had they all attacked as Pope had originally directed, the outcome of the contest on August 29 would have been different. The confusion with Sigel's command, the lateness of Kearny's command in getting into position, the uncertainty of the Union right flank, and Pope's misinterpreting the left, all led to mistakes that always mark a divided command. The situation would only fuel the finger-pointing and the ugly politics of Washington, D.C.

As for the concerns expressed by General Schurz of Sigel's Corps, in regards to Kearny's failure to support him, Schurz states the following: "One of your aides presented to me a letter which you had addressed to General Kearny, requesting him to attack at once with his whole force.... On my right, however, where General Kearny had taken position, all remained quiet, and it became clear to me that he had not followed your

XII. Manassas, August 29: Pope Engages

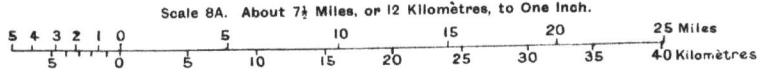

Campaign of Manassas (Library of Congress Geography and Map Division, Washington, D.C.).

request to attack simultaneously with me."[31] It seems that Carl Schurz is dismissing the fact that he did not directly correspond with Kearny in order to know of his precise whereabouts. He also fails to recall that David Birney of Kearny's division had, on his own initiative, gone in with his brigade to support the 1st New York, Schurz's Division. Schurz's report was

Major General Philip Kearny

written on September 15, a full two weeks after the battle, and appears to be somewhat disingenuous, considering Kearny was dead by then and of course could not respond.

It should be made clear that Schurz wrote a number of letters to Lincoln complaining of the army command. Schurz agonized over the fact that Lincoln had a number of opponents in his administration. Schurz was a political antagonist and Lincoln, to his credit, responded that both proponents and opponents had equal opportunity to fail or succeed in the command structure.

XIII

Manassas, August 30: Longstreet Attacks

On Saturday, August 30, the day rose clear and warm with the scattering of intermittent artillery and rifle fire coming from pickets toward Dogan's Ridge. The results of the previous day had to be disappointing to Kearny, who had anticipated success. On that Saturday morning, the army did not immediately attack. In fact, General Pope considered the enemy well in hand and the enemy forces at the railroad grade seemed to be on the defensive. General John Pope still insisted that the Confederates were in retreat, despite growing evidence that this might be a holding action by Confederate troops as Longstreet's Corps arrived.

Pope ordered III Corps Commander General Samuel Heintzelman to prepare the assault. In his report, Heintzelman put it this way: "It was decided that General McDowell should take his corps, mine, and General Porter's to make an attack on the enemy's left.... General McDowell and myself went to our right to reconnoiter more clearly the enemy's position preparatory to moving. We saw but few of the enemy."[1] It appeared that the Confederates may have withdrawn and were retreating. The Union forces had fallen for the bait: the Confederates were in fact not withdrawing anywhere, but preparing to engage and hold.

It occurred to no one, except General Kearny, that the determined defense the day before portended that the enemy had not gone anywhere. The muddled handling of the Union forces the day before did not disguise the fact that the Confederates had not given up ground. Pope believed that with Fitz John Porter's corps he could deal a blow to the Confederate army and follow it up with a concerted advance by all the Union force. Fitz John Porter did not want to commit his men, but did his duty and advanced. He had good reason for his skepticism, but this did not convince his superior. Much has been discussed about Fitz John Porter's inaction on the day of his assault, but it must be understood that the Army of the Potomac units attached were advancing to a confusing field.

Major General Philip Kearny

From the very beginning of this campaign, the initiative had always been in the hands of the Confederate Army of Northern Virginia. From the time Union forces camped on the shores of Harrison's Landing, opportunity literally had fallen into General Robert E. Lee's lap. From the time of the ominous drubbing the Confederate forces took at Malvern Hill and the shock that that battle had engendered in the mind of some of Lee's associates, the tide of battle was with the South. With a Union army now canvassing and operating in Northern Virginia around Fairfax and Manassas, the decision was made to confront them. It would become a masterful stroke that brought Thomas J. Jackson to that first day of combat on August 28, and on the 29th, General Longstreet would have his turn.

The Union Army of Virginia was initially confronted by General Jackson on August 9, 1862, at Cedar Mountain (Slaughter Mountain) in a sharp contest that Jackson found to be determined on the part of the Union forces, but was won by the Confederates. "The argument in Lee's mind pursued a circle, caution bringing him back to the waiting policy from which his desire to suppress Pope and his concern for the Virginia Central Railroad constantly were drawing him. He did the only thing he could do at a distance from a situation he could not fathom—he gave discretion to Jackson. Jackson did not wait for the discretionary orders."[2] This discretionary decision led to Cedar Mountain and finding Pope's intentions.

On August 15, in a meeting that included Corps Commanders James Longstreet and Thomas Jackson, along with Cavalry Commander Jeb Stuart, the plan of action of the Confederate forces was decided upon. Jackson's divisions had found Pope's van of the Army of Virginia astride the Rapidan and Rappahannock rivers. This presented the opportunity for Lee to let loose Jackson's corps, and he did just that. The result of the action of Cedar Mountain gave the Confederates an opportunity. Instead of falling back, Lee decided to push his lieutenant forward, giving Stonewall an opportunity that he was more than willing to fill. This mission was something that Philip Kearny could only dream about as his force moved up from the peninsula.

This became more important when Stuart's cavalry came across Pope's headquarters at Catlett's Station and acquired his dispatches and intentions. "Lee wrote [Confederate President Jefferson] Davis of his discoveries from Pope's correspondence and tactfully ordered the remaining units of the Army of Northern Virginia to rejoin him. Lee sent for Jackson to come to his headquarters. The conference that followed between

XIII. Manassas, August 30: Longstreet Attacks

the two was one of the most important Lee ever held. He told Jackson to take his command up the Rappahannock, to get in rear of Pope's army, and to cut his communications with Washington."[3] Jackson would then move within the hour, doing what he loved best: taking the offensive to the enemy.

General Jackson was true to his task and moved quickly. From the moment Lee and his generals decided to split his forces, he had information that allowed for this risky and bold action. "The disclosures of Pope's dispatch-book developed at once to Lee the practicability of turning the right of the Army of Virginia, getting in its rear, capturing its supplies and cutting it off from Washington. The execution of this hazardous stroke of generalship was confided to the audacious and ever-ready Jackson. It was nevertheless fraught with peril, and had Pope been reinforced, as he expected to be and should have been, the biter would have been bit."[4] Kearny had left Harrison's Landing on August 15 and made his way back down towards Yorktown. From there, with the command of George G. Meade's division, Kearny and his division made the way up the Chesapeake.

Turning the Army of Virginia's right flank presented a possibility of paying big rewards for the Confederacy. This had to be done as quickly as humanly possible to prevent the combination of the Army of the Potomac and the Army of Virginia. General Robert E. Lee was already aware of troop movements with that intention from the Peninsula. Kearny's Second Division was on Jackson's mind. "In other words, Jackson most considerately was warned that two Corps were to advance along the Warrenton Turnpike and were to concentrate on Manassas, presumably for an attack on him. He probably learned also that Maj. Gen. Phil Kearny, who had been with the Army of the Potomac, had joined Pope and was commanding a division."[5]

The fact that Kearny was mentioned by name, and the intelligence of the Confederate army was so well informed, made the movement of Jackson vital. Pope was aware of Jackson's presence, but not his ultimate destination. Jackson made his movement up to Thoroughfare Gap by way of Salem, Virginia. He was not detected by any Union forces and the right flank of Pope's army was exposed. "On August 27th two and a half miles from Salem the march was broken by the arrival of a courier. He brought from Jackson a dispatch that made every heart beat faster. By an astounding two days' march Jackson had covered fifty-four miles and the previous evening had reached Bristoe Station.... Jackson was precisely where Lee wanted him to be—in rear of the Federal army and between it and Washington."[6] Jackson sacked and looted the U.S. government stores at Manassas

Junction. This was the smoke that Kearny noticed in his roundabout march to Centreville.

The next task for Jackson was to position his forces to confront Pope's army. He decided on the hills of the old Manassas battlefield of 1861. Here, on August 28, Jackson noticed the movement of some of Pope's Army of Virginia moving east along the Gainesville road toward Centreville. With A.P. Hill's Light Division, including Richard Ewell and Isaac Trimble, Jackson decided to reveal the Confederates' presence. Pope now rushed his forces to Manassas to (as he had put it a few days earlier) "bag the whole crowd." The only question was, where were James Longstreet and the rest of Lee's Army of Northern Virginia?

Before long, General Lee and Longstreet were on the move, and were heading through the same Thoroughfare Gap that Jackson had passed through days earlier. Jackson had now found his tactical position. "Jackson has made the line of a half-finished railroad his defense and his men are behind the embankment and in the excavations."[7] Since then the Union Cavalry had placed itself astride the Thoroughfare Gap and forced Longstreet's infantry to dislodge them. "On the 28th, arriving at Thoroughfare Gap, he [Longstreet] found the enemy prepared to dispute his progress. General D.R. Jones' division, being ordered to force the passage of the mountain, quickly dislodged the enemy sharpshooters from the trees and rocks and advanced into the gorge."[8] Outnumbered and outflanked, the Union forces could do nothing but withdraw and immediately move east toward Gainesville. Lee understood that Jackson would have to absorb the constant attack of the Union forces and hold them in place.

James Longstreet and his veteran corps of battle-hardened troops were supposed to be the hammer to Jackson's anvil, with Pope's Army of Virginia to be struck in between. The problem was that, although Longstreet's forces had made good time overcoming Thoroughfare Gap, his lead elements began arriving on Jackson's right on August 29 as the battle was being joined on Jackson's left. "The whole operation had been conducted on Jackson's part without a serious mistake of any sort. His troops were weary and were sadly deficient in senior officers, but their spirit was high, and when they saw their old comrades of the Seven Days file into position, they turned again defiantly to the enemy, who was massing on the front as Longstreet came up."[9]

As Lee and Longstreet came up, the firing on Jackson's line was deafening. Situated along that unfinished rail cut and fill, the Confederate position was a good one. "The roar from the left now told of such a battle as even the Army of Northern Virginia had seldom fought. A.P. Hill, on Jack-

XIII. Manassas, August 30: Longstreet Attacks

son's left, had his six brigades in a double line. Against this line, now swinging to the right and now to the left, Pope threw his troops in successive charges from 3 o'clock until 6."[10] Lee asked Longstreet if he might consider moving his troops to the attack. Longstreet thought otherwise and wanted all his brigades to arrive before committing them to action. The roar that was talked about was the late afternoon assault that Kearny's division was making on Jackson's left, covered by Maxcy Gregg's South Carolinians.

On the morning of August 30, 1862, the day was ripe for the heat of battle. Longstreet's corps was taking up position at a right angle to General Jackson's line near Groveton up on the unfinished railroad. He now had all his men in place. "With Anderson's arrival and Hood's return, Longstreet had all his troops united and under the eye of Lee himself. Their position was one of exciting military interest. They were thrown diagonally across the Gainesville-Centreville Road in such a way that their line, following the best elevations, formed an angle of about 160 degrees with Jackson's front."[11] The question was whether Pope would send forces into the jaws of this formation.

In midafternoon, the Union struck exactly where the Confederates had hoped. As Longstreet was positioning his brigades for what was expected to be an assault, Fitz John Porter, commanding the Union corps, committed to the attack around 3:00 p.m., striking Jackson's far right flank. Longstreet had already positioned Stephen Lee's artillery batteries at a right angle to literally rack the oncoming blue army. "He immediately ordered up two batteries, and two others being thrown forward about the same time by Col. S.D. Lee, under their well-directed and destructive fire the supporting lines were broken and fell back in confusion. Their repeated efforts to rally were unavailing, and Jackson's troops, being thus relieved from the pressure of overwhelming numbers, began to press steadily forward, driving the enemy before them."[12] Now, at about 4:00 p.m., Longstreet ordered his legions forward and struck the hammer blow on Pope's Army of Virginia.

General Kearny and his division spent the morning of the 30th adjusting their line per the order by Heintzelman preparatory to attack. A friend of John Watt De Peyster caught up with him in the forenoon and remembered this exchange: "He was then much excited and mortified at the result of the failure to support the attack he had been directed to make from our right, on the day previous, on the enemy's left, and criticized Pope severely, as was, in fact, just, for such blundering I never witnessed. I said to him: 'Phil, this is the day which is to decide this battle, is it not?'

Major General Philip Kearny

'No,' said he. 'Don't say so to anyone else, but the chance of success was thrown away on yesterday. Had Pope supported my flank attack by a vigorous charge on the enemy's front, we must have overwhelmed Jackson's inferior force."[13] Kearny had misgivings and looked over the ground fronting him, waiting for the guns to open the action.

General Ricketts's Second Division, III Corps, Army of Virginia, came up to relieve Hobart Ward's 38th New York Regiment, and cover Kearny's left. In the official report, Kearny recalled: "On the morning of the 30th General Ricketts ... relieved one of my extra charges on the left of the road, and I again concentrated my command."[14] When word arrived that the division was to advance along with the rest of III Corps in support of the Union line, it did not venture far. The Union far left was already in attack. General Fitz John Porter's Corps had arrived and the sound of heavy rifle fire could be heard down the line. By late afternoon, as the ranks of Kearny began to move forward, the sound of massed artillery, seeming out of nowhere, exploded on the far left of the line.

It finally dawned on everyone that the enemy was not retreating. Heintzelman believed that the Confederates had withdrawn "from opposite our right ... to mass ... on our center and left."[15] He was partially correct. A large segment of the Confederate Army (Longstreet's Corps) had now arrived on the field, and their attack had begun. Even General Pope now realized he had missed an opportunity, for he too heard the artillery at the right of the enemy's line. He had pinned his hopes on Fitz John Porter to dislodge and drive the enemy. Instead it would be Porter who would be catching the full impact of the artillery fire and the assault of Longstreet's legions. The cannon fire was devastating as the smoke rose above the crowd of Union blue breaking their lines.

By 5:00 p.m., the impact of the attack was remarked on by General Sigel, who was near the Union center and reported: "We had the whole army of the enemy before us ... and showed clearly his plan of attack."[16] Kearny held his forces on Matthews Hill as the Army of Virginia started to trickle men toward the Union rear. Late on the afternoon of August 30, the Union left flank started to move toward the Union center. That trickle of men making for the rear soon descended into a flow of wild-eyed and dazed men stunned by what had happened. Officers on horseback cajoled and threatened soldiers as they simply continued to move off toward the makeshift Bull Run Bridge.

The reality now presented itself to the Union command. The left flank of the Army of Virginia was broken. The assault by Union General Fitz John Porter was crushed by the thunderous shell of Confederate artillery.

XIII. Manassas, August 30: Longstreet Attacks

For General Pope, the disintegration of the Army of Virginia was now beginning. There was only one thing to do: bring up as much artillery as possible to shore up the Union center. Concentrated on the crossroads near the Stone House, unit after unit of artillery sections were lined up almost wheel to wheel, belching flame in the smoking twilight.

Kearny was very much aware of the situation and recalled "a sudden and unaccountable evacuation of the field by the left center occuring."[17] The events that probably had been on Kearny's mind had come to pass. The Confederates had never given up the initiative, and had they attacked earlier in the morning, the entire Union Army might have been lost. As it was, it was late in the afternoon, and a mass of Yankee blue moved to and fro over the well-trampled ground near Matthews and Henry Hill. Early 19th-century military theorist Carl von Clausewitz, who saw war at its most raw, once stated that two armies facing one another appeared like slow-burning embers as unit after unit was burned away in attrition. Not only did the Union troops burn away, they simply started to move away in groups or individually, as order in the ranks soon began to break down.

Massed Union artillery now pulled into line, urgently positioning itself forward of the Sudley Church Road. Positioned near the Stone House Tavern crossroads below Dogan's Ridge, the Confederates came en masse toward and down the ridge at a right angle and over Chinn Ridge on their left. It was an irresistible surge, overwhelming everything in its path. Just after 5:00 o'clock in the evening, Colonel Orlando Poe of the Third Brigade observed that "everything was in confusion."[18] Kearny had Randolph's Battery E, 1st Rhode Island to take up position on Matthews Hill to cover his division's withdrawal. Centreville Road was now beginning to become crammed with soldiers headed east. The Union right was holding its own. Generals Kearny and Reno and later John Gibbon remained in position as the Union left crumbled.

As the Confederate left now began to move forward, Kearny directed another battery, trying to stem the enemy onslaught. "Lieutenant [possibly F.J.T. Blume or Wallace Hill] a German Officer of distinction, put at my disposal by General Sigel … covered our right flank and drove off the enemy's battery and regiments."[19] Colonel Poe remembered this unit firing down the ridge at the enemy as he began to extradite his brigade over Matthews Hill. Gradually Kearny removed his division back off the hills he had traversed the day before.

At around 10:00 p.m., with the stark reality of retreat looming, a rear-guard action was now necessary to cover the rest of the retreating army. Kearny realized the deteriorating situation and began to concentrate his forces as he received orders to help fend off the advancing enemy. "I massed my troops at the indicated point."[20] This point was probably near the Portici House on Matthews Hill. The hill presented a panoramic view over toward Dogan's Ridge, and Kearny viewed the slow movement of Jackson's Corps move up and over that ground, heading toward the crossroads at the Stone House. It was at this time that the rear guard of Kearny and Gibbon's divisions came to control the Army of Virginia's retreat to Centreville.

Kearny now moved his divisions to the left to present a better front with General Reno. Corps Commander Heintzelman recalled that he "he sent General Kearny's division to the left to close up a gap between my left and the main body of the army."[21] While making this necessary adjustment with his force, Kearny caught up with General Gibbon near Henry House Hill. John Gibbon was in command of the Black Hat Brigade of western men and was the one who had opened up the contest with Jackson on August 28. He too was led to believe, at that time, that the Confederates were retreating, but was realizing otherwise. "The Division was placed under the orders of MAJ. Gen. Fitz John Porter to aid in pursuit of the enemy, who was supposed to be retreating on the Warrenton Turnpike."[22]

Both Gibbon and Kearny would meet up on Matthews Hill. Kearny remained with his artillery and made a slow retreat with his division deployed. As the last of the remaining Union forces made its way toward the Bull Run fords, he vented his disappointment over events with some fellow rear-guard officers. This exchange between them was revealing and remembered by John Gibbon. "When Gibbon said he hoped it was not as bad as that, Kearny snapped perhaps not, Reno is keeping up the fight, he is not stampeded, I am not stampeded, that is about all, sir; my God, that is about all."[23] Late that evening near midnight, the rear guard of the Union army made its way across Bull Run and headed toward Centreville. Kearny recalled that his division arrived there around 2:00 a.m. on August 31, 1862. Once there, Kearny's division went into bivouacs around the forts at Centreville with the fate of the Army of Virginia still in doubt.

It had been a disappointing outing and the results were opposite of John Pope's design. Instead of bagging the whole crowd, as Pope had boasted, the Confederate force had nearly bagged Pope and the Union Army of Virginia. As one Union observer saw it: "The rebels came on and swept everything before them, completely turning the left wing of the army. There was no support whatever behind us, and somebody was evidently to blame; it looked to me as if it was left so on purpose to defeat

XIII. Manassas, August 30: Longstreet Attacks

Pope … commanders of the Army of the Potomac … not willing to cooperate with him."[24] Had it not been for the determined and disciplined troops of Kearny, Gibbon, and others, the outcome may have been worse than what it was. With the rear-guard actions of the Union force, the slowing momentum of the Confederate forces under Longstreet and Jackson, and the late hour of the day, the fight at Henry Hill was over.

XIV

Requiem

Kearny's division had performed its mission as the rear guard of the combined Army of Virginia. With little embellishment, he reported: "I maintained my position until 10:00 p.m. with, in connection with General Reno and General Gibbon.... I retired my brigade."[1] General Kearny moved his troops to Centreville along with the rest of the remainder of the Union army. He more than realized that the army had lost an opportunity. This army was mauled, and although he believed his division did well, it was for naught.

Located just to the east of Bull Run, only a few miles distant, lies the small crossroads town of Centreville. Occupying the approaches of Braddock Road, Warrenton Turnpike and the road to Fairfax Courthouse, Centreville had now become the regrouping and staging area for this retreating Union army.[2] Already located around the town was a series of small earthen forts that had been constructed earlier in the war. Built primarily by the Confederates, they now would serve as cover for the Army of Virginia.

Kearny and his Third Division of Third Corps were ordered to pitch his camp on the eastern slope on the rise of land that Centreville had been built upon. Kearny's troops were located to help watch the approaches from the Fairfax Court House Road (Germantown Road), which ran north of the town. Located nearby was a feeder road, more like a trail (Ox Road), which went toward the Little River Turnpike. As Kearny took time to make camp, his officers and men settled in to take time to make some food and get some rest. Kearny himself set up his headquarters at a small cottage just outside the village.

As little time as he allowed himself, Kearny too took some sleep at that small cottage. When he awoke early that Sunday morning, August 31, he called for his young orderly Gustave Schurmann. Schurmann was barely thirteen years of age when he became orderly to General Kearny. Having served the general since the Peninsula, Schurmann became a reliable

XIV. Requiem

and trusted orderly for the commander of the First Division and was always there when Kearny needed to compose an order or note for his lieutenants.

It was at Harrison's Landing that Kearny was in need of an orderly, and Schurmann, a drummer in the 40th New York, was identified as one who would be capable of filling the task. The test for the young Schurmann to become the general's orderly was an unusual one. The story goes that, while on horseback, the young lad jumped a ditch with the general, when the rest of his staff had decided on an easier route away from where he and the general jumped. This ability to keep pace with the general convinced Kearny that Gustave Schurmann was more than capable, and from here on he would serve as Kearny's assistant.

Brigadier General Orlando Poe replaced the reliable B.G. Hiram Berry to brigade command while serving under Kearny. His actions at Second Manassas and Chantilly raised some questions (Library of Congress Prints and Photographs Division, Washington, D.C.).

When young Schurmann arrived at division headquarters at Centreville, he found the general still resting on a bed with what seemed to be a fixed expression on his face and deep in thought. Schurmann remembered that the general instructed him to do a certain task. "He gave me some official documents, and a letter directed to Mrs. Kearny, which I believe was the last letter he ever wrote home, and three or four golden dollars and some silver, to defray my expenses and told me to post them in Alexandria."[3] For young Schurmann, it would be the last time he would see General Kearny. With his duty assigned, he left the cottage to make his way toward Alexandria. The upcoming engagement would be the first time Schurman would not be at Kearny's side.

The Warrenton or Fairfax Road connects with the Little River Turnpike at Germantown. Just about two miles to the east is the Fairfax County Court House. This was the objective of both General Pope and his adversary, General Thomas J. Jackson. The concentrated forces of the Union were now at Centreville, and among those forces was the command of Philip Kearny. With ominous weather stirring overhead, the troops on both sides would get no time to rest.

Pope found that he needed to withdraw and on September 1, 1862, ordered his army toward the forts around Washington, D.C. If the Confederates could reach the courthouse before the Union forces, Jackson could cut off Pope's army. General Jackson reported, "Early the next morning [September 1] we moved forward, and late in the evening, after reaching Oxhill, came in contact with the enemy, who were in position on our right and front.... I was ordered by the commanding general to turn that position ... in the direction of Fairfax Court House."[4] The plan was to cut into the Union forces, and it would be up to Pope to prevent it.

The weather had turned dark and threatening with thunder and lightning starting to streak the sky. With the warming air of late afternoon came with it the humid conditions prevalent in the Potomac and Chesapeake Bay region. Union and Confederate infantry began to adjust their lines as a cool air mass began its descent from the Appalachian Mountains. This cool front would cause instability in the atmosphere, leading to the torrential rain that would soak both armies on September 1, 1862. It would become a clash of nature and of men. Confederate division commander Ambrose Powell Hill remembered it this way: "This battle commenced under the most unfavorable circumstances—a heavy, blinding rain-storm directly in the faces of my men."[5]

Confederate General Jackson had his orders to "get possession of the turnpike at Fairfax Court House."[6] If he could do this, the Army of Virginia would be cut off and Washington exposed. It was in this lightning-filled atmosphere that Pope ordered his army eastward. With General Isaac Stevens's division leading, the Union set out in anticipation of making contact with the enemy. III Corps commander Samuel Heintzelman recalled in his official report: "I learned from General Pope that the enemy was threatening our rear, and he detached General Hooker ... to take command of some troops, near Germantown, to hold the enemy in check."[7] In the

XIV. Requiem

afternoon of September 1, General Heintzelman learned that the enemy was closer than he expected, and he needed to adjust his plan for immediate movement to support General Reno (Stevens), who had come across the enemy on the Union left, half a mile from the Union line of retreat.[8]

The weather had now started to become dark and threatening as lightning streaked overhead. Raindrops that had started out intermittent now began to get larger and heavier. With darkening skies and hard rain, the troops slogged their way along muddy and slippery roads. General Kearny moved along on horseback up and down the ranks, encouraging his men along. As he progressed, a rider soon rode up from the other direction and informed him of the need for his division to support General Stevens, who had contact with the enemy. Kearny told the rider that, by God, if Stevens needed his support, he would provide it. Lightning was now brightening the sky as Kearny rode on. The sounds of rifle and cannon fire would soon mix with the sounds of the heavens.

Up the road off to his left, the fight had already begun when Kearny reached the field. A narrow trail called Ox Road led to a place called Chantilly by the locals. The Confederates seemed to know the place, and H.J. Williams of the 5th Virginia described it: "Chantilly (the residence of Fullerville Stewart, esq.) ... to Ox Hill, a densely wooded crest overlooking the village of Germantown."[9] Ox Road intersected the Little River Turnpike just below the hill, and here the Confederates determined to send their lines forward to interdict the road toward Fairfax Court House.

The rider with the message met Kearny at around 4:30 p.m. His need was urgent, as General Reno's IX Corps was being hotly contested by the enemy just a mile or so from Kearny's present position. As noted, Kearny informed the man of his intentions, and turned the black horse he was riding to order his regiments to that point. He directed General David Birney to move forward with his First Brigade toward a point where General Stevens was now being engaged. With lightning everywhere in the skies, Birney moved his division to form line to cover Stevens's left. General Kearny rode slightly ahead to try to reconnoiter.

General Birney moved his troops up to initiate contact with the enemy. In his report he stated: "On reaching that point I found the division of General Stevens retiring in some disorder before the enemy.... I immediately ordered forward the Fourth Maine Regiment and it gallantly advanced.... I successively took forward the One Hundred and first New York, Third Maine, Fortieth and First New York."[10] Advancing obliquely to the left, the units filed in on Stevens's left flank. As they moved on their

Major General Philip Kearny

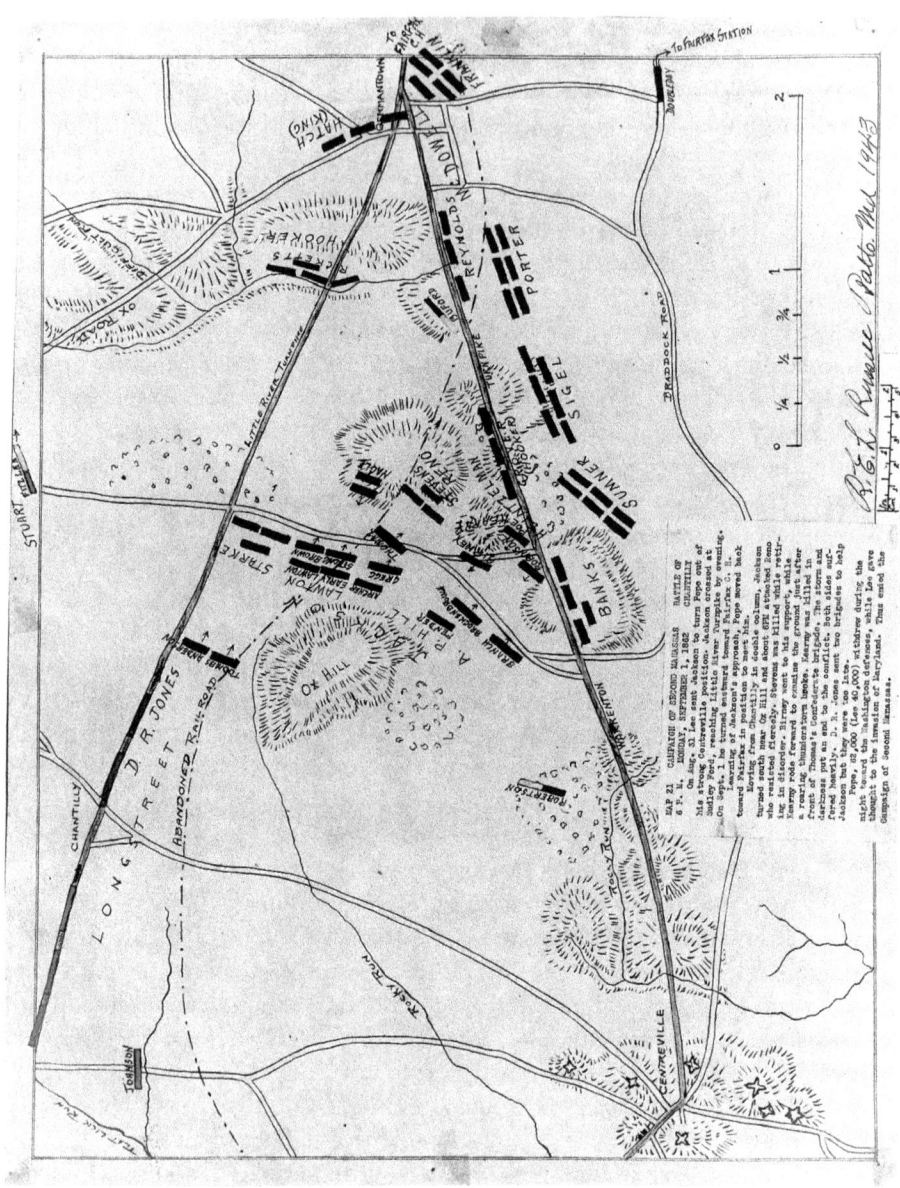

Map of Second Manassas Campaign from a series of 21 pen and ink maps showing details of battles of Gainesville, Groveton, Second Manassas, and Chantilly, August 28–September 1, 1862 (Library of Congress Geography and Map Division, Washington, D.C.).

XIV. Requiem

line, the regiments dressed and opened fire on the Confederates as thunder now mingled with the deadly fire of rifled muskets.

While keeping watch as General Birney moved his troops in position, General Kearny moved up his support artillery, the First Rhode Island Light Artillery, under the command of Captain George E. Randolph. Randolph recounted, "Under direction of General Kearny, I took a position on a knoll directly in rear of General Birney's line."[11] Realizing that the enemy was just beyond the wood line, Randolph's battery of four 12-pounder Napoleons began to fire sold shot into the tops of the trees, shattering and splintering shrapnel down upon the Confederates.

Randolph remembered in his report that he was unsure if the firing had any effect on the enemy. Birney remembered otherwise, as he saw Kearny place Randolph's battery, and said it "aided my brigade by a well-directed fire."[12] The Confederates did not return any artillery fire in response. In fact, the Confederates had not brought up much in the way of artillery support. This was probably because the weather had made road passage seriously problematical. It was likely that General Jackson had soon made the decision to simply hold their ground that had already been taken.

It was at about this time that it became clear how badly shot-up Stevens's division was. Overwhelming force was a key to dominating the battlefield and destroying the enemy, and this was already slipping away. In this situation, General Kearny was trying to bring the rest of his brigades into the contest to engage the enemy to the right and east of Birney's division. Kearny realized the urgency and believed he could interdict the advancing Confederates, thereby blunting their attack on the retreating Federal columns.

It was at this crucial moment that General Kearny directed Colonel Orlando Poe to move up the Third Brigade in support. Poe appears to have been unclear as to his orders and did not seem to move with celerity. In fact, Poe seemed to be more concerned with covering artillery than in supporting his general officer. General Kearny was concerned with the vacant position to Birney's right, and he was in need of troops to cover it. Kearny held up the reins of his horse, looked over his shoulder, and likely wondered where Orlando Poe and the rest of the division were.

It was at about this time that W.H. Paine of the U.S. Topographical Staff of the Army of the Potomac remembered encountering General Kearny. Paine related his experience that night in a letter written after the war. He noted that he observed that General Reno's forces had drifted toward the Union far right from what was probably David Birney's Brigade.

Major General Philip Kearny

"I found General Kearny, with his command, about to advance from the rear toward this vacated position ... and that his own left and front were uncovered by the movement of General Reno's troops."[13] Paine noticed that Kearny was surprised and thought that General Reno would not allow such action by his forces. With Poe and Robinson still not coming up, Kearny rode off to confer with General Birney.

As for Colonel Orlando Poe, his movements that evening still seem to be a mystery. It was not with persistence that he moved his troops up the same trail that Birney had just followed; as a matter of fact, Poe had halted his movement. As Kearny looked for Poe in the pouring rain, he decided that he needed to find regiments from whatever units were available nearby. But first he went to see how Birney's situation was progressing. Conferring with Birney, General Kearny was confident of his lieutenant's ability to hold his ground. Without Kearny's other regiments coming up, General Birney and General Kearny met soon after Kearny positioned Randolph's battery. General Birney relayed the following in his official report: "I pointed out to the General a gap on my right caused by the retreat of Stevens's division."[14] Kearny, as confirmed by two eyewitnesses, realized his predicament. He glanced down the road but failed to see any of the other two brigade commanders.

Where were Poe and Robinson? In his report, Poe related: "I received orders from General Kearny to form the brigade in line of battle on the road and move forward in the direction of the firing ... until our left connected with Robinson's right. We did so, and halted for a few minutes, when Lieutenant-Colonel Brown, aide-de-camp, brought me an order to move forward by a road which he would point out."[15] Poe now slowed his advance and simply waited. Why he was given conflicting orders has never been explained. This delay and misdirection would cost much.

Kearny had directed Birney and Randolph to the field. His intentions seemed to be to have Poe and Robinson to follow up and move on David Birney's flank. Since Robinson was behind Poe, he could not move any faster than Poe, and Poe had stalled. On horseback, Kearny and Birney discussed the predicament. With no support coming from his other brigade commanders, Birney and Kearny rode off to the Union right to reconnoiter the situation. Flashing cloud-to-cloud lightning illuminated the ground, making it hard to discern what forces were available and whether they were friend or foe in the shadowy light. General Kearny had no choice: he would have to reconnoiter on his own to find units to support his lieutenants.

While the two generals were riding and discussing the situation along

XIV. Requiem

the way, an incident occurred that stuck in Birney's mind and he would later remember. "At this time it was raining and smoke from the batteries [probably Randolph's cannons] hung low.... He accompanied me, and as we leaped a ditch his horse shied, and he remarked how disagreeable that a horse should behave so in battle. He then galloped to the right and I saw him no more."[16] Birney then returned to his brigades to adjust his lines, expecting to see his commander with the rest of the command coming up with units to support his right.

General Kearny was disconcerted at what he saw. There seemed to be no cohesive units anywhere in the gap in front of Birney, only the remains of Stevens's shattered division. These remnant units struggled to maintain their order as they moved off the field. The foul weather and the flight of Pope's Army of Virginia toward the forts around Washington presented a dismal picture. Now it was up to the thin line of Kearny and Stevens's divisions to prevent Jackson's Confederate legions from coming down and scattering that army. Fortunately for the Union troops, the Confederates were also having a hard time in the heavy rains. A.P. Hill had his orders, and he sent forward from his command the brigades of O.B. Branch and Brockenbrough to feel out what units might be facing him as the heavy rains continued to mask the front.

Second U.S. Artillery Commander Lieutenant Colonel Samuel M. Benjamin recalled some of events of that day as he watched what remained of Stevens's command moving past his position. It is unclear whether Lt. Col. Benjamin was aware of Steven's death; it is clear that at some point, through the unrelenting weather, he did see General Kearny, but only for a moment, galloping quickly by. "After a number of troops had passed and the road was clear, I saw General Kearny ride past at a swift gallop entirely alone, and turn down the road ... he passed within twenty feet of me, and in full light of my fire."[17] Benjamin relates that he called out to Kearny, probably to warn him, but Kearny seemed not to hear him, due to the rain and thunder, as he quickly rode by.

Kearny was now on a mission. The general rode through the pouring rain in search of Union forces that had not withdrawn. The waning light of the day and the heavy rain only added to his urgency. The remnants of General Stevens's command had not entirely scattered after their general fell. In fact, scattered elements were milling about as rain continued to pelt both Confederate and Union soldiers. Seeing a number of groups making their way toward the rear, General Kearny noticed, through the continuing rain, a larger unit, possibly of regimental size, holding in open ground very near his line of approach.

Major General Philip Kearny

Stone Church and Centreville, Virginia, 1862. It was near Centreville that Philip Kearny entered the American Civil War, and it was near here that his service ended (Library of Congress Prints and Photographs Division, Washington, D.C.).

Generals Kearny and Stevens truly wanted to get at the Confederates notwithstanding the weather, and strike the enemy before they could get at the federal army. Kearny realized better than most the need to shore up his line, which he believed would prevent the enemy from flanking him. With poor intelligence of the enemy forces, Kearny was basically improvising on the fly. In so doing, he also would continue to engage the Confederates and thereby keep them from turning the Union flank and destroying Pope's Army, or at least a part of it, which was actually Jackson's plan. It is possible that General Kearny recognized that if the Union force was having difficulties, maybe the Confederates were as turned as

XIV. Requiem

well. General A.P. Hill found as he deployed his units that his flank on Branch's brigade was exposed. Consequently, he brought forward in succession the brigades of Maxcy Gregg, Pender, Thomas and Archer in order to cover his lines.

Now going on 6:00 p.m. or sometime after, Kearny came across the 21st Massachusetts Infantry Regiment, formerly of Stevens's command. Under the command of Colonel William B. Clark, this unit had been mauled while in action with General Stevens, who had been killed in action. Remaining on the field in some semblance of order, it was the only unit Kearny found, and he was determined to have it support David Birney. Kearny now had to convince the 21st and Clark's second in command, Captain Walcott, that he was in urgent need of this unit, no matter what condition he thought his men might be in. Col. Clark was occupied elsewhere, and Captain Walcott did not expect and of course was not prepared for the encounter with the excited general that stormy day.

As Kearny rode up in the driving rain, he identified himself and inquired what unit this was. Walcott informed him if was 21st Massachusetts, formerly of Stevens's command, and advised Kearny of their poor condition after previous action that day. Kearny would hear none of it and informed the captain that it was his duty to come to the aid of his troops. Walcott, to his credit, was unsure of where Birney's right lay, and after being informed by Kearny of Birney's position in the field, Walcott warned the general that he thought that there were Confederates just over in the cornfield to his left. Kearny continued to insist that the 21st must come to his aid, and Captain Walcott finally relented. At some point, Colonel Clark returned; after talking with Walcott, he again described the confusing field to General Kearny, who remained adamant.

With rain coming in torrents, it was hard to discern just what forces might be in the field. The 21st Massachusetts was in a dilemma, and as his men moved to the left, Clark began to deploy his troops in line to form ranks. Kearny was incensed at the maneuver, but Colonel Clark had reason to be cautious. In the heavy rain, Walcott again warned the general that the enemy was there before him. "Kearny decided to do his own personnel reconnaissance. He spurred his horse into the cornfield and came upon an unrecognizable group of muddy soldiers near the wood line."[18] The lateness of the day and the continuing rain, coupled with the fact that Kearny was now trying to do everything himself since he had no aides and no escort, led him to make a fatal error.

As for the rest of Kearny's brigade commanders, Colonel Poe was now getting to the scene of action after considerable delay. Birney was

Major General Philip Kearny

already in action, and General Robinson was just coming up. Poe reported to General Reno, "who directed me to remain where I was until further orders."[19] General Robinson was soon posted on the right, where General Kearny most likely passed the artillery captain who had tried to hail him earlier. Robinson was in support of Graham's artillery and "was placed in line of battle on rolling ground to the left of the Centreville road."[20] Neither commander had any idea as to the whereabouts of their division commander, and for some reason, they failed to stay in touch with General Birney.

Young Gustave Shurmann was trying to move back toward his command after completing his postal assignment from General Kearny. He eventually ran into some straggling Union men that evening who warned him of the engagement just up the road. He recalled in a letter written after the war, "I proceeded as far as I dared, not knowing the position our men occupied, and remained ... under as heavy a shower as it has ever been my misfortune to be in."[21] It was at about this time that Lt. Col. Benjamin, just twenty minutes after encountering Kearny, heard what he described as musket fire, "a straggling volley of perhaps thirty shots or less."[22] This musket fire was coming from the direction in which General Kearny had ridden.

Up on the wood line, opposite the cornfield that the 21st Massachusetts Regiment had been trying to move through, lay the body of General Philip Kearny. In a flash of lightning, the general had come upon a body of wet and muddy Confederate soldiers just waiting to engage what they thought was a Union regiment. To their surprise, they encountered a lone rider who soon turned to flee. A captured Union officer shouted for him to stop: "'General Kearny, this is a Confederate line and we are both securely in their power. Please do not attempt to escape for your own and your country's sake!' Phil., looking around said gaily: 'Sir, I have a good horse here. I can depend on him every time. He'll carry me through!' Phil.'s black colt wheeled! Twenty shots rang out! Kearny falls! Just as a Confederate Officer reached him he murmured 'put me back on my horse.' Then his limbs gave one convulsive quiver and all was over."[23] The musket fire was still reverberating through the trees. The enemy rank and file moved forward and paused for a moment to look upon the quivering body they had just shot from his horse

These observers were the men of A.P. Hill's Light division, Edward Thomas's Brigade, 49th Georgia Regiment. Not knowing who it was that was before them, a Confederate officer brought forward a captured Union soldier, who believed that the dead officer was General Philip Kearny.

XIV. Requiem

Douglas Southall Freeman wrote of the Confederate reaction: "Kearny's body was recovered ... as it lay on the porch of a cabin a Confederate wrote, 'He is a very soldierly looking man.' Another ... remembered him as a spare, erect, military figure, looking every inch the soldier he was."[24] Jackson and A.P. Hill had a great deal of respect for the man whom their soldiers referred to as that one-armed devil. When Hill came upon Kearny's body, he was saddened at what he saw. A.P. Hill remarked, "Poor Kearny ... he deserved a better death than that."[25]

As Kearny was taking the bullet that tore into his spine and traveled through his abdomen, General Birney began to consider his situation now that his division commander was nowhere to be found. His official after-action report stated: "I assumed command of the division, and ordered forward Robinson's and Berry's (Poe) brigades, relieving my tired regiments and hold until 3 O'clock a.m. September 2."[26] By this time the opposing forces had been firing at the muzzle flashes in the darkness. These were the last acts of the battle at the time of Kearny's death. The antagonists broke off contact and the Union forces moved on toward Fairfax County Court House as they made their way to the forts of Washington.

For all intents and purposes, General Kearny had performed his duty and held the Confederate forces at bay, allowing for the rest of Union army to pass. The next day, General Robert

Ambrose Powell Hill was acquainted with Kearny before the Civil War and lamented the general's death before Hill's command at Ox Hill (Chantilly) helped arrange the return of his remains (Library of Congress Prints and Photographs Division, Washington, D.C.).

Major General Philip Kearny

E. Lee sent General Kearny's body in a Confederate ambulance to the Union lines under a guard of honor. "Under orders of Lee, I accompanied Kearny's body under a flag of truce. I felt only sorrow and sadness. He died as he wished to die as has become his heroic character. Walter Taylor, Adj. General."[27] It was soon transferred to Union cavalry, who took it to his division for preparations to send him to his home in New Jersey.

It is not surprising that Philip Kearny was admired by both Union and Confederate officers, possibly even more so by many of the Confederates. A.P. Hill saw the encounter and recorded: "The enemy obstinately contested the ground, and it was not until the Federal generals Kearny and Stevens had fallen in front of Thomas' brigade that they were finally driven from the ground. They did not, however, retire far."[28] Third Corps commander Heintzelman thought Kearny's action was a bit reckless, but General John Pope, of all people, praised Kearny, echoing what the Confederates had related: "He died as he could have wished to die as has become his heroic character."[29].

It is an inescapable irony that the Union officers who remembered Kearny after he was killed were the officers who probably would have been replaced by Kearny in command in that army. Kearny's most capable lieutenant, David Birney, recognized all this and more in his commander. "No unkind criticism of Kearny ever passed Birney's lips. He believed his old commander to be the embodiment of all that was gallant as an officer, brave as a soldier, and courteous as a gentlemen; and sharing his fortunes, identified himself, perhaps too much, with the unfortunate jealousies which, in 1862, existed in the Army of the Potomac between regular and volunteer officers."[30] Birney probably recognized all this because he came to experience those jealousies, and it was Kearny who came to his defense. Now Birney accepted the mantle of general of Kearny's division.

McDowell, McClellan and Pope had all been found wanting by the Lincoln administration and by Lincoln himself. It should be recalled that Lincoln had met young Kearny in Illinois country back in the 1840s. It is very probable that in conversation with Winfield Scott, Kearny's name along with others may have been brought up for command of the Army of the Potomac. In the Stephen Watts Papers, residing at the Missouri History Museum Archives, is a manuscript citing that Major General Philip Kearny had been selected to command the Army of the Potomac on the day he was killed in action. Even Alexander McReynolds, who had served with Kearny in Mexico at Churubusco, alludes to the fact that he recommended Kearny to the Lincoln administration in a testimonial.

In his 1937 book *General Philip Kearny: Battle Soldier of Five Wars*,

XIV. Requiem

Thomas Kearny states: "Civil War 1861–62. Killed, Chantilly, September 1862, day Lincoln appointed him to command Army of the Potomac."[31] Is this definitive proof that Kearny was to command the Army? Unfortunately, we cannot be sure that this happened, but it may have been the case. In reality, it is probably an indication that the process to confirm him was just beginning. Kearny himself would have had to accepted the position, and much like John Reynolds later in the war, he probably would have insisted on less interference from Washington itself.

At the time of the Manassas Campaign, dissension was rife in the officer ranks in the Union army. The fact that McClellan refused to cooperate with John Pope and was in constant disagreement with President Lincoln and most of his cabinet did not bode well for the outcome of the campaign. Lincoln didn't care what was thought about a commanding general just as long as he was successful against the enemy, and he believed Pope would have been successful. "Pope did well, but there was an army prejudice against him ... and if our generals, who were vexed by Pope, had done their duty ... all of our present difficulties and reverses have been brought upon us by these quarrels of the generals."[32] These "quarrels of the generals"[33] were long in the making, and they did not end with Pope or the eventual pillorying of generals like Fitz John Porter.

As early as April of that year, Lincoln encouraged McClellan to rein in and control his general staff and warned him of political ramifications of playing favorites. Kearny's replacing Hamilton probably was not popular, and Kearny was no fan of McClellan and his tactics. By the time of Manassas, the Union army was a split command between Pope and McClellan, and the mix of forces of the Army of the Potomac and Army of Virginia allowed for some confusion. It was very probable that Winfield Scott, the old former commander of the U.S. Army, was looking for someone to bridge the gap between the two armies and had recommended Philip Kearny to the president, knowing his expertise and experience.

Thomas Kearny is probably right, given the issues with the generals, as remarked by President Lincoln. The Army needed to be unified and the rift needed to be mended; it was a defining moment for the Union army. Lincoln needed a general, not a political opponent, and Philip Kearny was a very effective choice. Winfield Scott knew the man and his soldierly qualities from the army's early years and the Mexican War. On September 1, 1862, Lincoln appointed Kearny to command Army of the Potomac. If the statement by Thomas Kearny is true, it is most likely that Philip Kearny's views were beginning to get political attention by certain people in the military circles in Washington. Alexander McReynolds seems

Major General Philip Kearny

to support this possibility in a testimonial given after Kearny's death. In his statement, he claimed that he and other officers, former and active, met with President Lincoln at the time of the Second Manassas Campaign and discussed General Kearny's possible elevation to command the Army of the Potomac. This claim is problematic, for there is no verifiable evidence to prove that written orders were on their way for General Kearny's promotion.

An important piece of circumstantial evidence in favor of the claim of Kearny's promotion is that many in the political and military circle of President Lincoln, especially people like Secretary of War Stanton, wanted George McClellan gone. In fact, in a letter of condolence, Secretary Stanton indicates to Mrs. Kearny that her husband was probably being considered to command the Army of the Potomac:

"War Department Washington, Sept. 18, 1862.

Dear Madam:

Unwilling to intrude upon your grief in its first sacred moment, I postponed until now a testimonial of regret, and the calamity suffered by the Nation, in the death of Major General Philip Kearny. His high appreciation by this Department was shown in the rank he held which would have been acknowledged by still higher command if he had not fallen upon the field of Chantilly. His heroic courage and distinguished military skill had secured to him the confidence and admiration of the government, and endeared him to the people of the United States who mourn his loss; and among those who feel it most deeply as a public calamity is your friend,[34]

Edwin M. Stanton. (War Department)

This response from Stanton could very well be in response to Kearny's widow Agnes, who had sent a letter to President Lincoln previously. One should remember that this is a letter from a woman who had just lost her husband.

Bellegrove, Newark, Sep—13th 1862.

Mr. Lincoln.

It may seem unbecoming in this dark hour of my heavy affliction, to address you—and although too late for words to have effect, I must yield to conscience and have the privilege of saying, that my heroic husband, Gen. Kearny was sacrificed—sacrificed. The pang of sorrow is rendered more keen, from the knowledge, that he always felt, he would be sacrificed in this war—You have once spoken of him, as "your general"—why did you not firmly stand to him—and see that justice was done him? that after being called up in every battle, and in every crisis, he was not placed in the highest command—Could you name one other, unless Hooker, who has really done his service in this rebellion? Who has so undauntedly braved the foe while leading his men to victory? Pardon me, Sir, for intruding myself upon

XIV. Requiem

your notice—but a voice from Above, has been counselling my heart, to speak out, in justice for the blessed dead—"He lived a hero, and died a martyr."

Very respectfully yours
—Mrs. Philip Kearny.[35]

General Birney and his men reached the defenses of Washington, after a tedious march, on September 2, 1862. On the next day he issued the following order:

HEADQUARTERS KEARNY'S DIVISION Fort Lyon, Va. September 1862
[General Orders, No. 49]

The Brigadier-General commanding this division announces with deep sorrow the death of Major-General Kearny, its gallant commander. He died on the battle-field of Chantilly as his division was driving the enemy before it, the entire country will mourn the loss of this chivalric soldier, and officers and men of this division will ever hold dear his memory.

Let us show our regard for him by always sustaining the name which, in his love for the division, he gave it, viz., the "Fighting Division." As a token of respect for his memory, all the officers of this division will wear crape on the left arm for thirty days, and the colors and drums of regiments and batteries will be placed in mourning for sixty days.

To still further show our regard and to distinguish his officers as he wished, each officer will continue to wear, on his cap, a piece of scarlet cloth, or have the top or crown piece of the cap made of scarlet cloth.

By command of Brigadier-General D.B. BIRNEY

J.B. Brown
Acting Assistant Adjutant-General[36]

After the Battle of Chantilly, the army retired to the defenses of Washington. General Birney retained the command of the First Division of the Third Army Corps, which had devolved upon him on the death of General Kearny by right of seniority. General Kearny, before his death, had issued an order requiring the officers and men under his command to wear a badge or mark, by which they would be known wherever met. This badge was a piece of scarlet cloth, worn on the cap or hat, so as to be visible at all times. This was the first attempt to designate officers or men in our army by any distinctive mark or badge. The evident object of this order was to individualize the members of this division, and to designate the officers and men, should they lag on the march, or straggle in action. The Scarlet Patch referred to in the foregoing order was soon converted into a piece of red cloth or flannel, cut in the form of a diamond, and this for some time was known as the Kearny Patch.

The Kearny patch eventually evolved into badges for the Army of the Potomac. "When General Hooker assumed command of the Army of the

Major General Philip Kearny

Potomac, January 26th 1863, he found that its morale had never been so bad. The army had become despondent through repeated reverses and the incapacity of its leaders. Upon assuming command, General Hooker at once addressed himself to the task of elevating the character of the army...."[37] Following Kearny's lead, Hooker adopted the badges. First Corps, he gave the circle; Second Corps, trefoil; Third Corps, diamond; Fifth Corps, Maltese cross; Sixth Corps, Grecian cross; Eleventh Corps, crescent; and Twelfth Corps, star.

Epilogue

By the time the division under Birney arrived at the fortified works of Fort Lyon, young orderly Schurmann had finally caught up with division command. He was informed there of his general's demise, and in a letter remembered it this way: "I never saw the Generals body after it was sent into our lines, and conveyed to Alexandria by ambulance."[1] Schurmann was probably disappointed in not being able to say a proper goodbye, but he reported to David Birney, who took Schurmann as his orderly. He was assigned to another unit after the Battle of Fredericksburg, and after Gettysburg in 1863, he was mustered out of the service. He would not forget his General Kearny and wrote a letter after the war relating his experiences with him. (See Appendix D: Kearny Testimonials.)

Of interest were the letters that the young Schurmann was assigned to deliver to the post at Alexandria, the last letters written by Kearny to his wife and family. One of the letters gives some insight to the general's concerns and thinking after the battle at Manassas.

> August 31, 1862 Dearest Love:
>
> I wrote you yesterday morning. Since then there has been a sort of Bull Run episode. It is dangerous work to fight in this army; you have to fight ten times your share; and to expose yourself to prevent the demoralizing effect of almost cowardice in others. Hooker's Division is almost the only exception. This army ran like sheep; all but General Reno and General Gibbon. As for myself I was abandoned shamefully. My only salvation depended on holding a certain hill and house in the rear adjoining me.... My regiments behaved like perfect loves—so beautifully steady. I stayed for more than three hours after all the Americans but Reno and Stevens had left; and Reno was as much to the left as I was to the right behaving very handsomely.... This disaster is not Pope's fault but rather in the other generals in places they are not fit for.... I foresaw it all three hours before it took place. But I am sorry for our cause.
>
> Kisses for the children; love
Phil.[2]

It is interesting to note that in his last letters, General Kearny expresses his concern to his family of the events that had occurred over the

Epilogue

last twelve months. Kearny admits that he is taking greater chances and exposing himself to dangers that he admits is his nature. His frustration is evident in the letters and gives us an insight into why he took even greater a risk in the upcoming engagement outside of Fairfax Courthouse at Chantilly. Kearny seemed to portend that the Union armies could expect further setbacks if something in its leadership was not addressed.

Of the four brigade officers who served with Kearny, two would survive and two would lose their lives in combat. John Robinson and Orlando Poe would see future action, and both would live out their natural lives after the war. The questions about their support and confusion on September 1, 1862, would remain a question. To Orlando Poe's defense, it was a fluid situation; but in his after-action report, Colonel Poe remains vague as to his orders and does not explain why he was delayed other than taking pause! General Birney referred to Poe's brigade as Berry's brigade in his report, giving some indication of his disfavor toward Poe for his tardiness at Chantilly. Was this just a lapse of thought, or is this the way Birney actually thought of Poe? We just don't know, and Birney would not, unfortunately, survive the war to explain. As for Poe, he would not continue to serve under Birney's command. After the Antietam Campaign, he would be transferred into the new Ninth Corps.

Hiram Berry would actually serve under his collegial former division commander David Birney, now in command of the III Corps, at the Battle of Chancellorsville in May of 1863. On May 3 of that year, Berry commanded a division on the Union right flank near the Rappahannock River covering the fords. Also located at this position was the 1st Division of XII Army Corps, under the command of Alpheus Williams. Williams would be one of the last persons to see Berry before his end, and stated: "On the morning of May 3rd my line was ... connecting with the left of Berry's division."[3] In a letter to his daughter, Williams describes what took place as the enemy attacked. "As soon as the battle opened I rode to the right to consult with Gen. Berry.... Poor man! He was probably dead within fifteen minutes after I left him, killed by a rifle ball."[4] Gallant Berry died defending the Union right flank at the closing of the Chancellorsville Campaign.

General Birney had now lost two people in the war whom he probably considered friends, and unfortunately, Birney too would suffer a similar fate. The trusted lieutenant of General Kearny had served well under him, surviving a number of crucial battles, including Gettysburg, the Wilderness and Spotsylvania Court House, where he was wounded by a shell fragment, and Cold Harbor. It was in the trenches that grew

Epilogue

around Petersburg, Virginia, that General Birney found his end in 1864. Birney started in the Overland Campaign as a division commander in the II Corps, and eventually was given command of the X Corps in the Army of the James. During the siege of Petersburg, Birney became ill with diarrhea. At first, this was a minor complaint and he was able to remain in command, but in September his health started to get worse. Birney was reluctant to take a leave of absence and so tried to remain on duty, but he was so sick that he had to be transported in an ambulance. General Meade and General Grant soon requested that Birney be sent home at once, and he was taken to Philadelphia, where his health simply failed. On October 18, he died an agonizing death of what was probably typhoid fever. He was buried in Woodlands Cemetery.

Like Poe and Robinson, General Heintzelman would survive the war. After the Battle of Antietam, he would be assigned to various administrative duties, seeing no further combat. In his official report of what he referred to as the Battle of Little River Turnpike, he described the end of General Kearny this way: "General Kearny rode forward alone to reconnoiter, in his usual gallant, not to say reckless manner, and came upon a rebel regiment. In an attempt to escape he was killed."[5] Heintzelman had some mixed feelings about Kearny, which may have been aggravated because Kearny was being considered for higher command. To his credit, Heintzelman did go on to report that the army he served under would always have his name identified with its glory. Maybe Heintzelman knew of the rumors of Kearny's pending assignment to command the Army of the Potomac. We will probably never know.

John Pope was relieved of his command of the deactivated Army of Virginia and was assigned to duty on the frontier of the Dakotas. He took command of the American Indian situation that had caused problems in Minnesota and the Dakota Territory. His actions at Manassas would always follow him, and probably unfairly. George B. McClellan's stint as commander of the Army of the Potomac ended soon after the Battle of Antietam. McClellan remained an enemy of the Lincoln administration. After he left the army, he entered politics, and became the presidential nominee for the Democrats in 1864. He was promptly defeated in that election by his former commander in chief, Abraham Lincoln.

Once General Kearny's body was returned to the Union lines, it was David Birney who would see to it that his horse and personal effects, returned by the Confederates, would be forwarded to his wife Agnes in New Jersey. Birney also informed the division in General Order No. 49, "The Brigadier-General Commanding this division announces with deep sor-

Epilogue

row the death of Major General-Kearny.... He died on the battlefield ... as his division was driving the enemy before it."⁶ It was actually Birney's division that did most of the driving of the enemy. Kearny's body was buried in the famous Trinity Church Cemetery in New York City. It was here that many of the Kearny family were interred, along with a number of prominent citizens of early American society.

Ironically, Kearny's end came where he had skirmished with Confederates eleven months earlier. He was then commanding his beloved Jersey Blues when they drove off some Confederate cavalry on the Little River Turnpike. Those New Jersey soldiers who came under his disciplined approach to fighting never forgot their now dead former leader. When the Grand Army of the Republic (GAR) was founded shortly after the war, some of his former command started a movement to honor his memory in grand fashion. Sometime around 1866, in the City of Richmond, Virginia, a number of Civil War soldiers decided to form a GAR post. Here, in the former Confederate capital, the gathered veterans dedicated the post in the name of Philip Kearny, GAR No. 10.

The fact that the Grand Army of the Republic Post No. 10 was located in the old Confederate capital was significant. The fact that it was named after the revered General Philip Kearny was even more significant. Here was a general who was respected by both sides, and whose name was highly regarded by former adversaries who could well respect heroes. The end of the War Between the States could have gone differently had not the veterans of that war met to mend the fences long broken by the internecine strife. From a local Richmond newspaper: "The Blue and the Gray at Richmond—Confederate decoration and federal Memorial day was observed in Richmond yesterday with the usual programme. Public business was suspended. In the forenoon Phil Kearney Post, G.A.R., R.E. Lee Camp of Confederate Veterans and the United Veterans, escorted by Companies B and D of the First Virginia Regiment, proceeded to the battle ground of Fair Oaks, ode Seven Pines, where the graves of the federal dead in the national cemetery were decorated with flowers, flags and evergreens."⁷

The Phil Kearny Post in Richmond was initially established sometime in 1868. The post was reestablished in 1882, building on the traditions of the original established name. The GAR's purpose consisted of these three main premises: fraternity, charity and loyalty. Almost all former soldiers of the Union army joined this fraternal order. One of these former soldiers was Charles Hopkins, who was from New Jersey when the Blues were formed and served under Kearny's command. A survivor of Andersonville

Epilogue

Prison in Georgia, Hopkins became an assemblyman of the state legislature in New Jersey after the war. He believed he was indebted to General Kearny for shaping him into the man he became and the unit he served, helping him to survive the war.

Instrumental in organizing Kearny's recognition along with a number of others who served with Kearny, Hopkins led a movement to have Kearny's body disinterred so that it could be laid to rest at Arlington National Cemetery in Washington, D.C. With support from surviving family members, Kearny's remains were disinterred with much pomp and then removed, on a ceremonial caisson, from the New York Trinity Church. Making its way by train to Washington it arrived in April, and on April 12, 1912, Kearny was buried at Arlington, very near Mary Custis Lee's rose garden, with full military honors. The *Washington Post* reported:

> GRAVE HERE FOR HERO,
> Body of Maj. Gen. Kearny will be brought from New York,
> TRANSFER AFTER FIFTY YEARS.

A fitting soldier's monument encompassed a military service to his country: commissioned 2nd lieutenant of dragoons in 1836, serving at Forts Leavenworth, Gibson, Coffee, Jefferson Barracks. Military Roads Commissioners and member of commission studying Cavalry tactics. Attended French Cavalry School at Saumur, participated in French Colonial operations against Muslim insurgents in Atlas Mountains as part of Chasseur d'Afrique 1840. Cavalry tactics formulated by Kearny's commission adopted, as referenced in a letter, expeditions to Rocky Mountains under his Uncle Stephen Watts Kearny. Lost left arm in combat in Mexican War and made brevet major for gallantry. Duty in California and Oregon Indian War. In 1851 resigned his commission and moved to France. Served under French Military in its war with Austria over Italian independence and fought in battles at Magenta and Solferino, awarded Cross of Legion of Honor in 1860.

Two years after Kearny was interred at Arlington, an equestrian statue portraying the general on his horse was mounted on the grave site. Designed by Edward Clark, it remains there to this day, and is one of only two equestrian monuments at the world-famous cemetery. This bronze statue looks out over the walkway inside Arlington Cemetery, some of the most sacred ground in the United States. Standing prominently and dominating its surroundings, the general's statue peers out over the Potomac. A visitor who looks up at the statue will see a rider alert in the saddle with his back straight and his head slightly glancing towards the capital city, as

Epilogue

Dedicated in 1914, the Kearny Equestrian Monument at the site of Maj. Gen. Phil Kearny's final resting place at Arlington National Cemetery, Arlington, Virginia (author's collection).

if in the distance he hears gunfire and is ready to lead his troops toward the sounds of impending action. He is ready to say to his young orderly Gustave Schurmann, "One should never be afraid of anything."

Appendix A: Lost Letter of Lt. Philip Kearny

The following note presents to the reader the opening paragraphs—all that relates to military service, proper—of one of the missing reports of General (then Lieutenant) Kearny. After a long search, founded on the indications of Major-General George W. Cullum, it was discovered in one of the pigeonholes of the United States Ordnance Department. It is not the military report or statement, so often sought and alluded to, that entered into the details of all that Kearny witnessed while serving with the French Troops in Africa.

Algiers, July 1st, 1840. To Honorable J.B. Poinsett, Secretary of War.

Sir—I have the honor to inform you that I am just returned from the late expedition to Milianah in the province of Algiers, Africa, with the French Army, under the orders of Marshal Valee.

As I previously informed you, in a letter of May 8th, 1840, difficulties presented themselves on my first arrival in Africa, from the want of a proper authorization from the French Government, and also from the communication with the army, then in the field, being cut off by the number of Arabs in the plain of the Metidja. This prevented my taking part with the first expedition, in May, under the command of the Marshal and with which the Duc d'Orleans was also present, as lieutenant-general commanding a division. My time, however, was fully occupied in visiting the camps and advanced stations of this province, and in accompanying General Rostolan with a detachment of 1,500 men, sent to Mansajah in charge of a convoy. The 23d of May the army of Marshal Valee re-entered Algiers, but as the principal objects proposed in their expedition, the taking of Milianah and the occupation of the plain of Cheliff, had not been achieved, from a want of provisionment for a sufficient time, a second was immediately again set on foot, which opened on the 1st of June with an army of 12,000 men. This, through the intervention of General Schramm, Chief-of-Staff of the Army of Africa, and late Minister of War, I obtained permission to join, and was attached, accordingly, to a Regiment of Cavalry, the 1st Chasseurs d'Afrique. The considerations which first urged my going to Africa promised the study of the cavalry, that, by personal observation, I

Appendix A

might assure myself of the manner in which it was conducted in campaigns, as a component part of an entire army; the tactics it generally employed in its movements; and the various details by which a regiment regulated its system of interior police. This last was a study particularly interesting for us, since our cavalry being of but a few years' formation, however perfect might be our practice, there was an incertitude from the short period of our experience: and, if other inducements mingled with the above, it was the expectation in a war of the French with the Arabs, *from this resemblance that must ever exist between all wars with uncivilized nations, of finding something in the service generally that might be of utility to us in our Indian Wars*. Moreover, from the view in which I have looked on the selection of young officers for the mission abroad, I have ever considered that their individual instruction was even more the solicitude of government than the actual improvements they might introduce, and certainly no military information can be so generally instructive as that derived from being with a large army in the field, where large bodies of different Corps are united and wielded for the purposes of war, and where, by personal observation, one learns to appreciate and understand those nameless and many wants, the necessities of troops in campaign, which with an army cannot be dispensed with, and which, though not mingling immediately in the combat, tell the most in the general operations of the field, and yet can never be learned by mere theory or study.

That the utility of this measure of sending officers into Africa is recognized by other governments, is proved by the number of foreign officers who have been here previously, and that there are sixteen Belgian and two Danish officers present at this moment.

Your obedient servant,
P. KEARNY Junior Lieutenant 1st Regiment Dragoons, U.S. Army.

Major-General P. Kearny, at the age of twenty-two, accepted the commission of Second Lieutenant First Dragoons, and soon after was sent to Europe by the government to study and report upon the French cavalry tactics.

To accomplish this object he entered the military school at Saumur, France, and from thence went to Africa, where he joined the First Chasseurs d'Afrique, as a volunteer. By his daring exploits he attracted the attention of the French army, and was presented with the Cross of the Legion of Honor. *The Military and Naval History of the Rebellion in the United States*, by W.J. Tenney.

From John Watts de Peyster, *Personal and Military History of Philip Kearny, Major-General United States Volunteers* (1869).

Appendix B:
Extracts from Official Reports— Mexican War

Major-General Scott's Official Report, No. 5, of the "Battles of Contreras and Churubusco," Executive Documents, No. 1, page 304.

Arriving here, the 18th (August), Worth's division and Harney's cavalry were pushed forward a league to reconnoiter, and to carry or to mask San Antonio, on the direct road to the capital. This village was found strongly defended by field works, heavy guns, and a numerous garrison. It could only be turned by infantry to the left over a field of volcanic rocks and lava; for, to our right, the ground was too boggy. It was soon ascertained, by the daring engineers, Captain Mason, and lieutenants Stevens and Tower, that the point could only be approached by the front, over a narrow causeway, flanked with wet ditches of great depth. Worth was ordered not to attack, but to threaten, and to mask the place. "The first shot fired from San Antonio (the 18th) killed Captain S. Thornton, Second Dragoons, a gallant officer, who was covering the operations with his company. "The same day a reconnaissance was commenced to the left of San Augustin, first over difficult mounds, and farther on over the same field of volcanic rocks and lava which extend to the mountains, some five miles from San Antonio towards Magdalena. This reconnaissance was continued to-day by Captain Lee, assisted by lieutenants Beauregard and Tower, all of the engineers, who were joined in the afternoon by Major Smith, of the same corps. Other divisions coming up, Pillow's was advanced to make a practicable road for heavy artillery, and Twiggs' thrown farther in front to cover that operation; for, by the partial reconnaissance of yesterday, Captain Lee discovered a large corps of observation in that direction, with a detachment of which his supports of cavalry and foot, under Captain Kearny and Lieutenant Colonel Graham, respectively, had a successful skirmish.

Appendix B

Major-General Scott's Official Report, Ibid., No. 32, page 315.

As soon as the tete du pont was carried, the greater part of Worth's and Pillow's forces passed that bridge in rapid pursuit of the flying enemy. These distinguished Generals coming up with Brigadier-General Shields, now also victorious, the three continued to press upon the fugitives to within a mile and a half of the capital. Here Colonel Harney, with a small part of his brigade of cavalry, rapidly passed to the front, and charged the enemy np to the nearest gate. "The cavalry charge was headed by Captain Kearny, of the First Dragoon, having, in squadron with his own troop, that of Captain McReynolds, of the Third—making the usual escort to general headquarters but, being early in the day attached to general service was now under Colonel Harney's orders. The gallant Captain, not hearing the recall that had been sounded, dashed up to the San Antonio gate, sabering in his way all that resisted. Of the seven officers of the squadron, Kearny lost his left arm, McReynolds and Lieutenant L. Graham were both severely wounded, and Lieutenant R.S. Ewell, who succeeded to the command of the escort, had two horses killed under him. Major F.D. Mills, of the Fifth Infantry, a volunteer in this charge; was killed at the gate.

Major-General Pillow's Official Report Ibid., page 340–1.

Captain Kearny, of the First Dragoons, commanding a squadron composed of his own and Captain McReynolds' companies, was on duty with my division during the action, and made his way with great difficulty across the wide and marshy fields and deep ditches. Seeing no field for the action of his fine squadron until the tele de pont was carried, I had held him in reserve. I then let him loose. Furious was his charge upon the retreating foe, dealing death with the unerring sabre, until he readied the very suburbs of the city, and drew from the enemy's batteries at the Garita a heavy and destructive fire, by which the gallant Captain lost his left arm; and Captain McReynolds, Third Dragoons, who nobly sustained the daring movements of his squadron commander, was also wounded in the left arm. Both of these fine companies sustained severe losses in their rank and file also.

Colonel William S. Harney's Official Report, Ibid, page 347.

The reports of Major Sumner, commanding First Battalion, and Lieutenant-Colonel Moore, commanding Second Battalion, which I have the honor to forward herewith, will show in what manner the other troops

Extracts from Official Reports

and squadrons of my command were employed. The three troops of horse brought by me on the field, being ordered away in different directions, Major Sumner and I soon found ourselves without commands. I then employed myself with my staff in rallying fugitives and encouraging our troops on the left of the main road. Major Sumner, towards the close of the engagement, was placed by the general-in-chief in charge of the last reserve, consisting of the rifle regiment and one company of horse, and was ordered to support the left. This force was moving rapidly to take its position in line-of-battle, when the enemy broke and fled to the city. At this moment, perceiving that the enemy were retreating in disorder on one of the main causeways leading to the city of Mexico, I collected all the cavalry in my reach, consisting of parts of Captain Kerr's company, Second Dragoons, Captain Kearny's company, First Dragoons, and pursued them vigorously until we were halted by the discharge of the batteries at their gate. Many of the enemy were overtaken in the pursuit and cut down by our sabers. I cannot speak in terms too complimentary of the manner in which the charge was executed. My only difficulty was in restraining the impetuosity of my men and officers, who seemed to vie with each other whom should be foremost in the pursuit. Captain Kearny gallantly led his squadron into the very entrenchments of the enemy, and had the misfortune to lose an arm from a grape-shot fired from a gun at one of the main gates of the capital. Captain McReynolds and Lieutenant Graham were also wounded, and Lieutenant Ewell had two horses shot under him.

List of casualties
August 19 & 20, 1847
Harney's Brigade

KILLED:

1. Pvt. Patrick Mart, Co. F, 1st Dragoons.
2. Pvt. McBrophy, Co. F, 1st Dragoons.
3. Pvt. James McDonald, Co. F, 1st Dragoons.
4. Pvt. John Ritter, Co. F, 1st Dragoons.
5. Capt. Seth B. Thornton, Co. F, 2d Dragoons.
6. Pvt. Edward Curtis, Co. G, 3d Dragoons.
7. Pvt. Augustus Delsol, Co. G, 3d Dragoons.
8. Pvt. George DeDuve, Co. G, 3d Dragoons.

Appendix B

WOUNDED:

1. **Capt. Philip Kearny, Co. F, 1st Dragoons, severely, lost left arm.**
2. Lieut. Lorimer Graham, 10th Infantry attached to 1st Dragoons, severely.
3. Capt. A.T. McReynolds, Co. K, 3d Dragoons, severely.
4. Private Cowden, Co. K, 3d Dragoons.

The Sword Presentation to General Kearny After His Return from Mexico, by members of the New York Union Club.

To Major Kearny of the 1st Regiment, United States Dragoons:

On your return from the war in Mexico, where, in a gallant and successful charge at the very gates of the Capital, you lost an arm in your country's service, your friends and fellow townsmen, members of the Union Club, felt desirous to testify their sense of your deserts, by offering you an appropriate testimonial in honor of your noble bearing in that arduous campaign. Too national in our feelings not to proffer a general tribute of admiration where all employed on the service have deserved so high a need of praise, we are still free to confess that, as New Yorkers, we feel a special pride when our city's sons are enabled to contribute to our country's fame.

You followed the career of arms as one leading to honorable distinction, and you have liberally applied your means and zealously devoted your energies to the profession of your choice.

When called to the field a soldier inquires not into the causes of the war, but looks to the issue of the contest, being mindful only of the honor of his country's flag. You and your companions in arms planted our National banner in a foreign soil; it there became the symbol of our glorious Union, the type and emblem of home, of country and of fame. On every field it waved defiance to the foe, in every conflict it proved the harbinger of victory. Let this sword, which I have the honor of being charged to present for your acceptance, when it reminds you of a war in which you shared alike the glories and the sufferings, be not valued the less since peace has followed in the train of victory; nor yet let the weapon rust in its scabbard during a night of repose, lest another day should again summon you to the battle. We ask of you, for our sake, to regard the sword as a trophy that you both sought and won. Wear it in peace as in war, as a token of our admiration and (your) modest merit. Accept it as a testimonial from the friends whose esteem you possessed in the relations of peace, and who now acknowledge with pride your conduct in war.

New York, 3d November, 1848.

General Kearny's Reply,
New York, November 1848

Sir, The sword of honor which I have this day received at the hands of my fellow townsmen members of the Union Club is an overwhelming mark of distinction. It has been conferred by you in language the kindness of which renders the gift doubly interesting. You bid me to consider this sword in the light of a distinction of a trophy. Indeed, sir, such I most sensibly feel it, I behold in it the mark of regard of gentlemen whose esteem is not the view of the mere enthusiast but the approval of men calmly weighing actions as they pass before them in the moving panorama of life. Yet could I scarcely in due modesty admit to myself this full meaning of so honorary but that silence might be interpreted into insensibility. I am also aided in this avowal by the consideration as you sir have so happily expressed it that the insignia with which I am this day endowed are given to me as your townsman shared amidst others far more esteemed and prominent, who, forming part of our late army, planted our country's banner in Mexico, and now receive its ennobling tribute of admiration—a host whom our country sent forth to exemplify in the eyes of all nations those qualities which every individual of the United States is ready to bring forward as an offering when the public welfare may require.

For myself, sir, when on returning from Mexico, with other crippled remnants of the victorious army, I shared, in the hospitable city of New Orleans, those distinguished marks of attention which none knew better how to bestow than the generous Southerner, whose whole being vibrates in unison at the touch of honor, I was rewarded.

When, on arriving in my native city, I felt the pulse of sympathy beat high, and was received with cordiality by gentlemen whom I realize the honor of calling my friends and associates in the Union Club, my heart was touched.

This day, on being presented with a sword of honor, I confess that my cup of ambition is filled to the brim and overwhelming, and that most amply am I repaid, whatever of peril and suffering I have encountered.

In presenting me with this sword, sir, you charged me not to value the gift less now that "peace has followed in the train of victory." In our country, where military ardor is dangerous unless controlled, the soldier may

Appendix B

well prefer the sword, no longer baton; in marshalling to the fight, now trophy of victories passed, emblem of a successful war achieved. Still, with the predilections of a youth spent in my present profession, must I ever as strongly bear in mind that a republic particularly applies the motto "Dulce et decorum est pro patria mori." With a tear to the memory of cherished comrades, who, having already fulfilled the noble role, have passed from a death-bed of fame to a still more glorious rest, and with a profession of readiness, if at any future period my services be needed, joyfully once again to follow our country's banner on the war-path, I have the honor to conclude my thanks to you as Chairman of the Committee of Presentation.

But, sir, the associations connected with this day have no conclusion; they will extend, with this sword, which you have put in my power, after proudly wearing during my own life, to bequeath, a sparkling memento, to a succeeding generation of republican soldiers.

(Signed) KEARNY.

Appendix C: Documents, Reports, etc.— American Civil War

Centreville, Virginia, August 31, 1862

Colonel George D Ruggles, Chief of Staff to Major General John Pope

Colonel I report the part taken by my division in the battles of the two previous days.

On the twenty ninth on my arrival, I was assigned to the holding of the right wing my left on the Leesburg road. I posted Colonel Poe with Birney's Brigade in first line General Robinson First Brigade on his right, partly in line and partly in support, and Birney's most disciplined regiments reserved and ready for emergencies. Towards noon I was obliged to occupy a quarter of a mile additional on left of said road from Schurz' troops being taken elsewhere. During the first hours of combat General Birney on tired regiments in the centre falling back, of his own accord rapidly pushed across to give them a hand to raise themselves to renewed fight.

In early afternoon General Pope's order per General Roberts, was to send a pretty strong force diagonally to the front to relieve the centre in the woods from pressure. Accordingly I detached on that purpose General Robinson with his Brigade the Sixty third Pennsylvania Volunteers Colonel Hays the One Hundred and Fifth Pennsylvania Volunteers Captain Craig the Twentieth Indiana Colonel Brown and additionally the Michigan Marksmen under Colonel Champlin. Gen. Robinson drove forward for several hundred yards, but the centre of the main battle being shortly after driven back and out of the woods, my detachment thus exposed so considerably. In front of all others both flanks in air was obliged to cease to advance and confine themselves to holding their own. At five o clock thinking though at the risk of exposing my fighting line to being enfiladed that I might drive the enemy by an unexpected attack through the woods,

Appendix C

I brought up additionally the most of Birney's regiments the Fourth Maine Colonel Walker and Lieutenant Colonel Carver the Fortieth New York, Colonel Egan, First New York, Major Burt and One Hundred and First New York Lieutenant Colonel Gesner and changed front to the left, to sweep with a rush the first line of the enemy. This was most successful the enemy rolled up on his own right: it presaged a victory for us all; still our force was too light. The enemy brought up rapidly heavy reserves, so that our further progress was impeded. General Stevens came up gallantly in action to support us, but did not have the numbers.

On the morning of the thirtieth General Ricketts, with two brigades, relieved me of my extra charge of the left of the road and I again concentrated my command. We took no part in the fighting of the morning, although we lost men by an enfilading fire of the enemy's batteries. A sudden and unaccountable evacuation of the field, by the left and centre, occurring about five p.m., on orders from General Pope. I massed my troops at the indicated point, but soon re- occupied with Birney's Brigade, supported by Robinson's a very advanced block of woods. The key point of this new line rested on the Brown house towards the creek; this was held by regiments of other brigades; soon however, themselves attacked, they ceded ground and retired without warning us. I maintained my position until ten p.m., when, in connection with General Reno and General Gibbon—assigned to the rear guard—I retired my brigades.

My command arrived at Centreville in good order at two a.m. this morning and encamped in front of the Centreville forts. My loss in killed and wounded is over seven hundred and fifty, about one in three, in some regiments engaged a great deal severer; in the Third Michigan, one hundred and forty out of two hundred and sixty; none taken prisoner, except my engineer officer, who returned to the house supposed to be held by the troops alluded to.

It makes me proud to dwell on the renewed efforts of my Generals of Brigade, Birney and Robinson. My regiments all did well, and the remiss in camp seemed as brightest in the field. Besides my old tried regiments, who have been previously noted in former actions and maintained their prestige, I have to mark the One Hundred and First New York Volunteers and Fifty seventh Pennsylvania Volunteers, as equaling all that their comrades have done before; their commanders Lieutenant-Colonel Gesner, with the One Hundred and First New York Volunteers and Major Birney, with the Fifty seventh Pennsylvania Volunteers, have imparted to them the stamp of their own high character. The Sixty third Pennsylvania and Fortieth New York Volunteers, under the brave Colonel Egan suffered the most. The gallant Hayes is badly wounded. The loss of officers has been great; that of Colonel Brown can hardly be replaced. Brave, skillful, a disciplinarian full of energy and a charming gentleman, his Twentieth Indiana must miss him. The country loses in him one who promised to fill worthily high trust. The Third Michigan, ever faithful to their name, under Colonel Champlin and Major Pierce, lose one hundred and forty out of two hundred and sixty combatants. Colonel Champlin is again disabled. The staunch Fourth Maine, under Walker, true men of a rare type, drove on through the stream of battle irresistibly. The One Hundred and Fifth Pennsylvania Volunteers was not wanting. They are Pennsylvania's Mountain Men; again have they been fearfully decimated. The desperate charge of these regiments sustain the past history of this division.

Randolph's Battery of Light Twelves was worked with boldness and address. Though narrowly reached by three long reaching enfilading batteries of the enemy, Randolph's Battery constantly silenced one of theirs while shelling and ricocheting its shot into the reinforcements moving from the enemy's heights down into the woods. On the 27th with two sections and Robinson's First Brigade, Captain Randolph had powerfully contributed to General Hooker's success at Bristow Station.

Captain Graham, First United States Artillery, put at General Sigel's disposition, as repeatedly drove the enemy hack into the woods, as the giving way of that infantry left the front unobstructed. This practice was beautifully correct and proved Irresistible. On the 31st, Captain Graham, not being required on the right, was sent to the extreme left, and rendered important service with General Reno firing until late in the night.

Lieutenant _____, a German officer of distinction, put at my disposal by General Sigel, with two long range Parrots, covered our right flank and drove off an enemy's battery and regiments. I name these gentlemen as ornaments to their branch of the service.

I must refer to General Hooker to render justice to the part taken by my First Brigade under General Robinson, and Randolph's Battery in the affair of the 27th at Bristow Station.

Again am I called on to name the efficiency of my staff. Captain Mindil., often cited brave and intelligent, was the only military aide present to assist me; but Dr. Pancoast Division- Surgeon-General, not only insured the promptness of his department but with heroism and aptitude carried for me my orders.

Very respectfully
Your obedient servant Commanding Division
Lieutenant-Colonel C McKeever Chief of Staff Third Army Corps.

Appendix C

*Indorsement on the Foregoing Headquarters,
First Division, Third Corps (Army of the Potomac,
Fort Lyon, September 4, 1862)*

Respectfully forwarded as the official report drawn up by the late Major-General Philip Kearny and intended to have been signed by him the day of his death

(Signed) D.B. BIRNEY, Brigadier-General Commanding Division.

Official:

Lieutenant-Colonel C. McKeever Chief of Staff Third Army Corps

Appendix D: Kearny Testimonials

Kearny's Charge in Mexico

A[lex] McReynolds, Grand Rapids, Michigan, July 12th, 1869
To General De Peyster:

My Dear Sir—Your favor of the 24th ultimo (informing me that you contemplated writing a life of your cousin, the late Maj. Gen. Philip Kearny, killed at Chantilly, and requesting me to give you particulars of his charge at the San Antonio Gate, City of Mexico, in which I participated, and any other incident of interest connected with him that might occur to me), reached me by due course of mail.

When the army, under the command of Lieut. Gen. Scott, reached Puebla (Mexico), where we remained some four weeks for the purpose of reorganizing and awaiting reinforcements previous to entering on the campaign of the valley, having for its objective point the City of Mexico; an order issued from headquarters detaching Captain Kearny and myself, with our troop, from our respective regiments, the 1st and 3d dragoons, and attaching us to headquarters in squadron organization, as escort or body guard to the General-in-Chief (Captain Kearny being the senior and I the junior captain), which position our squadron occupied during the campaign of the Valley and until our flag floated in triumph over the Halls of the Montezuma's, and the Conqueror of Mexico was relieved from the command of an army that by his matchless military-genius he had immortalized. Although attached to headquarters, yet such was the impulsive ardor and heroic daring of the lamented Kearny, that no opportunity was lost by him where dragoons could operate against the enemy; this, too, with the sanction of our chief, and our adventures in that direction were frequent and successful. I well remember, that on the morning of the 19th of August, 1847, and previous to the battle of Contreras of that day, our

Appendix D

squadron, together with three companies of infantry, under the command of Major (Lt. Col. Wm. Montrose) Graham, I think, of the (11th U. S.) infantry, was detailed to accompany Captain Robert E. Lee, then of the headquarters staff (the Lieut. Gen. Lee of the Confederate Army), who had been ordered by Gen. Scott to reconnoiter the enemy's works at Contreras, for the purpose of ascertaining their strength and position.

("Official account of the Mexican War," Ex. Doc. No. 1,304) Gen. Valencia, in command of the Mexicans, anticipating the object of our movement, sent a force of five hundred lancers to drive us back. They moved by a circuitous route, and, undiscovered by us, until they reached a position on our right flank under cover of a prominence. Our dragoons were in the advance; our infantry, not keeping pace with us, were a short distance in our rear. When we approached within range the Mexicans opened fire upon us, when Kearny, whose keen military eye was quick to see an opportunity and prompt to embrace it, without waiting for our infantry, promptly gave proper form to our squadron and ordered a charge, when the enemy, as promptly, retreated to a point where the ground was broken and covered with Pedregal or lava, the result of an eruption of the earth, where they fancied our dragoons could not conveniently operate. But Kearny, ever equal to an emergency, immediately ordered our dragoons to dismount, and advancing on foot, killed, wounded and captured quite a number, and drove the remainder to flight. The infantry-major, in command of our detachment, was quite indignant that Kearny should have acted without his orders and thus bear off the laurels that, of right, belonged to him; he being the senior in command: but Kearny never stood on the order of his going; when opportunity offered he always went. The great conflict of the day (the battle of Contreras) followed. The struggle was terrific, and when night closed upon the gloomy scene the victory was with neither army; but, at the dawn of the following morning, by a desperate and sanguinary charge upon the enemy's strong works they were carried in triumph, and nearly the entire force of Valentia either killed or captured. The slaughter was terrible; little did we then dream, that within a few hours we should be again engaged in the crowning battle of the war—the battle of Churubusco—distant some three or four miles from Contreras. There, General Santa Anna, with his entire available army, was in strong position, evidently anticipating the utter annihilation of our noble little army, and well he might, when the great strength of his position and his superiority of numbers, at least four to one, is considered. This battle was a surprise, as the first intimation we had of his presence in that immediate vicinity, was a furious and destructive fire opened on our advance. Then it was, that the military genius of "the great Captain of the age" was again invoked, and after a conflict of nearly four hours duration, as sanguinary and bloody as ever had taken place on the American Continent, the last stronghold of the Mexicans, the great Tete-de-pont—was stormed by our noble army and the battle won. At this opportune moment, our squadron was in the right place, and as the Mexicans retreated on the causeway that led to the City of Mexico, distant about two miles, with Santa Anna at their head, the gallant Kearny saw his opportunity and made the charge that terminated at the base of the battery that covered the San Antonio Gate, and that is faithfully described in the newspaper article that I send you; which, after diligent search among my papers, is the only one I could find that gives particulars: and, being a participant, I prefer that others than myself should speak. Disclaiming, however for myself, any other merit than that of following my gallant leader, as to him all the credit of the movement belongs, I write with less diffidence. I would here remind you of the impression the charge made on the mind of Santa Anna, when in his report to his congress, exculpatory of his fresh disasters, he said, "what might we expect when a mere handful of the enemy's dragoons had the temerity to mount the Very Rampart of our defences;" and, again, when on the occasion of a large assembly of officers at Willard's Hotel in Washington city, congratulatory to Gen. Scott, at the close of the Mexican war, I chanced to be of the number; the General, in introducing me to Gen. Dearborn, of Massachusetts, stated that I had participated in Kearny's charge at the gates of Mexico, and in his emphatic manner added: "Sir, it was the boldest charge I have ever seen or read of. " Maj. Gen. Pillow made an official report of the charge, in which I remember he pictured it in glowing colors. I did not preserve it, but presume it will doubtless be found in the War Department at Washington.

It was my fortune to be again associated with Gen. Kearny in the early days of the late rebellion. Indeed, I was present when President Lincoln conferred upon him his first commission as Brigadier-General. A committee of gentlemen from New Jersey, of whom Governor Newell was one, was sent to Washington for the purpose of securing the appointment of Brigadier-General of the 1st New Jersey Brigade for Gen. Kearny. I was then in the city and was invited by them to accompany them and state to the President that I knew of General Kearny's military qualities. I gladly consented; indeed, it was a labor of love as well as duty, and I had the pleasure of hearing the President grant their request; and during that fall and winter (1861 and 1862) we were organized in the same division (Franklin's), with our quarters adjoining each other near the Alexandria

Appendix D

Seminary, Va.; during which time our intercourse was daily and of the most intimate and friendly character, and so continued during the war and until he fell, nobly defending the flag of his country that he loved so well. He was the soul of chivalry, generosity and hospitality: well may it be said of him that he was "bravest of the brave" and generous as he was brave. I knew him well, and here permit me to seek to correct a somewhat popular error in reference to his qualities as a soldier. To the casual observer he seemed to be recklessly impulsive in his movements, and such was the impression of many. This, in my humble judgement, is a grave mistake. In military movements his perceptive faculties were intensely acute, he saw quickly, reached conclusions rapidly, and under the inspiration of the military genius with which he was by nature endowed and a Spartan heroism that never failed him, executed promptly and vigorously. Thus it was, that movements that were the result of rapid deliberations (if I may be permitted the expression) were by some deemed to be reckless and without aim. In my humble judgment neither army, during the rebellion, produced his superior in all the qualities that constitute the true and accomplished soldier, and had his life been spared and the opportunity given him, none would have eclipsed him in the brilliancy of his achievements.

(Signed) ALEX. T. McReynolds

From Joseph Lane; Roseburg, Oregon April 27th 1868
To John Watts DePeyster

Sir I regret my inability to furnish you a copy of the letter you mention in yours of the 21st of January, but I would like to give you pleasure to supply as well as I can from memory, a brief statement of the conduct, in Oregon, of the late General.

During the summer of 1851 Major Phil Kearny received orders to proceed with two companies of United States Dragoons Captains Stewart and Walker, from Oregon to some point in California, en route he was informed of a recent attack of the Rogue River Indians in which they succeeded in killing quite a number of miners and doing other mischief. These Indians were at that time the most warlike and formidable tribe on the Pacific coast. Never having known defeat they were exceedingly bold in their depredations upon the miners and settlers and were the terror of all. Major Kearny determined if possible to give them battle and finally found them three hundred strong in the occupation of an excellent position. He ordered an attack and after a sharp engagement succeeded in dislodging them killing wounding and capturing fifty or more. It was here

that the lamented brave and brilliant Stewart fell. The Indians retreated across Rogue River and feeling that they had not been sufficiently chastised the major concluded to pursue them and whilst in the prosecution of this purpose, I joined him. He followed until the Indians made a stand quite favorable to themselves on Evans Creek about thirty miles distant from the scene of their late disaster. Here he again attacked them killed and wounded a few and captured about forty among the latter a very important prisoner in the person of the Great Chiefs favorite wife. By means of this capture and these successes an advantageous peace was obtained. Being an eyewitness in part of Kearny's movements and action I can with great truth and do with no less pleasure bear testimony to his gallantry as a soldier and his ability as an officer. I was then and still am sensible of the great good secured to Oregon by his achievements at that particular time.

Very respectfully your obedient servant,

Joseph Lane, formerly Governor of Oregon

General of the Army Winfield Scott

West Point Sept 7 1862

Dear Sir I am much grieved that I did not know of the time and place of the funeral of Major General Kearny till the receipt of your note yesterday about noon when it was impossible for me to reach New York in time as crippled as I am I should certainly have made every effort to be present to assist in doing honor to the memory of an old staff officer of mine and recently a highly distinguished General the bravest among the brave whom the whole Union admired in the field when living and now mourns among the dead look upon his fall in the present great crisis of the war as a national calamity.

Respectfully yours Winfield Scott

Letter of Gustave Schurmann

The letter, by Phil. Kearny's Little Bugler, is too characteristic and interesting to be omitted. It speaks equally well In favor of the General who could inspire a lad of twelve years with such sentiments of admiration and devotion, and of the drummer boy who, at the age of sixteen, could inspire such a grateful and agreeable memorial of his old commander.

New York, July 23, 1868.

I will try and detail, in the smallest possible compass, as far back as

Appendix D

I can recollect, my experience with General KEARNY. In the first place, I will begin with my enlistment. In the early part of 1861, I was drumming recruits in Chatham Square, New York city, for the Forty-second Regiment Volunteers (Tammany), for a couple of months, when my father enlisted in the Fortieth N.Y. Volunteers (Mozart) at Yonkers. When the Forty-second, not treating me well, I left them, not being mustered in, and tried to join the Fortieth; but its commander, Colonel Riley, would not take me, on account of my being too small, and also too young, being only eleven years old. As soon as the Colonel said no, I began to cry, and turned away from the tent; but my father went and spoke to him, when he called me back and take the drum and beat on it. All the men commenced to laugh, because the drum was nearly as big as myself.

But nevertheless, the Colonel said I would do. So I was mustered in on the 26th June, 1861, and discharged on the 26th of June 1861. Our regiment was guarding the railroad during the first battle of Bull Run. I was with the regiment from the Battle of Williamsburg, our first fight, until we came to Harrison's Landing, when a Corporal Brown, clerk at General Kearny's headquarters, and also a member of our regiment, came to me one day, stating that General Kearny ordered him to get him a drummer from our regiment to serve as an orderly for one day, as General McClellan was to review the army the next day.

I reported myself next morning early. He received me kindly, gave me his gray horse (Baby), one that he brought from Mexico. During the review, the General had occasion to jump a very large ditch. I jumped it with him, but a great many of the officers had to cross further up. I think my jumping this ditch brought me favorably to his notice. Accordingly, when I reported myself in the evening, after the review, so as to return to my regiment, he said, "no; but go and bring my baggage over to headquarters, and consider yourself my Orderly in the future."

From that day until his death, I was always with him. It was his habit to ride outside of the picket-guard every day at Harrison's Landing, only taking me with him. Many a time I would have to ride on top of the horse, lengthwise, so as not to knock my legs against the trees. He would go so fast through them, one time my hat was knocked off; the General never stopping, so by the time I was in the saddle again, there was no General to be seen, but I gave "Baby" his own way, when in less than five minutes he brought me up to him. I have known that same horse to kick at him as he went in the gate. The General would then "damn" me for not holding the horse tight; but for all that, the General always treated me the same as my own father would have done, and no one mourned his untimely death more than I did.

Kearny Testimonials

The first affair of any note in which I was with the General, was the skirmish near Black River, or Water. The rebel cavalry made a charge on our skirmishers, but we gave them one volley, when they retreated, but came very near making a prisoner of General D.B. Birney, near the skirmishers at the time. He managed to kill one with his pistol, and flung it in the face of another. Nothing of note took place on our march from Harrison's Landing to Alexandria, except at the second Battle of Bull Run, when during the engagement the General had occasion to write orders, which he did on his knee, while I steadied the paper with my fingers. When noticing that I trembled some he asked me "what was the matter." I replied, "Nothing, only I was a little frightened." He said, "I must never get frightened at anything;" any other man but him, would have acted just the same as I did, for the way the rebels were throwing shell and minie-ball in that particular spot was a caution.

During another part of the fight, several officers had congregated in a group—a few Generals and aides-de-camp—when one of the enemy's batteries fired a piece of railroad iron at us, and struck on my left, the General said "it was aimed at him," but did no harm except scattering dirt and gravel all around us. That place, getting a little too hot to hold us, we moved further on. At another time, he went outside the line of battle—the men all having lain down—to view the enemy, which went within an inch of costing him his life, for we had no sooner got outside when their sharpshooters commenced making a target of us. Some of the men called him in, but he took his time, until he saw all he could see, when he condescended to turn his horse's head, and show the enemy his rear.

After we retreated to Centerville, early on the morning of the 31st of August, 1862, he called me into his room; he was then quartered in a small cottage. I found him in bed; he gave me some official documents, and a letter directed to Mrs. Kearny, which I believe was the last letter he ever wrote home, and three or four golden dollars and some silver, to defray my expenses, and told me to post them in Alexandria. This was the last time I ever saw the General alive or dead. Inclosed you will find the pass he gave, which you will return after you have examined it. I proceeded to Alexandria, but came near being cut off by the enemy, who were then trying to surround us, which, I think, led to the battle of Chantilly. Having obeyed orders I commenced to retire, the afternoon of September 1st. Understanding from some stragglers that our troops were engaged—this was in the evening—I proceeded as far front as I dared, not knowing the position our men occupied, and remained there, in there in the road, under as heavy a shower as it has ever been my misfortune to be in, until next

Appendix D

morning, when I moved on, and inquired for the General's headquarters, when I was told that he was either dead or a prisoner. I found out all that I could about it, which was, that the previous evening General Kearny had asked General * * * to reconnoiter a certain gap which was left unguarded, but General * * * advised him not to go; he said "he would go anyhow," which he did, and that was the last time I was ever seen of him alive.

A great many seem to think that the General rode a gray horse at the time; but the one he rode was a coal black. I never saw the General's body after it was sent into our lines, and conveyed to Alexandria in an ambulance. I then reported to General Birney, was with him some time, when General Stoneman, taking command of the Third Army Corps, I went with him, and was with him in the Battle of Fredericksburg, when he being ordered to the command of the Cavalry of the Army of the Potomac, General Sickles then had, the command, and I was under him in the Battle of Gettysburg, which was the last engagement I was in—making ten battles in all, and never received a scratch.... I also received the Maltese (Kearny) Cross from General Birney.

I remain your obedient servant,
Gustave A. Schurmann.

Appendix E: Kearny and First New Jersey Regiment

Organization of the Division of the Potomac, August, 1861:

Division of the Potomac:

First New Jersey Brigade: Brigadier General Philip Kearny

First New Jersey Regiment, Col. William Montgomery
Second New Jersey Regiment, Col. George Mclean
Third New Jersey Regiment, Col. George Taylor
Green's Battery (G) Second U.S. Artillery and Company G Second U.S. Cavalry

New Jersey State Legislature Resolutions: Trenton New Jersey

That New Jersey highly appreciates the disinterested fidelity of General Philip Kearny, in declining proffered promotion rather than separate himself from the command of Jerseymen entrusted to him.

On the 28th of the same month, a set of resolutions was passed, in the following terms:

Resolved, That to the New Jersey Volunteers belongs the praise not only of checking the retreat of the Federal Forces retiring from Bull Run, and greatly aiding in the preservation of the National Capital from capture, but also of advancing, unsupported, on the Rebel stronghold at Manassas, and compelling its precipitate abandonment; and that General Kearny deserves the warm approval and thanks of the Nation for his boldness in making this advance, and this skillful strategy he displayed in its execution.

Resolved, That having already testified our high appreciation of the self-sacrifice and fidelity to his trust, which led General Kearny to decline

Appendix E

promotion rather than leave his Brigade, we now express our regret at the existence of any such necessity, and respectfully suggest to those in authority the propriety (unless it be inconsistent with the public interest) of combining all the New Jersey Troops on the Potomac into one Division, and placing the same under the command of General Kearny, whose devotion to his soldiers, care for their comfort and discipline, and brilliant qualities as an officer, entitle the country to his services in a higher position than the one he now occupies.

Resolved, that a Copy of these Resolutions be forwarded to the Honorable the Secretary of War.

Appendix F: Kearny Assigned to III Corps, 3rd Division

Army of the Potomac, General George McClellan Commanding

Brigadier General P Kearny was relieved from command of the New Jersey Brigade and assumed command of the 3d Division formerly Hamilton's 3d Army Corps May 2 1862

Name of Division changed to 1st Division August 13 1862

First Brigade Brigadier General Chas D Jameson commanding until June 13 1862 Brigadier General JC Robinson commanding from June 14 1862 to September 1862
57th Pennsylvania Vols. Transferred to 2d Brigade August 12 1862
63d Pennsylvania Vols.
105th Pennsylvania Vols.
87th New York Vols. Relieved from duty with Division August 23 1862
20th Indiana Vols. Joined Brigade June 10 1862

Second Brigade, Brigadier General DB Birney commanding
38th New York Vols.
40th New York Vols.
101st New York Vols. Joined Brigade June 9 1862
3d Maine Vols.
4th Maine Vols.
99th Pennsylvania Vols. Joined Brigade July 5 1862
57th Pennsylvania Vols. Joined from 1st Brigade August 12 1862

Third Brigade, Brigadier General Hiram G Berry commanding until August 19 1862 Colonel Orlando M Poe 2d Michigan Vols. commanding from August 20 1862 to September 1862
2d Michigan Vols.

Appendix F

3d Michigan Vols.
5th Michigan Vols.
37th New York Vols.
1st New York Vols. Joined Brigade June 3 1862

Artillery of Division, Company G 2d United States Artillery Relieved July 18 1862 Company B
1st New York Artillery Relieved June 5 1862 Company E 1st Rhode Island Artillery Company K
3d United States Artillery Joined July 18 1862

Appendix G: Union and Confederate Order of Battle (Selected Units)

Union Order of Battle Peninsula Campaign (Selected Units)

Army of the Potomac Maj Gen George B. McClellan
Commanding in the field: BG Edwin V. Sumner

III Corps: BG Samuel P. Heintzelman

Second Division: BG Joseph Hooker

First Brigade, BG Cuvier Grove
2nd New Hampshire: Gilman Marston
1st Massachusetts: Col Robert Cowdin
11th Massachusetts: Col William E. Blaisdell
26th Pennsylvania: Col William F. Small (w), Maj Casper M. Berry

Second Brigade, Col Nelson Taylor
70th New York: Col William Dwight (w&c), Maj Thomas Hold
72nd New York: Ltc Israel Moses
73rd New York: Col William R. Brewster
74th New York: Ltc Charles H. Burtis

Third Brigade, BG Francis E. Patterson
5th New Jersey: Col Samuel H. Starr
6th New Jersey: Ltc John P. Van Leer (k), Maj George C. Burling
7th New Jersey: Ltc Ezra A. Carman (w), Maj Francis Price, Jr.
8th New Jersey: Col Adolphus J. Johnston (w), Maj Peter H. Ryerson (k)

Third Division: Brig. Gen. Philip Kearny

First Brigade, BG Charles Davis Jameson

Appendix G

57th Pennsylvania: Col Charles T. Campbell
63rd Pennsylvania: Col Alexander Hays
105th Pennsylvania: Col Amor A. McKnight
87th New York: Col Stephen A. Dodge

Second Brigade, BG David B. Birney
38th New York (Mozart): Col J. H. Hobart Ward
40th New York (Scotts Life Guard): Col Edward J. Riley
3rd Maine: Col Henry G. Staples
4th Maine: Col Elijah Walker

Third Brigade, BG Hiram G. Berry
2nd Michigan: Col Orlando M. Poe
3rd Michigan: Col Stephen G. Champlin
5th Michigan: Col Henry D. Terry
37th New York: Col Samuel B. Hayman

Artillery, Cpt James Thompson
Battery B, 1st New Jersey Light Artillery: CPT John E. Beam
Battery E, 1st Rhode Island Light Artillery: CPT George E. Randolph
Battery G, 2nd U.S. Artillery: CPT James Thompson

Order of Battle Manassas Campaign (Selected Units)

Union Army of Virginia: Major General John Pope
Union Army of the Potomac (Attached units)
Maj Gen George McClellan

III Corps Major General Samuel P. Heintzelman

First Division: Major General Philip Kearny
First Brigade, BG John C. Robinson
20th Indiana: Col William L. Brown (k), Maj John Wheeler
30th Ohio (6 cos.): Lt. Col Theodore Jones
63rd Pennsylvania: Col Alexander Hays (w), Capt James F. Ryan (w)
105th Pennsylvania: Lt. Col C.A. Craig (w), Maj J.W. Greenwalt

Second Brigade, BG David B. Birney
3rd Maine: Capt Moses B. Lakeman
4th Maine: Col Elijah Walker
1st New York: Maj Edwin Burt
38th New York (Mozart): Col John Henry Hobart Ward
40th New York (Scotts Life Guard): Col Thomas W. Egan

Union and Confederate Order of Battle (Selected Units)

101st New York: Lt. Col Nelson A. Gesner
57th Pennsylvania: Maj. William Birney

Third Brigade, Col. Orlando M. Poe
37th New York: Col Samuel B. Hayman
99th Pennsylvania: Col Asher S. Leidy
2nd Michigan: Lt. Col Louis Dillman
3rd Michigan: Col S.G. Champlin (w), Maj Byron R. Pierce
5th Michigan: Capt. William Wakenshaw

Artillery Battery E, 1st Rhode Island: Capt George E. Randolph
Battery K, 1st United States: Capt William M. Graham

Confederate Order of Battle (Selected Units)

Army of Northern Virginia Lt. Gen Robert E. Lee

Jackson's Corp. Maj Gen Thomas J. Jackson

A.P. Hill's Light Division
Maj. Gen. Ambrose Powell Hill
Gregg's Brigade
BG Maxcy Gregg
1st South Carolina: Maj Edward McGrady Jr. (w), CPT George W. McCreary
1st South Carolina (Orr's Rifles): Col J. Foster Marshall (k), Ltc Daniel A. Ledbetter (k), CPT Joseph J. Norton Capt George McD. Miller
12th South Carolina: Col Dixon Barnes
13th South Carolina: Col Oliver E. Edwards (w), CPT David R. Duncan
14th South Carolina: Col Samuel McGowan (w), Ltc William D. Simpson

Archer's Brigade
BG James J. Archer
5th Alabama Battalion: Capt Thomas Bush (k), Lt Charles M. Hooper
19th Georgia: Capt Frank M. Johnston
1st Tennessee (Provisional Army): Col Peter Turney
7th Tennessee: Maj Samuel G. Shepard
14th Tennessee: Col William A. Forbes (mw), Maj James W. Lockert

Branch's Brigade
BG Lawrence O. B. Branch
7th North Carolina: Capt Robert B. MacRae

Appendix G

18th North Carolina: Ltc Thomas J. Purdie
28th North Carolina: Col James H. Lane
33rd North Carolina: Col Robert F. Hoke
37th North Carolina: Col William M. Barbour

Ewell's Division
MG Richard S. Ewell (w) BG Alexander R. Lawton

Early's Brigade
BG Jubal A. Early
13th Virginia: Col James A. Walker
25th Virginia: Col George H. Smith (w)
31st Virginia: Col John S. Hoffman
44th Virginia
49th Virginia: Col William Smith
52nd Virginia
58th Virginia: Col Samuel Letcher

Definitions (k) killed (w) wounded (c) captured

Chapter Notes

Preface

1. *A Street Guide to Civil War Alexandria*, Fort Ward Museum and Historic Site, 1995.
2. Freeman, Douglas Southall. *Lee's Lieutenants* (New York: Scribner, 1942–43), Vol. 1, p. 371.
3. De Peyster, John W. *Personal and Military History of Philip Kearny, Major General United States Volunteers* (New York: Rice and Gage Publishers, 1869), p. 27.

Chapter I

1. Freeman, Vol. 1, p. xxiv.
2. *Ibid.*
3. Freeman, p. xxii.
4. De Peyster, John, p. 39.
5. *Ibid.*, p. 41.
6. De Peyster, p. 48.

Chapter II

1. *The 1820 Journal of Stephen Watts Kearny*, ed. Valentine Mott Porter (Missouri State Historical Society, 1908).
2. ed. Kane, Lucile, Holmquist, June and Gilman, Carolyn, *The Northern Expeditions of Stephen H. Long* (St. Paul: Minnesota Historical Society Press, 1978), p. 347. The location of the fort on the bottoms was abandoned a month after Kearny left, and Leavenworth was assigned elsewhere. The new commander, Colonel Josiah Snelling, relocated the post on a promontory above the confluence of the St. Peters and Mississippi rivers, just where Stephen Long suggested in his report in 1817.
3. *Ibid.*
4. *Ibid.*, p. 14.
5. *Ibid.*, p. 20.
6. *Ibid.*, p. 152.
7. *Ibid.*, p. 40.
8. *Ibid.*, p. 45.
9. *Ibid.*
10. *Ibid.*, p. 152.
11. Jefferson Barracks Community Council, *History of Jefferson Barracks*, 2011. General Wilkinson was implicated in espionage and as an agent acting for Spain during the Burr investigation.
12. *Life of Black Hawk* (Chicago: Dover, 1994), p. 69. It was a young officer named Jefferson Davis who escorted the leader of the Sac and Fox, Black Hawk, to the post of Jefferson Barracks, after his capture. Black Hawk praised Jefferson Davis for his treatment and kindness toward him and his warriors.

Chapter III

1. Stephen Watts Kearny Papers, Box 18, Journal of S.W. Kearny, Missouri History Museum Library.
2. *St. Louis Republican*, Stephen Watts Kearny collection, Missouri History Museum Library.
3. De Peyster, p. 53.
4. *Ibid.*, p. 71.
5. *Ibid.*, p. 88.
6. *Ibid.*, p. 99.
7. Stephen Watts Kearny Papers, Box 1, Missouri History Museum Library, St. Louis.
8. *Oregon Trail, Oregon National Historic Trail/Missouri to Oregon*, National Park Service, 2008.
9. De Peyster, p. 112.
10. *The 1820 Journal of Stephen Watts Kearny*, p. 4.

Chapter Notes

11. ed. Kane, Holmquist, and Gilman, p. 11.
12. De Peyster, p. 112.
13. *Ibid.*, pp. 112–113.
14. *Ibid.*, p. 115.
15. *Ibid.*, p. 117. Preeminent American historian Francis Parkman would traverse the trail in 1846 with Henri Chatillon of the American Fur Company, based in St. Louis. He later wrote an exceptional account about the Oregon Trail.
16. *Ibid.*, p. 116.
17. *Ibid.*, p. 117.
18. Western National Parks Association, *Fort Scott National Historic Site*, p. 9.
19. De Peyster, p. 120.
20. *Ibid.*
21. *Ibid.*
22. Thornbury, William, *Principles of Geomorphology* (New York: John Wiley & Sons, 1969), pp. 116–117.
23. De Peyster, p. 121.
24. Western National Parks Association, *Fort Scott National Historic Site*, p. 5.
25. Kearny papers. On October 31, 1848, S.W. Kearny died in St. Louis and was buried in Col. O'Fallon's Vault Bellefontaine Cemetery.

Chapter IV

1. Morison, Samuel E. *The Oxford History of the American People* (New York: Oxford University Press, 1969), p. 559.
2. *Ibid.*, p. 561.
3. De Peyster, p. 124.
4. *Ibid.*, p. 125.
5. *Ibid.*, p. 125.
6. *Ibid.*, p. 126.
7. *Ibid.*, p. 128.
8. *The West Point Atlas of American Wars*, ed. Esposito, Vincent (New York: Henry Holt and Company, 1995), p. 15.
9. De Peyster, p. 131.
10. *Ibid.*, p. 133.
11. *Ibid.*
12. *Ibid.*, p. 134.
13. Report of the Survey of the Valley of Mexico. www.history.army. Mil, p. 304.
14. To Mexico City with Scott. Chapter 7. www.history.army, p. 195.
15. Official Report of the Battles of Contreras & Churubusco www.dmwv.org/mex.war.
16. *Ibid.*
17. Official Report of the Battles of Contreras and Churubusco. Major General Winfield Scott, www.dmwv.org.
18. De Peyster, p. 141.
19. Official Report of the Battles of Contreras and Churubusco. Major General Winfield Scott, www.dmwv.org.
20. De Peyster, p. 146.
21. Kearny, Thomas, *General Philip Kearny: Battle Soldier of Five Wars* (New York: Putnam & Sons, 1937), pp. 148–149.
22. *Ibid.*, p. 155.
23. De Peyster, p. 157. See Appendix D for the full letter of Governor Lane.
24. De Peyster, p. 146.

Chapter V

1. Phil Kearny and the Battle of Solferino, contributed by William Styple, www.geocities.com.
2. *Ibid.*
3. De Peyster, p. 190.
4. Sears, Stephen, *To the Gates of Richmond* (New York: Mariner Books, 2001), p. 23.
5. *Official Record of the War of the Rebellion* (Washington, DC: U.S. Government Printing Office, 1880), Vol. 5 Chapter, XIV, p. 113. Hereinafter O.R.
6. Life Stories of Civil War Heroes: The Biography of Corporal Charles Hopkins, www.geocities.com.
7. O.R., p. 16.
8. O.R., p. 13.
9. O.R., p. 537.
10. *Ibid.*
11. Kearny Papers.
12. O.R., p. 539.
13. *Ibid.*
14. De Peyster, p. 254.
15. *Ibid.*, p. 255.
16. De Peyster, p. 258.
17. O.R., p. 72.
18. O.R., p. 129.
19. Luvaas, Jay, ed. *Guide to the Battle of Antietam* (Lawrence: University Press of Kansas, 1996), p. 258.
20. *Ibid.*, p. 265.
21. *Ibid.*, p. 271.

Chapter VI

1. O.R., Volume 11, Chapter XXIII, p. 15.
2. Miller, William J., "Federal Logistics," p. 141.
3. De Peyster, p. 258.
4. O.R., p. 136.
5. O.R., p. 155. Lincoln did travel to Ft. Monroe on May 8 to observe and visit the army as McClellan moved up the Peninsula.
6. O.R., p. 139.
7. *Ibid.*
8. O.R., p. 20.
9. O.R., p. 458.
10. Sears, p. 75.
11. De Peyster, p. 272.
12. *Ibid.*, p. 291.
13. *Ibid.*
14. Ruegsegger, Bob, "Confederate, Union Forces clash near Williamsburg," *Gazette Extra*, May 2012.
15. Sears, p. 78.
16. O.R., p. 492.
17. Davis, Oliver Wilson, *Life of David Bell Birney, Major-General U.S. Volunteers* (Philadelphia: King & Baird, 1867), p. 40.
18. *Ibid.*, pp. 40–41.

Chapter VII

1. Sears, p. 108.
2. Schneider, James J., "A New Form of Warfare," www.cgsc.army.mil.
3. O.R., Volume 11, Chapter XXIII, pp. 184–185.
4. Miller, "Federal Logistics," p. 154.
5. Freeman, p. 225.
6. De Peyster, p. 362.
7. O.R., p. 838.
8. *Ibid.*
9. O.R., p. 843.
10. *Ibid.*
11. Life Stories of the Civil War Heroes: Kearny at Seven Pines, by Edmund Clarence Stedman, www.geocities.com/stdragoons.
12. Kearny Papers.
13. O.R., p. 850.
14. O.R., p. 851.
15. Kearny at Seven Pines.
16. O.R., p. 843.
17. Davis, pp. 44–45.
18. O.R., p. 856.
19. De Peyster, p. 366.

Chapter VIII

1. O.R., Vol. 11, Ch. XXIII, p. 133.
2. O.R., p. 841.
3. *Ibid.*, p. 835.
4. *Ibid.*, p. 222.
5. Harwell, Richard, *Lee: An Abridgement* (New York: Touchstone Books, 1997), pp. 195–196.
6. O.R., p. 836.
7. *Ibid.*
8. *Ibid.*, p. 224.
9. *Ibid.*, p. 223.
10. *Ibid.*, p. 836.
11. *Ibid.*, p. 225.
12. *Ibid.*, p. 98.
13. *Ibid.*
14. Harwell, pp. 207–208.
15. O.R., p. 61.

Chapter IX

1. O.R., Vol. 11, Ch. XXIII, p. 40.
2. De Peyster, p. 361.
3. *Ibid.*, p. 362.
4. O.R., pp. 210–211.
5. O.R., p. 213.
6. *Ibid.*
7. O.R., pp. 215–216.
8. O.R., p. 184.
9. O.R., p. 254.
10. *Ibid.*
11. O.R., p. 268.
12. O.R., p. 161.
13. O.R., p. 99.
14. O.R., p. 181.
15. O.R., p. 797.
16. Freeman, p. 567.
17. De Peyster, p. 349.
18. O.R., p. 99.
19. O.R., p. 162.
20. *Ibid.*
21. De Peyster, p. 341.
22. O.R., p. 100.
23. O.R., p. 163.
24. O.R., p. 164.
25. O.R., p. 101.
26. Kearny Papers.

Chapter Notes

Chapter X

1. De Peyster, p. 330.
2. *Ibid.*
3. *Ibid.*, p. 498.
4. O.R., Volume 11, Chapter XXIII, p. 103.
5. Sears, Stephen W., "General Lee and Malvern Hill," *North & South Magazine* 10, No. 5 (March 2008): p. 27.
6. De Peyster, p. 497.
7. O.R., p. 186.
8. O.R., p. 165.
9. *Ibid.*
10. De Peyster, p. 352.
11. O.R., p. 66.
12. O.R., p. 292.
13. O.R., p. 379.

Chapter XI

1. De Peyster, p. 402.
2. O.R., Volume 12, Chapter XXIV, p. 12.
3. *Ibid.* pp. 11–12.
4. *Ibid.*, p. 13.
5. *Ibid.*, p. 37.
6. *Ibid.*
7. *Ibid.*, p. 35.
8. Foote, Shelby, *The Civil War* (New York: Random House, 1958), p. 625.
9. Gibbon, John, *Personal Recollections of the Civil War* (Dayton, OH: Morningside Bookshop, 1988), p. 54.
10. *Ibid.*
11. Ludolf Longhenry Diary.
12. J.H. Brunemer, *Fennimore Times*, September 7, 1907.
13. O.R., Volume 12, Chapter XXIV, p. 38.
14. O.R., p. 412.
15. *Ibid.*

Chapter XII

1. O.R., Volume 12, Chapter XXIV, p. 411.
2. De Peyster, p. 425.
3. Esposito, p. 57.
4. O.R., p. 415.
5. Foote, p. 621.
6. O.R., p. 51.
7. *Ibid.*
8. Fisher, Edwin, "Military Intelligence 1861–1863," p. 91.
9. Esposito, p. 61.
10. *Ibid.*
11. O.R., p. 37.
12. Hennessy, John J., *Return to Bull Run* (Norman: University of Oklahoma Press, 1999), p. 195.
13. *Ibid.*, p. 221.
14. O.R., p. 415.
15. O.R., p. 267.
16. Davis, p. 63.
17. O.R., p. 434.
18. De Peyster, p. 426.
19. *Ibid.*
20. O.R., Volume 12, Chapter XXIV, p. 430.
21. O.R., p. 416.
22. O.R., p. 430.
23. O.R., p. 416.
24. O.R., p. 421.
25. Patchan, Scott C., "Second Manassas," *Blue & Gray Magazine* 29, No. 2 (2012): p. 48.
26. Freeman, p. 235.
27. O.R., Volume 12, Chapter XXIV, p. 421.
28. Patchan, p. 48.
29. O.R., Volume 12, Chapter XXIV, p. 431.
30. De Peyster, p. 417.
31. O.R., p. 298.

Chapter XIII

1. O.R., Volume 12, Chapter XXIV, p. 413.
2. Freeman, p. 227.
3. *Ibid.*, p. 233.
4. De Peyster, p. 397.
5. Freeman, pp. 105–106.
6. Freeman, p. 234.
7. De Peyster, p. 413.
8. Robert E. Lee's report of 2nd Manassas, *The Longstreet Chronicles*. www.chickasaw.com.
9. Freeman, pp. 237–239.
10. *Ibid.*, p. 239.
11. Freeman, p. 121.
12. De Peyster, pp. 416–417.
13. Robert E. Lee's report of 2nd Manassas.
14. O.R., Volume 12, Chapter XXIV, p. 416.
15. O.R., p. 413.
16. O.R., pp. 268–269.

17. O.R., p. 216.
18. O.R., p. 435.
19. O.R., p. 417.
20. O.R., p. 416.
21. O.R., p. 414.
22. O.R., p. 379.
23. Foote, p. 640.
24. De Peyster, p. 412 (p. 152, "Soldiers' Letters," edited by Lydia Mjenturi).

Chapter XIV

1. O.R., Volume 12, Chapter XXIV, p. 416.
2. *Ibid.*
3. De Peyster, p. 426.
4. O.R., p. 647.
5. O.R., p. 672.
6. De Peyster, p. 43.
7. O.R., p. 414.
8. *Ibid.*
9. Major H. J. Williams's Official Report, vol. 19, www.civilwarhome.com.
10. O.R., p. 418.
11. O.R., p. 420.
12. O.R., p. 418.
13. De Peyster, p. 459. Paine Letter.
14. O.R., p. 418.
15. O.R., p. 436.
16. De Peyster, p. 461.
17. *Ibid.*, p. 452.
18. Kearny's Death, www.espd.com.
19. O.R., p. 436.
20. O.R., p. 423.
21. De Peyster, p. 426. (See Appendix D for Schurman's letter).
22. *Ibid.*, p. 463.
23. Kearny Papers.
24. Freeman, p. 133.
25. Foote, p. 644.
26. O.R., Volume 12, Chapter XXIV, p. 418.
27. Kearny Papers.
28. O.R., p. 672.
29. O.R., p. 48.
30. Davis, p. 33.
31. Kearny Papers.
32. National Park Service booklet series, *The Vortex of Hell*, p. 20.
33. *Ibid.*
34. Kearny, Thomas, p. 436.
35. Abraham Lincoln papers: Series 1. General Correspondence. 1833–1916: Agnes M. Kearny to Abraham Lincoln, Saturday, September 13, 1862 (Death of her husband), Manuscripts, Library of Congress.
36. Davis, pp. 73–74.
37. De Peyster, p. 367.

Epilogue

1. De Peyster, p. 426.
2. Kearny, Thomas, pp. 407–408.
3. Luvaas, Jay, and Nelson, Harold, *Guide to the Battles of Chancellorsville & Fredericksburg* (U.S. Army War College Guide, Lawrence: University Press of Kansas), p. 264.
4. *Ibid.*, p. 267.
5. O.R., Volume 12, Chapter XXIV, p. 414.
6. De Peyster, p. 369.
7. Anonymous Richmond newspaper clip, Phil Kearny Post, G.A.R.

Bibliography

Books, Manuscripts, Papers

Black Hawk. *Life of Black Hawk*. Chicago: Dover, 1994.
Catton, Bruce. *American Heritage Picture History of the Civil War*. New York: American Heritage, 1982.
Davis, Oliver Wilson. *Life of David Bell Birney, Major-General U.S. Volunteers*. Philadelphia: King & Baird, 1867.
De Peyster, John. *Personal and Military History of Philip Kearny Major General United States Volunteers*. New York: Rice and Gage Publishers, 1869.
Esposito, Vincent J., ed. *West Point Atlas of American Wars*, vol. 1. New York: Henry Holt and Company, 1995.
Foote, Shelby. *The Civil War*. New York: Random House, 1958.
Freeman, Douglas Southall. *Lee's Lieutenants*, vols. 1 & 2. New York: Scribner, 1942–43.
Gibbon, John. *Personal Recollections of the Civil War*. Dayton, OH: Morningside Books, 1988.
Harwell, Richard. *Lee: An Abridgement*. New York: Touchstone Books, 1997.
Hennessy, John J. *Return to Bull Run*. Norman: University of Oklahoma Press, 1999.
Kane, Lucile, June Holmquist, and Carolyn Gilman, eds. *The Northern Expeditions of Stephen H. Long*. St. Paul: Minnesota Historical Society Press, 1978.
Kearny, Stephen Watts (1794–1848). *The 1820 journal of Stephen Watts Kearny, comprising a narrative account of the Council Bluff–St. Peter's military exploration and a voyage down the Mississippi River to St. Louis* [from old catalog]. St. Louis, reprinted from Missouri Historical Society collections, vol. III, 1908. Combined Arms Research Library, Ft. Leavenworth, KS.
Kearny, Thomas. *General Philip Kearny: Battle Soldier of Five Wars*. New York: G.P. Putnam & Sons, 1937.
Luvaas, Jay, and Harold Nelson. *Guide to the Battles of Chancellorsville & Fredericksburg*. U.S. Army War College Guide. Lawrence: University Press of Kansas, 1994.
Morison, Samuel E. *History of the American People*. New York: Random House, 1965.
Sears, Stephen. *To the Gates of Richmond*. New York: Mariner Books, 2001.
Stephen Watts Kearny Papers: Missouri Historical Museum Archives: (Collections) St. Louis, MO.
United States War Department. *The Official Military Atlas of the Civil War* by George B. Davis, Leslie J. Perry, Joseph W. Kirkley; compiled by Calvin D. Coles; intro by Richard Sommers. New York: Grammercy Books, 1983.
———. *Official Record of the War of the Rebellion*. Washington, DC: Government Printing Office, 1880.
Utley, Robert M. *Fort Scott National Historic Site*. Tucson, AZ: Western National Parks Association, 1991.

Bibliography

Magazines

Hardy, Michael C. "McClellan's missed opportunity." *America's Civil War Magazine*, March 2007.

Kolakowski, Christopher L. "Sedgwick Saves the Day." *Hallowed Ground* 6, No. 3 (Fall 2005).

Laurant, Darrell. "On the B-List: Top 10 Most Overlooked Battles of the Civil War." *America's Civil War Magazine*, November 2015.

Longstreet, James. "From Manassas to Appomattox." *The War Times Journal*, www.wtj.com/longstreet

Miller, William J. "The Peninsula Campaign of 1862." *Hallowed Ground* 6, No. 3 (Fall 2005).

Patchan, Scott C. "Second Manassas." *Blue & Gray Magazine* 29, No. 2 (2012).

Sears, Stephen W. "General Lee and Malvern Hill." *North & South Magazine* 10, No. 5 (March 2008).

Newspapers/Papers

"Biographical Sketch of General Stephen Watts Kearny, Nov. 3, 1848." *St. Louis Republican*. Stephen Watts Kearny collection, St. Louis History Museum Library, St. Louis, MO.

Brunemer, J.H. "The Battle of Gainesville." *Finnimore Times*, September 11, 1907.

Fairfax County Virginia Civil War Sesquicentennial. "Battle of Ox Hill." Commemorative event paper, September 1, 2012.

Fisher, Edwin. "Military Intelligence 1861–1863."

Longhenry, Ludolph. "Diary." Antietam National Battlefield, National Park Service (collections).

Miller, William J. "Federal Logistics."

National Park Service. *The Vortex of Hell: From Richmond to Manassas in 1862*, 2012.

Ruegsegger, Bob. "Confederate, Union Forces Clash Near Williamsburg." *Gazette Extra*, May 2012.

A Street Guide to Civil War Alexandria, Fort Ward Museum and Historic Site, 1995.

Online Sources

Clausewitz, Carl von. *On War*. Book I, Chapter 1, www.clausewitz. J.J. Graham translation.

A Continent Divided: The U.S.-Mexico War. University of Texas Arlington, https://library.uta.edu/usmexicowar/.

CWSAC Battle Summaries, www.nps.gov.

Documents & Letters, *The Longstreet Chronicles*, www.chickasaw.com.

General Kearny, www.espd.com.

Library of Congress Abraham Lincoln papers: Series 1. General Correspondence. 1833–1916: Agnes M. Kearny to Abraham Lincoln, Saturday, September 13, 1862 (Death of her husband), https://www.loc.gov.

Library of Congress Abraham Lincoln papers: Series 2. General Correspondence. 1858–1864: Philip Kearny to Oliver S. Halsted, Thursday, May 15, 1862 (Complains about General McClellan), https://www.loc.gov.

Life Stories of Civil War Heroes: The Biography of Corporal Charles Hopkins, www.goecities.com.

Bibliography

Life Stories of Civil War Heroes: Kearny at Seven Pines, by Edmund Clarence Stedman, www.geocities.com.
Maps-Pictures-Sketches, Library of Congress, http://www.loc.gov/pictures/collection/civwar/.
Richmond National Battlefield Park, www.nps.org.
Southern Oregon History, Philip Kearny Diary, http://truwe.sohs.org/files/index.html.
United States War Department. Official Report of the Battles of Contreras & Churubusco, www.dmwv.org.
United States War Department. *War of the Rebellion: A Compilation of the Official Records of the Union and Confederate Armies*. Washington, DC: Government Printing Office, http://cdl.library.cornell.edu/moa/browse.monographs/waro.html.
Williams, H.J. Official Report, www.civilwar.com.

Index

Abd-El-Kader, Mahdi Kader 19–20; Muslim insurgents 20, 159
Africa 22; Constantine Province 19–20, 161–162; French Africa 29; North Africa 19, 21–22, 35
Alexander, Confederate Brig. Gen. Edward 95
Alexandria, VA 1, 47, 51, 114, 155, 175, 180
Algeria 18–21, 25–27, 29, 41–42, 46; Algiers 18–20, 161
Arabs 18–21, 48, 161–162
Archer, Confederate Brig. Gen. James 147, 187
Arkansas River 16, 22, 24, 28–29
Arlington National Cemetery 159–160
Army of Northern Virginia 77, 81, 89, 104, 106, 113, 115, 123, 130, 132, 187
Army of the Peninsula 69
Army of the Potomac 48–50, 52–53, 55–56, 59, 66–70, 76–79, 84–86, 88–89, 91–92, 95–99, 101–102, 104–105, 107, 114, 129; units detached 131, 137, 143, 150–153, 157, 172, 180, 183, 185–186
Army of the South 36–37
Army of the Valley 104
Army of the West 6, 16, 30
Army of Virginia 102–105, 111–112, 114–118, 120, 123, 130–136, 138, 140, 145, 151, 157, 186
Atkinson, Gen. Henry 10; Black Hawk War 15, 18; Yellowstone-Missouri Expedition 23
Atlas Mountains 19–20, 25, 27, 29, 35, 41, 159
Austria 46–47, 159

Baby 113–114; Grey Horse of 178
Ball's Bluff 49
Beaver Dam Creek (Mechanicsville) Battle of 78–80, 88
Benjamin, Lt Col. Samuel 145, 148
Berry, Brig. Gen. Hiram 52, 64–65, 71–74, 87–88, 91–92, 94, 101, 116, 118, 139, 149, 156, 183, 186
Birney, Maj. Gen. David Bell 52, 64–66;

Chantilly 141, 143–144, 147–149; death of 155–158, 169–172, 179–180, 183, 186–187; Division Command 150, 153; Kearny defends 73–75, 87, 90–92, 94, 100; Second Manassas 113, 116, 118, 120–122, 125–127
Black Hawk 15–16, 136
Boatswain's Swamp 78–82
Bourmont French Gen. Louis Auguste Victor 19
Branch Confederate Brig. Gen. Lawrence O.B. 79, 145, 147, 171, 187
Buck Hill 120
Bull Run 48–49, 106, 112, 114–117, 120–122, 124, 126, 134, 136, 138, 155
Bullitt, Diana 43–44

California 1, 30, 41–43, 159, 176; San Francisco port of 40, 43
Camp Cold Water 11–12, 14
Casey, Brig. Gen. Silas: Division 70–74; Redoubt 69–70, 74
Cedar Mountain, Battle of 105, 115, 130
Centreville, Va. 50, 107–112, 114–117, 119, 132–133, 135–136, 138–140, 146, 148, 169–170
Chantilly (Ox Hill) 123; Battle of 139, 141–142; death of Kearny 147–149, 151–153, 156, 173, 179
Charles City Road 84, 88, 90–92, 94–95, 102
Chasseur a' Cheval 18; Chasseurs d'Afrique 20, 46, 159, 161–162
Chickahominy River 67–71, 77–78, 80–84, 86–88, 113
Churubusco Battle of 36–38, 150, 163–164, 174
Clark, Edward (sculptor) 159, Equestrian Monument of Kearny 159–160
Clark, William 10, 14, 23
Clark, Col. William B. 147
Clausewitz, Carl 50, 67, 87, 135
Columbia University 7, 9–10, 41
Couch, Maj. Gen. Darius 73–74, 98, 100–101
Council Bluffs 23, 27

Index

De Peyster, John Watts 3; cousin 8, 59, 62, 75, 86, 133, 173
Devils Gate 27–28
Dogan's Ridge 121, 129, 135–136
Dragoons 17–18, 25, 28, 33–35, 39, 42, 159, 162, 173–174; First 16–17, 25, 39, 46, 162, 164–166, 173; Second 163, 165; Third 37, 164–165, 166, 173; U.S. 9, 25, 46

Elm City 51
Ewell, Confederate Maj. Gen. Richard (Dick) 25, 104, 108–109, 132, 164, 165, 188

Fair Oaks (Seven Pines) 68–69; Battle of 74–75, 77, 83, 86–87, 89, 158
Fairfax Courthouse 50, 138, 140–141, 149, 156
Fairfax Station 50, 130
First Manassas 107, 115
Fort Belle Fontaine 10, 14–15
Fort Laramie 24, 26–27
Fort Leavenworth 17, 21–22, 24–25, 29, 41
Fort Lyon 153, 155, 172
Fort Monroe 49, 51, 53, 59, 64–65, 113
Fort Stephen Watts Kearny 31
Fort Vancouver 41
France 19–20, 22, 43–47, 96, 159, 162; Duc de Orleans 20, 161; French Military observers Comte de Paris 60; Royal School of Cavalry 18
Franco-Austrian War 44, 47
Freeman, Douglas Southall 2, 5–6, 90, 149
Fullerville, Stewart 141

Gaines Mill, Battle of 77–86, 88, 105
Gainesville 107, 109, 111, 132–133, 142
GAR (Grand Army of the Republic) 158
Garnett & Golding Farm 83–84, 89
George Washington Memorial Parkway 1
Gibbon, Maj. Gen. John 2, 108–111, 135–138, 155, 170
Glendale (Frazier's Farm) 90–91; Battle of 93, 95–97, 121
Glendale Crossroads 90–91, 93, 96
Graham, Capt William 148, 171, 187
Great Divide Basin 23, 27–28
Gregg, Confederate Brig. Gen. Maxcy 79–82, 94, 121, 123–125, 133, 147, 187
Groveton Battle of 111, 133, 142; Brawner Farm 108

Halleck, Maj. Gen. Henry (Chief of Staff) 104, 114
Hamilton, Brig. Gen. Charles 51, 57, 59, 151, 183
Hancock, Maj. Gen. Winfield Scott 65
Hanover Court House 69
Harney, Col. William S. 34, 36–37, 163–165

Harrison, William H. 14, 91
Harrison's Bar 113, 130–131, 139, 178–179
Harrison's landing 91–92, 98; Berkley Plantation 101–102, 104
Heintzelman, Maj. Gen. Samuel 57, 63–64, 68, 71–72, 74–75, 83–84, 86–89, 91, 94–96, 98–99, 102, 105, 107–108, 112–114, 117, 121, 129, 133–134, 136, 140–141, 150, 157, 185–186
Henry Hill 135, 137
Hill, Confederate Maj. Gen. Ambrose P. 78–85, 93–95, 132, 140, 145, 147–150, 187
Hill, Confederate Brig. Gen. Daniel Harvey 69, 83
Hooker, Joseph Maj. Gen. 61–63, 65, 75, 77, 107–108, 112, 124, 140, 152–155, 171, 185
Hopkins, Charles 49, 158–159
Humphreys Brig. Gen. Andrew 98

Indian Frontier 16–17, 21–22, 25, 28–29
Indian Plains tribes: Arapahoe, Cheyenne 26; Ojibwa 11; Philip visits Ioway 17; Sac and Fox 14–16; Sioux 11, 14, 27
Iron Brigade 2, 108
Iron Gates 19, 27
Italy 46–47, 159

Jackson, Confederate Maj. Gen. Thomas 79, 82, 97, 104–109, 111–112, 115–118, 126, 130–134, 136–137, 140 143, 145–146, 149, 187
James River 68, 80, 84, 89, 91, 96–98, 101–102, 104, 113
Jameson, Brig. Gen. Charles 52, 57, 65, 71–73, 123, 183, 185
Jefferson Barracks 3, 9; Kearny assigned to 15–18, 22, 130, 159
Jersey Blues 50, 95, and 158
Johnston, Confederate Lt. Gen. Joseph E. 49, 68–69, 77, 83
Jones Confederate Maj. Gen. David R. 100, 132

Kearny, Maj. Gen. Philip 1–3, 6–11; Chantilly (Ox Hill) 138–141; death of 143–158; Legion of Honor 159; letter of 161–168; Mexican War 31–37; in North Africa 17–22; in Paris 43–45, 46–53; Peninsula Campaign 55–57, 59–103; Plains Expedition 25–27, 29; recovered 40–42; Second Manassas 104–108, 110–137; testimonials 172–183, 185–186; wounded 36–39
Kearny, Philip, Sr. 7
Kearny, Gen. Stephen Watts 3; death of 29–31; family 9–12, 15–17, 21–23, 25; Grand Expedition 22–23, 25–26; Mexican War 30; War of 1812 6–7, 33, 40, 150
Kearny, Thomas 150–151

200

Index

Kennedy, Capt Archibald 7
King, Maj. Gen. Rufus 107–109, 111

Lane, Oregon Gov. Joseph 41–42; letter of 176–177
Lawton, Confederate Brig. Gen. Alexander 188
Leavenworth, Col. Henry 10, 12–14, 16–17
Lee, Confederate Lt. Gen. Robert E. 3, 9, 77–82, 83–84, 90, 95, 103–106, 113, 115–117, 130–138, 149–150, 94, 174, 187
Lee's Mill 59, 61–62, 64
Lewis and Clark 10, 14, 23
Lincoln, US Pres. Abraham 6, 33, 56, 59–60, 84, 102–104, 128; Agnes letter to 150–152, 157, 175; quarrels of the generals 151
Lincoln Memorial 1
Long, Maj. Stephen 11, 13–14, 28
Longstreet, Confederate Maj. Gen. James 9, 61, 82, 84, 93, 95, 116, 119, 129–134, 137
Louis-Phillipe (king of France) 19
Louisiana Purchase 10–11, 14

Magruder, Confederate Brig. Gen. John B. 44, 57, 61–62, 81
Malvern Hill, Battle of 85, 95–99, 101, 103, 130
Manassas 56, 69, 116, 119, 127, 132, 157; First Manassas 107, 115–116, 132; Second Manassas 2, 106, 111, 132, 139, 142, 151–152
Manassas Gap Railroad 123
Manassas Junction 50, 69, 106–107, 111, 114, 131–132
Matthews Hill 120–121, 126, 134–136
Maxwell, Agnes 44–45; letter to Lincoln 152–153
McCall, Brig. Gen. George 92, 94–95
McClellan, Maj. Gen. George 2, 6, 36, 49–51, 53, 55–57, 59–61, 65–70, 77–89, 91, 95–96, 98; Kearny protest 101–103, 104–107, 113–115, 150–152, 157, 178, 183, 185–186
McDowell, Maj. Gen. Irvin 106–108, 111, 129, 150
McReynolds, Capt. Alexander 37, 164–166, 150–151; letter of 173–174
Mechanicsville 78–79, 82
Meigs, Brig. Gen. Montgomery 52
Mexican-American War 16, 25, 30, 32–37, 39, 48, 53, 151, 159; O.R. 174–175
Mexico City 16, 29–30, 34–37, 40; the Pedregal 36, 174
Mississippi River 9–15, 17, 23
Missouri 3–4, 10, 14, 16, 118; Independence 21; New Madrid 104
Missouri River 15, 17, 21, 24
Morris, General 46

Naglee, Maj. Gen. Henry 71
Napoleon III 18–19; Emperor of France 46
New Jersey: Bellegrove 43–45, 152; Kearny family 2, 10, 48–51, 78, 94–95, 150, 157–159, 171, 181–183
New Mexico 16, 24–25, 29
New Orleans 17, 33, 167
New York NY: Broadway 7, 10–11, 17, 40, 43–45; Mozart & Scott's Life Guards 57, 64–65, 71, 74, 125, 134, 178
Northwest Ordinance 15; Pacific Northwest 2, 11, 21, 24, 27, 40, 42

Oak Grove, Battle of 77–78, 80, 88–89
Oregon 22, 26–27, 41–42, 176–177; Oregon Indian War 159; Rogue River Indian War 40–43, 176–177
Oregon Trail 21–23 25–27, 31

Paris 18; Kearny living in 43–44, 46–47
Pender, Confederate Brig. Gen. Dorsey 79, 147
permanent Indian Frontier 16–17, 22, 25, 29
Pierce, Brig. Gen. Franklin 40
Pike, Maj. Zebulon 11, 22–23, 28
Pillow, Maj. Gen. Gideon 37, 39, 163–164, 175
Platte River 24–27, 31
Poe, Col. Orlando 65, 116, 118, 120–121, 124, 126, 135, 139; Chantilly (Ox Hill) 143–144, Poe delayed 147–149; Poe's report 156–157, 169, 183, 186, 187
Poinsett, Secretary of War Joel Robert 18, 21, 29, 42; letter to 161
Polk, US Pres. James K. 22, 28, 32
Pope, Maj. Gen. John 2, 9, 102–103, 104–108, 111–121, 123–127, 129–137, 140, 145, 150–151, 155; relieved of command 157, 169–170, 186
Porter, Maj. Gen. Fitz John 77–79, 81–83, 95–96, 101, 103, 107, 111–112, 129, 133–134, 136, 151
Portillo (Mexican general) 35
Potomac River 1, 49–50, 53
Powhite Creek 80
Puebla, Mexico 34–36, 173

Randolph, Capt George: Chantilly (Ox Hill) 143–145, 171, 186–187; 1st Rhode Island Artillery 99; Second Manassas 135
Rapidan River 104–105, 130
Rappahannock River 104, 106, 130–131, 156
Reno, Maj. Gen. Jesse 106–107, 135–136, 138, 141, 143–144, 148, 155, 170–171
Richmond, Virginia 59, 66, 68, 72, 79–80, 86–87, 102; Philip Kearny G.A.R. Post 158
Richmond and York Railroad 55, 59, 68, 73–74, 87, 89

201

Index

Rio Grande 32–34
Robinson, Brig. Gen. John 87–88, 91–94, 101, 116, 118, 120–121, 123–125; Chantilly (Ox Hill) 144, 148–149, 156–157, 169–171, 183, 186
Robinson, Col. William 109–110
Rocky Mountains 21–24, 27–28, 159
Rodes, Confederate Brig. Gen. Robert E. 71–72

St. Louis 9–10, 15–16, 25, 30–31
St. Peters River 11–14, 23
San Antonio Gate (Churubusco) 36–37, 39, 163–164, 173, 175
Santa Anna, Pres. Antonio Lopez de 21; Mexican War 32, 34–36, 39, 174–175
Santa Fe Trail 16, 21–23, 25, 29–30; Bents Fort on 16
Saumur Cavalry School 18, 20, 162
Savage Station 68, 70, 73, 83–84, 89, 102
Schurmann, Gustave 114; Chantilly (Ox Hill) 138–139, 148, 160; letter of 177–180; Second Manassas 120–121
Schurz, Brig. Gen. Carl 120–122, 126–128
Scott, Lt Gen. Winfield 10, 22; letter of 177; Mexican War 33–37, 40, 150–151, 164, 173–175
Seven Pines (Fair Oaks) Battle of 68–69, 70–71, 73, 76–77, 80, 86, 83, 87–89, 97, 158
Shenandoah 104, 123
Sigel, Maj. Gen. Franz 106–107, 112; Kearny dispute 117–121, 126, 134–135, 171
Slocum Maj. Gen. Henry 92, 96
Solferino, Battle of 47, 159
South Pass 23–24, 28, 33
Stanton, Secretary of War Edwin 84; letter to Agnes 152
Stevens, Brig. Gen. Isaac 140–141, 143–147, 155, 163, 170
Stone House 115, 119, 121–122, 135–136
Sudley Church 121, 124, 126; Sudley Church road 120, 126, 135
Sudley Springs 108, 120; road 112, 120–122, 124
Sumner, Brig. Gen. Edwin 50, 61, 83, 86, 96, 185; Mexican War 164–165

Tammany Hall 44, 178
Taylor, Maj. Gen. Zachary 32–34, 94
Thompson, Capt. James 92, 94, 99, 186
Thornton, Capt Seth 163, 165
Thoroughfare Gap 106–108, 111, 116, 131–132
Trinity Church NY 158–159
Twiggs, Brig. Gen. David 163

Valee, Marshal of France Sylvain Charles 19–20, 161
Van Vliet, Brig. Gen. Stewart 51, 53, 56–57, 103
Vera Cruz, Mexico 33–34, 36
Victor-Emmanuel (king of Sardinia) 46

Walcott, Capt. 147
War of 1812 3, 6, 10, 13, 15, 34
Ward, Col. J. Hobart 65, 75, 86, 89, 123, 134, 186
Warrenton, Va. 107, 140
Warrenton Junction 107, 114–115, 117
Warrenton Turnpike 107, 111, 117, 122, 131, 136, 138
Washington DC 1–2, 16, 18, 22, 41, 38, 48–49, 53–54, 56, 69, 85, 102–105, 108, 114, 126–127, 131, 140, 142; forts of 145, 149, 151–153, 159, 175
Watts, John 7–8
Watts, Susan 6, 7
West Point NY 3, 53, 108; General Scott letter 177; West Point Landing 66, 77
White House Landing 55, 59, 88
White Oak Swamp 68, 73–74, 84, 88, 90
Wilkinson, Gen. James (territorial governor) 14, 16
Williams H.J. 141
Williamsburg Va. 55, 178 97, 103, 113 Battle of 59, 61–62, 66
Williamsburg Road 68–73, 75, 77, 87
Worth, Brig. Gen. William 37, 39, 163

York Peninsula 1, 52, 115
York River 49, 53, 59
Yorktown 55–57, 59, 61–62, 66–67, 131

www.ingramcontent.com/pod-product-compliance
Ingram Content Group UK Ltd.
Pitfield, Milton Keynes, MK11 3LW, UK
UKHW042005140426
5217IPUK00015B/1000